New Economics as Mainstream Economics

International Papers in Political Economy Series

Series Editors: Philip Arestis and Malcolm Sawyer

This is the seventh volume of the new series of *International Papers in Political Economy (IPPE)*. The new series will consist of an annual volume with five to six papers on a single theme. The objective of the *IPPE* will continue to be the publication of papers dealing with important topics within the broad framework of Political Economy.

The original series of *International Papers in Political Economy* started in 1993 and has been published in the form of three issues a year with each issue containing a single extensive paper. Information on the old series and back copies can be obtained from Professor Malcolm Sawyer at the University of Leeds (e-mail: mcs@lubs.leeds.ac.uk)

Titles include:

Philip Arestis and Malcolm Sawyer (*editors*)

NEW ECONOMICS AS MAINSTREAM ECONOMICS

PATH DEPENDENCY AND MACROECONOMICS

CRITICAL ESSAYS ON THE PRIVATISATION EXPERIENCE

POLITICAL ECONOMY OF LATIN AMERICA
Recent Economic Performance

ALTERNATIVE PERSPECTIVES ON ECONOMIC POLICIES IN
THE EUROPEAN UNION

FINANCIAL LIBERALIZATION
Beyond Orthodox Concerns

21st CENTURY KEYNESIAN ECONOMICS

International Papers in Political Economy
Series Standing Order ISBN 978–1–4039–9936–8

You can receive future titles in this series as they are published by placing a standing order. Please contact your bookseller or, in case of difficulty, write to us at the address below with your name and address, the title of the series and one of the ISBNs quoted above.

Customer Services Department, Macmillan Distribution Ltd, Houndmills, Basingstoke, Hampshire RG21 6XS, England

---

New Economics as Mainstream Economics

Edited By

Philip Arestis
University of Cambridge and University of the Basque Country

and

Malcolm Sawyer
*Professor of Economics and Head of the Economics Department,
University of Leeds, UK*

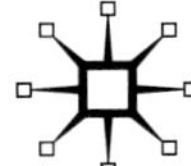

First published 2011 by
PALGRAVE MACMILLAN

Palgrave Macmillan in the UK is an imprint of Macmillan Publishers Limited,
registered in England, company number 785998, of Houndmills, Basingstoke,
Hampshire RG21 6XS.

Palgrave Macmillan in the US is a division of St Martin's Press LLC,
175 Fifth Avenue, New York, NY 10010.

Palgrave Macmillan is the global academic imprint of the above companies
and has companies and representatives throughout the world.

Palgrave® and Macmillan® are registered trademarks in the United States,
the United Kingdom, Europe and other countries.

ISBN 978–0–230–29877–4   hardback

This book is printed on paper suitable for recycling and made from fully
managed and sustained forest sources. Logging, pulping and manufacturing
processes are expected to conform to the environmental regulations of the
country of origin.

A catalogue record for this book is available from the British Library.

Library of Congress Cataloging-in-Publication Data
New economics as mainstream economics / [edited by] Philip Arestis,
Malcolm Sawyer.
  p. cm.
Includes index.
ISBN 978–0–230–29877–4 (hardback)
1. Neoliberalism.   2. Macroeconomics.   I. Arestis, Philip, 1941–
II. Sawyer, Malcolm C.
HB95.N46 2011
330.1—dc22   2011007013

10   9   8   7   6   5   4   3   2   1
20 19 18 17 16 15 14 13 12 11

Printed and bound in the United States of America

Contents

List of Tables

List of Figures

Notes on Contributors

Philip Arestis is Honorary Senior Departmental Fellow, Cambridge Centre for Economics and Public Policy, Department of Land Economy, University of Cambridge, UK; Professor of Economics, Department of Applied Economics V, University of the Basque Country, Spain; Distinguished Adjunct Professor of Economics, Department of Economics, University of Utah, USA; Senior Scholar, Levy Economics Institute, New York, USA; Visiting Professor, Leeds Business School, University of Leeds, UK; Professorial Research Associate, Department of Finance and Management Studies, School of Oriental and African Studies (SOAS), University of London, UK; and current holder of the British Hispanic Foundation 'Queen Victoria Eugenia' British Hispanic Chair of Doctoral Studies. He is Chief Academic Adviser to the UK Government Economic Service (GES) on Professional Developments in Economics. He has published as sole author or editor, as well as co-author and co-editor, a number of books, contributed in the form of invited chapters to numerous books, produced research reports for research institutes, and has published widely in academic journals.

Terry Barker is Director of the Cambridge Centre for Climate Change Mitigation Research (4CMR), Department of Land Economy, University of Cambridge. He is also Chairman of Cambridge Econometrics Ltd and Founder of the Cambridge Trust for New Thinking in Economics. He was a Co-ordinating Lead Author (CLA) for the Intergovernmental Panel on Climate Change's (IPCC) Third and Fourth Assessment Reports 2001 and 2007, taking responsibility for the chapters on greenhouse gas mitigation from a cross-sectoral perspective. He is an applied economist with over 100 articles and book chapters published mainly on the topics of economic modelling, international trade, and climate change mitigation. His research interests are in developing large-scale models of the energy–environment–economy (E3) system designed to address the issue of global decarbonisation and he has led teams developing models at the UK, European and global scales.

Gary A. Dymski is Professor of Economics at the University of California, Riverside. From 2003 to 2009, Gary was the founding Executive Director of the University of California Center, Sacramento. Gary's most recent books are *Capture and Exclude: Developing Nations and the Poor in Global*

Finance (2007), co-edited with Amiya Bagchi, and *Reimagining Growth: Toward a Renewal of the Idea of Development*, co-edited with Silvana DePaula (2005). Gary has published articles, chapters, and studies on banking, financial fragility, urban development, credit-market discrimination, the Latin American and Asian subprime financial crises, exploitation, housing finance, the subprime lending crisis, and economic policy.

Jesús Ferreiro is Associate Professor in Economics at the University of the Basque Country, in Bilbao, Spain, and an Associate Member of the Centre for Economic and Public Policy, University of Cambridge. His research interests are in the areas of macroeconomic policy, labour market and international financial flows. He has published a number of articles on those topics in edited books and in refereed journals such as *American Journal of Economics and Sociology*, *Economic and Industrial Democracy*, *Économie Appliquée*, *Ekonomia*, *European Planning Studies*, *International Journal of Political Economy*, *International Labour Review*, *International Review of Applied Economics*, *Journal of Post Keynesian Economics*, and *Transnational Corporations*.

Eckhard Hein is Professor of Economics at the Berlin School of Economics and Law. Previously he was a Senior Researcher at the Macroeconomic Policy Institute (IMK), Hans Boeckler Foundation, Duesseldorf, and a Visiting Professor at Carl von Ossietzky University Oldenburg, the University of Hamburg and at Vienna University of Economics and Business. He is a member of the coordination committee of the 'Research Network Macroeconomics and Macroeconomic Policies' (FMM) and a managing co-editor of *Intervention. European Journal of Economics and Economic Policies*. His research focuses on money, financial systems, distribution and growth, on European economic policies and on Post-Keynesian macroeconomics. He has published in *Cambridge Journal of Economics*, *European Journal of the History of Economic Thought*, *International Review of Applied Economics*, *Metroeconomica*, *Review of Political Economy*, and *Structural Change and Economic Dynamics*, among others. His latest monograph, *Money, Distribution Conflict and Capital Accumulation: Contributions to 'Monetary Analysis'*, was published by Palgrave Macmillan.

Malcolm Sawyer is Professor of Economics, Leeds University Business School, University of Leeds, UK. He was until recently Pro-Dean for Learning and Teaching for the Faculty of Business, University of Leeds, UK. He is managing editor of *International Review of Applied Economics*, on the editorial board of a range of journals and editor of the series

New Directions in Modern Economics. He has published widely in the areas of Post Keynesian and Kaleckian economics, industrial economics and the UK and European economies. He has authored 11 books and edited 18, has published over 70 papers in refereed journals and contributed chapters over 100 books.

Felipe Serrano is Professor in Economics at the University of the Basque Country, in Bilbao, Spain. He is the Head of the Department of Applied Economics V at the University of the Basque Country. His research interests are in the areas of social security, the welfare state, labour market, innovation and economic policy. He is the author of a number of articles on those topics in edited books and in refereed journals such as *Economies et Sociétés, Ekonomia, European Planning Studies, Industrial and Labor Relations Review, International Labour Review, International Review of Applied Economics*, and *Journal of Post Keynesian Economics*.

Irene van Staveren is Professor of Pluralist Development Economics at the Institute of Social Studies of Erasmus University Rotterdam. She is a feminist economist who engages in books and journal articles as well as teaching and policy advice with a variety of schools of economic thought from a gender perspective. She has published books on ethics and economics, including a recent *Handbook of Economics and Ethics* (2009) and *The Values of Economics – an Aristotelian Perspective* (2001). She has published widely in feminist economics, including an edited volume *The Feminist Economics of Trade*, the article 'Post-Keynesianism meets feminist Economics' in *Cambridge Journal of Economics* vol. 34 (2010) and an article on gender norms operating as institutions at different levels for women in Ethiopia in *World Development* (2010).

Achim Truger is Senior Researcher for Public Economics and Tax Policy at the Macroeconomic Policy Institute (IMK), Hans Boeckler Foundation, Duesseldorf, Germany. He is a member of the coordination committee of the 'Research Network Macroeconomics and Macroeconomic Policies' (FMM) and a managing co-editor of *Intervention. European Journal of Economics and Economic Policies*. He has taught Public Economics and Macroeconomics at the Universities of Cologne and Oldenburg, Germany. His research interests include macroeconomic policy, fiscal policy and tax reform. He is currently researching actively in the areas of economic forecasting and the German economic policy and tax reform debate. He has co-authored five books and co-edited more than 20. He has published a number of papers in refereed journals and more than 100 articles in economic policy oriented journals and books.

Preface

This is the seventh volume of the new series of *International Papers in Political Economy* (*IPPE*). The new series will consist of an annual volume with five to six papers on a single theme. The objective of the *IPPE* will continue to be the publication of papers dealing with important topics within the broad framework of Political Economy.

The original series of *International Papers in Political Economy* started in 1993 until the new series began in 2005 and was published in the form of three issues a year with each issue containing a single extensive paper. Information on the old series and back copies can be obtained from the editors: Philip Arestis (e-mail: pa267@cam.ac.uk) and Malcolm Sawyer (e-mail: mcs@lubs.leeds.ac.uk).

The theme of this seventh volume of six papers is New Economics as Mainstream Economics in terms of both theory and applications. The papers in this volume were initially presented at a two-day conference in Cambridge, UK, 28–9 January 2010. The conference was organised by the Department of Land Economy under the aegis of the Cambridge Trust for New Thinking in Economics; the latter fully supported and financed the conference. The papers were subsequently presented at the 7th International Conference, entitled 'Developments in Economic Theory and Policy', held at Universidad del Pais Vasco, Bilbao, Spain, 1–2 July 2010, which fully supported and funded the special session to which the papers included in this volume were presented. We are grateful to the organisers of the Bilbao conference and to the Cambridge Trust for all the help and funding provided.

1
Economic Theory and Policies: New Directions After Neoliberalism

Philip Arestis
University of Cambridge and University of the Basque Country

Malcolm Sawyer
University of Leeds

Abstract

This contribution attempts to go beyond the recent and current trends in terms of economic theory and policy. It is the case that the New Consensus Macroeconomics theoretical framework has dominated macroeconomic analysis in recent years and has in effect underpinned many macroeconomic policies. However, given the current experience with the 'great recession' crisis, the question arises whether there is not a better paradigm and set of economic policies that can lead the economy to an improved economic performance. This is precisely the focus of this contribution. Our response is very much that there is. In this contribution we propose another theoretical framework before moving to economic policy questions. The general background to the theoretical framework is that the analysis is of a monetary production economy in which finance and credit play a significant role. It relates to an economy, which has degrees of instability, and there is often inadequacy of aggregate demand. The level and distribution of productive capacity can often be inadequate for underpinning the full employment of labour.

Keywords: Economic theory, economic policy, new directions, after neoliberalism

JEL Classifications: E12, E60, E61

1 Introduction

Economic policies arise out of and can only be understood by reference to the theoretical framework that underpins the analysis undertaken and the ways in which the economy operates and works in the real world (Arestis and Sawyer 2010a, 2010c; see, also, Arestis, 2010). The links between the mainstream policies of the past two decades (in the areas of macroeconomics, inflation targeting by an 'independent' Central Bank and fiscal consolidation with labour market 'flexibility' and financial liberalisation) and the 'New Consensus in Macroeconomics' (NCM for short; see, for example, Arestis, 2007, 2009b; Arestis and Sawyer, 2008) are one confirmation of that. But the financial crisis and the 'great recession' have thrown the NCM and the associated policies into disarray, and we would suggest that important and significant changes are paramount. This is precisely the focus of this contribution. Given the experience with the 'great recession' crisis, the question arises whether there is not a better paradigm and set of economic policies that can lead the economy to a better economic performance. Our response is very much that there is. In this contribution we propose to discuss further our theoretical framework before moving on to economic policy questions. In terms of the latter we argue that an important policy dimension, which has been ignored in the past is financial stability.

Our purpose here is to set out an alternative macroeconomic framework and draw out a range of macroeconomic policy implications. The general background to the theoretical framework is that the analysis is of a monetary production economy in which finance and credit plays a significant role. It relates to an economy which has degrees of instability in the sense of being subject to the ups and downs of the business cycle and prone to crisis. There is often an inadequacy of aggregate demand (relative to what would be required for full employment of labour). The level and distribution of productive capacity can often be inadequate for underpinning the full employment of labour.

We begin our discussion with the essential elements of the theoretical framework that underpins relevant economic policy proposals, before we turn our attention to the economic policies themselves. So after this short introduction we turn our attention in Section 2 to the theoretical background of what might replace economic theory after neoliberalism. We discuss in Section 3 the economic policies that follow from this theoretical framework. In the final part of this contribution, Section 4, we summarise and conclude.

2 Theoretical background[1]

The theoretical framework, which underpins the analysis of this contribution, draws on a number of ingredients and we turn our attention to them in what follows in the next subsection.

2.1 Main theoretical elements

The general background to the theoretical framework outlined here is the emphasis on an economy of a monetary production type in which finance and credit play a crucial role, and the analysis of macro-economies cannot be reduced to studies of economies without money and finance. It relates to an economy which has degrees of instability in the sense of being subject to the ups and downs of the business cycle and prone to crisis.[2] The theoretical framework which underpins this analysis draws on five main elements. This model is constructed by putting together five building blocks which form a coherent whole; we outline and discuss these five building blocks below. The focus of all five blocks is on four propositions: (i) aggregate demand is always important for the level of economic activity though the supply potential of the economy has to be fully incorporated; (ii) distributional effects matter; (iii) money is endogenous, credit driven; and (iv) (appropriate) government deficits do not present financial risks. We discuss the five blocks to begin with, followed, in Section 3, by a discussion of the economic policy implications of the model that emerge.

The theoretical framework, put forward in this contribution, draws on the following main elements. In terms of the demand side of the economy, which relates to expenditure, income and employment, the focus is on the level of economic activity, which is set by aggregate demand. There is no existing market-based mechanism to propel the level of aggregate demand to any specific level of output. Investment has a dual characteristic in this model: it is a relatively volatile component of aggregate demand, and it is also a promoter of future productive potential. This establishes interdependence of the demand side and the supply side, which is closely related to ideas on path dependency (see, Arestis and Sawyer, 2009). The foreign sector is viewed as another relevant and significant constituent element of the model. A relevant aspect of this importance is that imports and exports are included in the aggregate demand equation, reflecting the effects on demand (and hence employment) of variations in the exchange rate.

The supply side is reflected in a range of ways. The level of economic activity (as set by the level of demand) relative to the supply potential of the economy impacts on investment and pricing decisions. The supply potential depends on the size and structure of the capital and the labour force, and that supply potential evolves over time as investment occurs. The relationship between wages and prices, and the inflationary forces in the economy depend on the nature of what may be termed the supply side of the economy and how that supply side interacts with demand.

In an inflationary process inflation is viewed as multi-causal and the sources of inflationary pressure vary over time and economy. The range of factors, which impact on the rate of inflation, includes: struggle over income shares; the level and rate of change of the level of aggregate demand and cost-push factors emanating notably from the foreign sector (change in import prices and the exchange rate).

The money, credit and finance sector is also an important element to this way of thinking about the macroeconomy. Money is endogenously created within the private sector with loans provided by banks themselves generating bank deposits. The central bank sets the key policy interest rate, which governs the terms upon which the central bank provides the 'base' money to the banking system.

Cycles and fluctuations in economic activity occur frequently and full employment is at best a rather infrequent occurrence. Changes in economic activity impact the rate of change of prices and wages, and consequent changes in the distribution of income between wages and profits. Changes in the distribution of income have effects on the level of aggregate demand, with the nature of the effects depending on whether there is a wage-led or a profit-led regime. These interactions contribute to the generation of cycles.

The constituent elements of the model we put forward are discussed below, along with the functional relationships implied by the description provided. The model is divided into five blocks for convenience of exposition. With these general principles as the necessary background we turn our attention in Section 2.2 to discuss and develop more extensively the macroeconomic model that underpins the general principles just put forward.

2.2   Main ingredients of the model

The main ingredients of such a model are discussed below, along with the relationships implied by the description provided. The model is divided into five blocks as follows.

2.2.1   *Block I: aggregate demand and aggregate supply*

This block is based on the idea that the level of economic activity, as proxied by the level of national income, is set by the level of aggregate demand, which is the sum of intended consumer demand, investment demand and government expenditure plus net exports, as in equation (1):

$$Y = C + I + G + (X - Q) \tag{1}$$

where Y is national income, C is consumption, I is investment, G is government expenditure, X is exports and Q is imports, and thus (X − Q) is net exports (NE). Aggregate demand is important in both the short run and in the long run for the level of economic activity and for the evolution of the economy. There is no mechanism whereby market forces would propel the level of aggregate demand to any supply-side determined equilibrium. Investment expenditure in this model has a dual role. It is a relatively volatile component of aggregate demand; and it is also a creator of productive potential (see, for example, Arestis et al., 1985–6).

We examine the components of aggregate demand next, beginning with consumption as in (2):

$$C = C[(W \cdot E(1-tw), \Pi(1-t\pi), B, R, \Delta BLP_h] \tag{2}$$

where W is wage rate, E employment so WE is the wage bill, tw is the tax rate on wages, Π is total profits, $t\pi$ is the tax rate on profits, B is social security benefits and other transfer payments, R is the rate of interest on loans, and ΔBLP_h is changes in bank lending to households. The availability of credit to households influences consumer expenditure since expenditure has to be financed and households are credit constrained. With the equations presented, the independent variables are presumed to have a positive effect on the dependent variable unless otherwise stated. In the case of equation (2), R has a negative effect.

Investment expenditure is taken to be:

$$I = I(\Pi/K, Y/Ya, R, \Delta BLP_f) \tag{3}$$

where the symbols are as above with the addition of K, which is capital stock, ΔBLP_f is changes in bank lending to firms and Ya, which is a measure of desired capacity output (discussed below). For simplicity the rate of interest on loans to households and to firms are taken as closely related such that the use of a single rate of interest on loans in equations (2) and (3) is justified. In equation (3), R is anticipated to have a negative effect on investment.

Government expenditure is treated as a policy variable, and in the formulation of the model treated here as exogenous.

Net exports in demand terms are taken to be

$$NE = X(WT, RER) - Q(Y, \Pi, RER) \tag{4}$$

where WT is world trade, RER is real exchange rate, and the rest of the symbols are as above with all these variables in real terms, with RER having a negative effect on exports and a positive effect on imports.

The allowance made for the cost and availability of finance should be noted. It has generally been assumed that banks would supply loans to creditworthy firms and individuals, but ideas of credit rationing, application of the 'principle of increasing risk' (Kalecki, 1937), and the recent 'credit crunch' experience, indicate that some allowance should be made for the availability of finance and the degree of credit rationing. The cost of finance is also important and is reflected in the interest rate term. The rate of interest on loans is linked with the key interest rate set by the Central Bank as in equation (15) below.

On the supply side of the economy, the potential level of output at the level of the firm depends on, in a production function manner, the inputs of labour, capital and so on which can be deployed by the firm and the state of technology. At the aggregate level, it is assumed that there is a comparable relationship, but it must be recognized that there are severe issues of aggregation and that the structure of the capital stock will also influence the supply potential. This aggregate supply output Ys which could be produced depends on employment of labour, capital stock and state of technology: in conventional form this can be written as: Ys = Ys(E,K,T), where E is employment (in person hours), K some measure of capital stock, and T is state of technology. Actual output produced is taken to be demand-determined, and the production equation can be inverted to give employment for a given level of (demand determined) output as in equation (5):

$$E = E(Y, K, T) \tag{5}$$

In this formulation, the capital stock and technology have a negative effect on employment for a given level of demand. It is useful to define a benchmark level of output from a supply perspective, and Ya, which is a capacity measure corresponding to the 'desired' level of operation is used, and Ya = Ya(K, T), and would change over time as capital stock and technology change. There is a level of employment corresponding to Ya which would be Ea = E(Ya, K, T). Ya is taken as a benchmark for firms' investment decisions; and as indicated above: when Y > Ya firms feel themselves to be working at over-capacity and encouraged to invest, when Y < Ya they are thereby discouraged from investment. For a given level of K and T, it is envisaged that the relationship between productivity Y/E and E is such that Y/E initially rises as E rises, then flattens out, and eventually declines.

In the model presented above there is no market mechanism which can be taken to ensure that the level of demand is consistent with any specified level of output such as the one which corresponds to the full employment of labour or to the non-accelerating inflation rate of unemployment (NAIRU). By contrast, we follow the tradition that suggests that aggregate demand and aggregate supply are not necessarily moved towards each other in the long run by the market mechanism. Indeed, and as Hein and Stockhammer (2007) indicate, how aggregate demand evolves over time depends on the parameters involved. The latter are influenced by a number of factors, such as: wage and price changes, along with the consequent changes in the distribution of income between wages and profits. In addition, the differential effects of wages and profits on the level of demand, and whether that is a movement towards or away from any supply-side equilibrium, are all-important determinants of the parameters involved. As noted above, aggregate supply also evolves over time and depends on the parameters as shown in equation (5), and discussed therein, in a way that is completely independent of those of aggregate demand.

In this analysis distributional aspects are thereby relevant and important. We turn to this aspect next.

2.2.2 Block II: distributional aspects and the inflationary process

The interaction of price and wage determinants produces the distributional aspects of the theoretical framework put forward in this contribution (Arestis, 1986). Four observations are important: (i) the interaction of prices and wages does not take place in the arena which is labelled the 'labour' market, and specifically the real wage cannot be taken as determined by an equilibrium between the demand for and the supply of labour; (ii) the emphasis is on the role of the productive capacity in the price-setting mechanism; (iii) any supply-side equilibrium does not act as an attractor to the actual level of economic activity; and (iv) the pricing of the supply of output is influenced by the prices of the factors of production and the level of demand, and the costs of production will vary with the level of output, and by the rate of change of demand.

Wages are determined in a variety of ways, and there are numerous theories on the determination of wages. For macroeconomic analysis we seek a relatively simple representation, which summarises the main factors involved in the determination of wages. However, in terms of the algebraic representation of an underlying relationship between real wages and employment, many of the approaches that are compatible with ours lead to similar outcomes – for example, trade union bargaining models, efficiency wage models (for more details see Sawyer, 2002, and Layard, Nickell and Jackman, 1991, especially chapters 8 and 9). The key elements of this approach are that real wages and employment are positively related and that money wages adjust to the experience of inflation as well as containing elements of seeking to adjust the real wage.

$$W/P = f(E/E^*) \cdot Q \tag{6}$$

where P is the price level, Q labour productivity, E^* is the size of labour force.

The wage inflationary process then draws on elements of responses to price inflation, adjustment of real wage to the underlying relationship, so that equation (7) is obtained:

$$w = w((f(E/E^*) \cdot Q - W/P), p) \tag{7}$$

where w is proportionate rate of change of W, and similarly p is proportionate rate of change of P.

There are numerous ways in which firms approach pricing decisions. But most theories of pricing decisions can be represented in terms of price as a mark-up over some forms of average or marginal costs. The mark-up itself and the average or marginal costs vary with the level of output. Here we represent the pricing decisions in terms of price relative to money wage and varying with the level of output.

The pricing decisions of firms aggregated provide a relationship such as:

$$P/W = g(Q, PM/ER \cdot W) \tag{8}$$

where Q as labour productivity is equal to $Y^s(E, K, T)/E$. Labour productivity can be seen to rise initially with the level of employment, but then to decline at some stage. Thus the relationship between the level of employment and P/W in this equation may well be one of an initial negative slope, a portion where is it close to horizontal and then a rapidly rising section. PM is the price of imported materials on the world market (in dollars), ER is the nominal exchange rate and hence PM/ER the price of imported materials in domestic currency terms.

Equation (9) for price inflation is taken to be:

$$p = p[(g(Q, PM/ER \cdot W) - P/W, pm, er)] \tag{9}$$

where er is the rate of change of the nominal exchange rate, and pm the rate of change of material/commodity prices on the world market, and hence here the sign of er is negative in this equation.

Equations (6) and (8) can be brought together, along with the relationship between employment and output given above. From (6) and (8), $f(E/E^*) \cdot Q \cdot g(Q, PM/W) = 1$, and this can in principle be solved (with a clear possibility of multiple solutions) for the employment rate in terms of the other variables involved since Q is as given above. Let us write this as $E^\wedge/E^* = h(K,T)/E^*$. The employment rate $E^\wedge/E^*$ is a form of NAIRU/supply-side equilibrium in that it is an employment rate at which wage and profit claims are mutually compatible, and would (provided that the coefficients on price change terms in (7) and in (9) sum to unity) correspond with constant inflation. Let us call this employment rate a (conditional) CIER (constant inflation employment rate); from the production relationship there is a corresponding level of output. Let us write this as $Y^\wedge = Y(E^\wedge, K, T)$, and in particular focus on $Y^\wedge/Ya$ that is output normalised by the 'desired' level of output, the constant inflation output ratio (CIOR).

There are a number of significant aspects of this approach. First, the CIER and the CIOR are akin to an inflation barrier in that if the economy were operating at the CIER CIOR, provided that the wage: price ratio was at a corresponding level (that is, for example, the real wage is that given by $W/P = f(E^\wedge/E^*).Q$, the price inflation would be constant.

Second, there is no presumption that the economy will actually operate at the CIER, CIOR: it is rather that the CIER and CIOR are where wage and profits claims would be compatible. When the economy is not operating at the CIER, CIOR (that is, virtually all of the time), the model above would provide indications what would be developing with wage and price inflation. It is further the case that there is no presumption that there are market forces which guide the economy in the direction of the CIER CIOR.

Third, the CIER, CIOR depend on the size of the capital stock, and would evolve over time as the capital stock changes. The capital stock changes as investment occurs, and in that way the CIOR would be continuously changing – though the changes may be rather small and difficult to detect. But when there are significant changes in capital formation, as, for example, during a recession, there would be substantial changes in the CIOR.

Fourth, the CIER depends on the size of the labour force E^*, and that changes over time not only through demographic factors but also through 'push and pull' factors which draw people into the workforce and which 'expel' people.

Finally, the CIER, CIOR depend on the wage claims and the profit claims made, reflected in the f and g functions above. Over time, as the strength of labour and the market power of firms change so will those claims and hence the CIER, CIOR.

To complete this block, the rate of change of the prices of raw materials is determined as in equation (10).

$$p_{rm} = p_{rm}(er, WT) \tag{10}$$

Equation (10) endogenises the rate of change of the prices of raw materials, making it a function of the rate of change of the nominal exchange rate (er) and world trade (WT).

2.2.3   Block III: money and credit

Money is endogenously created within the private sector with loans created by banks generating bank deposits. The willingness or otherwise of banks to provide loans and the terms upon which they are provided impact on the level and structure of demand. Consequently, since money comes into existence via the credit process, the ways in which credit is created impacts on investment, and thereby the productive potential of the economy. Money is thereby created through the credit system, where the manner in which loans are provided by the banking system becomes central to the analysis: banks provide credit 'off their own bat'. Commercial banks decide upon the amount of loans they are ready to grant funding, within regulatory requirements, and worry later about their liquidity position. The central bank, as 'lender of last resort', is generally obligated to provide required reserves, albeit at a penalty in the form of a higher bank rate (BR). It is clear, then, that the willingness or otherwise of commercial banks to provide loans and the terms upon which they are provided impact on the level and structure of aggregate demand. Money is, then, created as a by-product of the loans provided by the banking system. Consequently, since money comes into existence via the credit process, the way in which credit is created impacts on investment, and thereby the productive potential of the economy. Credit money is a requirement of the economic system; it is not a parasite on the system and it is certainly not a veil. The central bank sets the key policy interest rate, which governs the terms upon which it provides the 'base' money to the banking system. Money is an output of the system with its endogenous behaviour governed by a number of factors. The latter include the borrowing needs of firms, households and the government and the portfolio behaviour of financial institutions and of the personal sector (see, also, Arestis, 1987–8).

The expansion of the stock of money is driven by the demand for loans, which leads to the expansion of bank deposits in so far as the demand for loans is met by the banking sector. Changes in the money supply can then come about through changes in bank deposits to the government and to the public. We can, thus, have in equation (11):

$$\Delta M = \Delta BDGC + \Delta BDP \tag{11}$$

Equation (11) defines changes in the money supply (ΔM) as the sum of changes in bank deposits to the government including currency ($\Delta BDGC$) and changes in bank deposits held by the public (ΔBDP). We endogenise ΔBDP as in equation (12):

$$\Delta BDP = \Delta BDP(\Delta Y, \Delta R) \tag{12}$$

We postulate in equation (12) that the behaviour of ΔBDP depends on changes in the level of income (ΔY), reflecting the flow of funds into the banking sector as a result of changes in the level of economic activity. It also depends on changes in the market rate of interest (ΔR), where the determination of R is as in equation (15) below. The market rate of interest is hypothesised to account for possible portfolio effects: it proxies the relative attractiveness of alternative financial assets available to depositors as the market rate of interest changes.

The other variable in equation (11) is $\Delta BDGC$. This is a small fraction of the total money supply and we treat it as the residual in the identity described in (13).

$$\Delta BDGC = \Delta BLP + \Delta BLG + \Delta BLES - \Delta BDP \tag{13}$$

Equation (13) defines $\Delta BDGC$ as the sum of changes in bank lending to the public (ΔBLP) and to the government (ΔBLG) as well as of changes in bank lending to the external sector including other non-bank lending ($\Delta BLES$), minus ΔBDP. $\Delta BLES$ is treated as an exogenous variable and with ΔBLG endogenised in Block IV, the rest of the variables of equation (13) are endogenised as explained immediately below. We begin with ΔBLP as in equation (14).

$$\Delta BLP = \Delta BLP(\Delta Y, \Delta R, \Delta CR_R) \tag{14}$$

where $BLP = BLP_h + BLP_f$, and ΔBLP, which aggregates the bank lending needs to industry, consumers and other (non-commercial bank) financial institutions, is hypothesised to depend on changes in the level of income (ΔY) reflecting requirements for funding as the level of economic activity changes. It also depends negatively on the cost of borrowing captured by changes in the rate of interest (ΔR), a variable that is thought particularly important in the case of consumers relative to industry. And it depends negatively on the variable ΔCR_R which stands for policy variables which can affect credit directly. The best example for this variable is credit rationing by the authorities. This possibility can occur when the demand for bank lending exceeds the available supply or the case when commercial banks refuse to lend to more-risky customers who are judged as imprudent in terms of their borrowing behaviour. Still, bank lending to the public is essentially demand-determined, with the monetary authorities having little influence over the level.

Next we consider the determination of the market interest rate. We treat the bank rate (BR) as set by the monetary authorities; it is, therefore, treated as a policy variable determined by the decisions of the central bank. Changes of BR directly influence changes in the market interest rate on loans (ΔR) via a mark-up. We may, thus, express ΔR as in equation (15), where in addition to the bank rate we have two more variables.

$$\Delta R = \Delta R(\Delta BR, \Delta PDC, \Delta EF) \tag{15}$$

The two further variables are: ΔPDC, which stands for sales of public debt to the non-bank public including currency; this is included to capture the influence of open market operations on market interest rates; and ΔEF to account for changes in external flows that can have an impact on market interest rates (ΔR).

2.2.4   *Block IV: government sector*

We begin this block by looking at the bank lending to the government (ΔBLG) variable from equation (13), which is portrayed in equation (16) as follows.

$$\Delta BLG = PSBR + \Delta EF - \Delta NBC \tag{16}$$

It is clear from equation (16) that the banking sector provides the residual, namely the difference between the sum of the public sector borrowing requirement (PSBR) and overseas finance (ΔEF, which stands for changes in external financing, and domestic finance (ΔNBC, which stands for sales of public debt to non-bank public including currency). ΔBLG is thus determined through the government budget identity. This reflects institutional arrangements, such as in the UK, where normally that part of the government's borrowing requirement which is not financed by the sale of debt outside the banking system is met by the sale of debt – in particular, Treasury bills – to the banking system. The latter acts, thereby, as the residual source of borrowing for the government. We treat ΔEF and ΔNBC as exogenous and discuss PSBR next.

The PSBR in equation (17) is simply defined as the difference between government expenditure (G) and tax revenues (T):

$$PSBR = G - T - OGR \tag{17}$$

We hypothesise G and T to be determined as shown below in equations (18) and (19) respectively. Equation (17) is an important ingredient of Block IV, which integrates the banking system with the government sector. The existence of a banking system implies that money is provided to the private sector through credit creation. The government supplies currency to the private sector by 'financing' government expenditure.

The commercial banks have interest-free reserves with the central bank, which come from government spending or lending. Of course, the central bank sets the terms of advancing the credit. One of the terms is the bank rate (BR); another is that the central bank demands collateral for the credit in the form of actual securities; still another possibility in this context is for the central bank to vary the required interest-free reserves, which they must supply.

Government expenditure is treated in this approach as a decision variable of government and within this model as exogenous. We do not attempt to endogenise government expenditure. Government expenditure G is expanded as:

$$G = Gc + Gi + B \tag{18}$$

Where G is government expenditure in real terms, Gc government consumption expenditure, Gi public investment and B social security benefits. The scale of public investment and some components of government consumption expenditure (notably education and health) would impact on the productive potential of the economy, and in a complete model the feedback of public investment onto supply potential should be incorporated. The level of social security benefits (expressed in real terms) would depend on the benefit levels as set by government, but would also vary with the level of economic activity (notably unemployment benefits).

The tax rates are treated as policy decision variables, and the tax revenue treated as endogenous in the following manner:

$$T = twW + tpP \tag{19}$$

(in a more extended model, allowance could be made also for rentier income; it is implicitly assumed that a tax rate such as tw reflects direct and indirect taxation which could be deemed to fall on wages). Equation (19), therefore, represents tax policy, in terms of tax rates, and also could be used for distribution of income purposes.

2.2.5 Block V: open economy aspects

This block comprises the rest of the relationships hypothesised in this model and is essentially concerned with the foreign sector in an open economy. We begin with the variable ΔEF, that is changes in external financing as in (20), which provides essentially the main ingredients to Block V.

$$\Delta EF = CB + \Delta KM - OEF \tag{20}$$

where ΔEF is equal to the current balance of international payments (CB) plus capital movements (ΔKM) minus other external financing (OEF) – this variable includes external lending to the public sector plus domestic bank lending to the public sector in foreign currencies. We treat OEF as exogenous and endogenise CB and ΔKM. We begin with CB based on the trade balance equation (3)

$$CB = X(WT, RER) - Q(Y, RER) + NI \tag{21}$$

where the signs involved have been discussed above.

Next, we endogenise ΔKM as:

$$\Delta KM = \Delta KM[(R/R_W), er] \tag{22}$$

The ratio of domestic interest rates (R) to world interest rates (R_W) is included on the assumption that capital flows are sensitive to the returns available internationally. These returns, however, are not captured simply by interest rates but, perhaps more importantly, by expected exchange rate movements, hence the inclusion of changes in the nominal exchange rate variable (er). There are many other factors influencing capital flows which should be borne in mind. The capital flows linked with foreign direct investment would depend on those factors influencing FDI both inward and outward. These capital flows, and especially those linked with portfolio investment, are subject to rapid changes as 'confidence' and 'sentiment' of the financial markets change.

Under a floating exchange rate system, the exchange rate would be determined from CB + KM = 0; in other exchange rate systems modifications would need to be made to reflect government interventions, whether seeking to maintain a fixed exchange rate or to influence its evolution. From that equality condition, the exchange rate can be solved to give the real exchange rate:

$$RER = RER[(R/R_W), Y, WT, NI, er] \tag{23}$$

where the variables, with the exception of domestic income Y, having a positive impact on the exchange rate. However, note the role of changes in the exchange rate which would bring some cyclical behaviour into the exchange rate, and that factors such as 'confidence' have relevance.

It should, however, be noted that the effects of exchange rate variations on prices will depend on the extent of pass through. The pass-through effect of a change in the exchange rate first on import prices and subsequently on the generality of prices, both goods and services, has weakened since the late 1980s (see. for example, Angeriz and Arestis, 2007a). Consequently, the stronger real exchange rate has had less offsetting effect on domestic prices than in earlier periods. The argument normally used to justify appreciation in the exchange rate that such a move slows inflation is no longer valid under such circumstances. The impact of interest rate changes may have become more ambiguous. Evidence seems to show that capital movements are based more on equities than on other assets (Angeriz and Arestis, 2007a, for example). A change in interest rates then may have the opposite effect on capital movements than otherwise. A further argument is that the capital flows can be subjected to sudden change, and that those flows may depend on, inter alia, on changes in the exchange rate. It is for these reasons that this approach to the exchange rate does not reflect the observed volatility of the exchange rate. But no other modelling of the exchange rate has been successful in accurately capturing movements in the exchange rate. It is for this very reason that ultimately we would suggest that a secondary instrument in the form of direct intervention may very well be necessary.

3 Economic policy implications

It is our firm starting point for the discussion of macroeconomic policies that the overall focus of macroeconomic policies should be on sustainable and equitable economic development and growth. A specific part of that general focus is the objective of the achievement of full employment of the labour force. Achieving such an objective requires the maintenance of both a high level of aggregate demand and the provision of sufficient productive capacity. The development and analysis of macroeconomic policies arise from interactions between those macroeconomic objectives and the theoretical framework outlined above.

3.1 Objectives of economic policy

There are a number of policy implications that follow from our discussion in Section 2. We begin by briefly commenting on the objectives of economic policy. The objectives of economic policy should be: (i) full employment of the available labour supply, and thus sustainable growth; (ii) a constant rate of inflation consistent with output growth rather than the target rate of inflation; and this in view of the evidence that inflation and output move together up to around 10–15 per cent inflation rate, as discussed below; and (iii) financial stability.

The instruments of economic policy may be briefly summarised:

(i)   Fiscal policy is crucial. We consider the operation of fiscal policy in terms of movements in the fiscal stance in the short run and also in respect of the long-run setting. In the short term, variations in the fiscal stance can be used in conjunction with automatic stabilisers to offset fluctuations in economic activity arising from, inter alia, variations in private sector aggregate demand. In the longer term, the general fiscal stance should be set to underpin the desired level of output and employment;

(ii) Interest rate policy should be set so that the real rate of interest is as low as possible in line with the trend rate of growth. In this sense, a real rate of interest in line with the perceived trend rate of growth could be targeted so that the nominal rate is set by the central bank equal to the target rate plus the expected rate of inflation. Further, the operations of the central bank should ultimately be directed towards financial stability and this objective of financial stability should be placed as the most significant one for the Central Bank, requiring the development of alternative policy instruments alongside the downgrading of interest rate policy and of any notion of inflation targeting;

(iii)   Exchange rate policy is also important. Changes in the exchange rate affect the domestic economy: primarily in terms of the level of demand and hence economic activity and, rather weakly, in terms of inflation. Intervention by the central bank in the foreign exchange market with the specific aim to stabilise the exchange rate may be important in this respect as argued above, where we suggested control and direct manipulation of the exchange rate by the central bank. In what follows we elaborate in these economic policies.

In view of the importance given to inflation and to the objective of price stability over the recent past, it is important to offer a few comments on the matter. Inflation is a non-monetary phenomenon with a complex of causes, including conflicts over the distribution of income. We take the view that it need not be the focus of economic policy in view of the fact that the causes of inflation vary and also that inflation is not always harmful to growth. In more general terms, the empirical evidence on this issue is actually not very supportive of inflation targeting and the surrounding theoretical model. Roger Ferguson, then Vice Chairman of the Board of Governors of the Federal Reserve System, argues that

> Unfortunately, the empirical evidence for industrial countries available to date generally appears insufficient to assess the success of the inflation-targeting approach with confidence. For example, it is unclear whether the announcement of quantitative inflation targets lessens the short-run trade-off between employment and inflation and whether it helps anchor inflation expectations. In addition, some research, controlling for other factors, fails to isolate the benefits of an inflation target with respect to the level of inflation or its volatility over time, and output does not seem to fluctuate more stably around its potential for countries that have adopted numerical targets. (Ferguson, 2005, p. 297)[3]

The control of inflation should be regarded as a side issue unless inflation is exhibiting tendencies to continue to rise and to exceed something of the order of 10 per cent (on the basis that inflation above 10 per cent begins to distort decision-making and that the evidence on the relationship between inflation and growth does not indicate detrimental effects of inflation on growth at rates less than (say) 10 per cent). This is reinforced by the evidence on the relationship between inflation and output, which suggests that it is not necessarily negative for at least single figures (Ferguson, 2005 summarises the argument; see, also, Ghosh and Phillips, 1998; Fischer, 1993; Bruno and Easterly, 1996; Levine and Renelt, 1992; Khan and Senhadji, 2001). There is, thus, no need to develop policies to tackle inflation unless it reaches high levels. Such an approach involves the development of an incomes policy to contain inflation when it reaches unacceptably high rates.

The instruments of economic policy summarised above to achieve the objectives, also alluded to above, are discussed in what follows beginning with fiscal policy.

3.2 Fiscal policy

Since the forces ensuring that the level of aggregate demand is in line with the productive potential (or full employment) are, at best, weak, there is a requirement for aggregate demand policies. Fiscal policy is a much more potent instrument than interest rate policy for setting the level of demand (Arestis and Sawyer, 2003, 2010b; Angeriz and Arestis, 2009). The operation of fiscal policy is considered in both a long-term setting and in terms of movements in the fiscal stance in the short term. In the short term, variations in the fiscal stance can be used to offset fluctuations in economic activity arising from, inter alia, variations in private sector aggregate demand. At the extreme this leads to the fine-tuning of fiscal policy. In the longer term, the general fiscal stance can be set to support the level of aggregate demand consistent with a high level of economic activity.

For the long term we adopt the approach of Lerner (1943) and Kalecki (1944) and aim to achieve a budget position to achieve a high target level of economic activity (labelled here Y_f). This is represented as a budget deficit in equation (24):

$$G - T = S(Y_f) - I(Y_f) + Q(Y_f) - X(Y_w) \tag{24}$$

where the variables are as above, with the exception of Y_f which stands for the target level of income.

A budget deficit would not be required when there is a high level of private aggregate demand such that investment equals savings at a high level of economic activity (and a surplus would be required when investment exceeds savings at the desired level of economic activity). The budget deficit required to achieve Y_f can be clearly seen to depend on the propensities to save, invest, import and the ability to export, and these over country and across time. The underlying budget position should then be set in accordance with the perceived underlying values of the propensities to save, invest, import and export (see Sawyer, 2009a, 2009b). This approach to fiscal policy can be said to incorporate a clear rule: set the underlying budget deficit compatible with the desired level of output. But it is clear that the estimation of the relevant budget stance would involve substantial difficulties and disputes. Although whether the latter difficulties are any greater than the estimation of key variables in the current orthodoxy such as the 'equilibrium rate of interest' and the 'non-accelerating inflation rate of unemployment' is an interesting question.

We maintain, therefore, that fiscal policy is paramount in both the short run and in the long run (see, also, Arestis, 2009a; Arestis and Sawyer, 2006, 2010b). We consider the operation of fiscal policy in terms of movements in the fiscal stance in the short run and also in respect of the long-run setting. In the short term, variations in the fiscal stance can be used in conjunction with automatic stabilisers to offset fluctuations in economic activity arising from, inter alia, variations in private sector aggregate demand. In the long run, the general fiscal stance should be set to underpin the desired level of output and employment. This approach raises the issue of sustainability of the deficit (see Arestis and Sawyer, 2006, 2009), which we view as not a significant issue for two basic reasons. First, in this approach, and in the model above, governments borrow because the private sector wishes to lend; if there were no potential excess of savings over investment, then there would be no need for a budget deficit. Savings (over and above investment) can only be realised if there is a budget deficit or overseas lending, which absorbs those savings. Second, a total budget deficit of d (relative to GDP) is always sustainable in the sense that the corresponding debt to GDP ratio (b) stabilises at: b = d/g with g as the growth rate. The budget deficit, which is relevant for the level of demand, is the overall budget position rather than the primary deficit (or surplus). To the extent that a budget deficit is required to offset an excess of private savings over investment, then it is the overall budget deficit which is relevant. Bond interest payments are a transfer payment and add to the income of the recipient, which is similar in that respect to other transfer payments (though the propensity to consume out of interest payments is likely to be less than that out of many other transfer payments). In terms of sustainability, then, of a fiscal deficit the condition is generally readily satisfied; this being the requirement of a positive nominal growth rate. Consequently, we may summarise the argument by suggesting that a budget deficit (including interest payments), which bears a constant relationship to GDP, is sustainable. In fact, it leads to a debt/GDP ratio equal to the deficit/GDP ratio divided by the growth of nominal GDP.

Since the forces ensuring that the level of aggregate demand is in line with the productive potential (or full employment) are, at best, weak, there is a requirement for aggregate demand policies. Fiscal policy is a much more potent instrument than interest rate policy for setting the level of demand (see, also, Arestis and Sawyer, 2003). The operation of fiscal policy is considered both in terms of movements in the fiscal stance in the short term and also in a long-term setting. In the short term, variations in the fiscal stance can be used to offset fluctuations in economic activity arising from, inter alia, variations in private sector aggregate demand. At the extreme this leads to the fine-tuning of fiscal policy. In the longer term, the general fiscal stance can be set to support the level of aggregate demand consistent with high level of economic activity.

A few words on fine-tuning are necessary at this stage. The ultimate in fine-tuning would arise when the budget stance was changed continuously in response to variations in economic activity. This would be comparable to the fine-tuning that is currently attempted through interest rate changes, with decisions on interest rates being made on a frequent (e.g. monthly) basis, even if the decision is one of no change. The problems of fine-tuning are well known in terms of the various lags involved, including those of recognition, decision making, implementation and effect. However, the automatic stabilisers of fiscal policy already perform part of that task in the sense that a downturn is met by reduced tax and increased expenditure, which modify – but do not eliminate – the degree of fluctuations in economic activity. The tax and expenditure regime could be designed in such a manner as to increase the extent of stabilisation and a more progressive tax system would enhance the stabilisation properties. But that should be argued for on grounds of equity and income distribution, albeit that there would be the additional benefits for stabilisation.

Automatic stabilisers of the traditional form (that is, tax revenues varying through movements in the level of output) are rather useful in this regard and depend on the progressivity of the tax system (and expenditure) and the scale of government. There is a good case for the enhancement of these automatic stabilisers.[4] Although the question remains as to whether a more progressive system, increased scale of government activities or through changes in tax rates triggered by prespecified changes in the level of economic activity should be the ultimate aim (Baunsgaard and Symansky, 2009).

There are other ways in which government policy may be able to influence the level of demand. Interest rate policy is one of those, but we would argue that such a policy is not an effective one as compared with fiscal policy (Arestis and Sawyer, 2003). Kalecki (1944) addressed the issue of an insufficiency of aggregate demand through 'Three Ways to Full Employment'. The three ways were the use of budget deficits, stimulating consumer expenditure (and hence reducing overall propensity to save) through the redistribution of income and stimulation of investment. These are alternative policy responses to the inadequacy of aggregate demand. This approach is based clearly on the notion that there are no strong (or even weak) market forces, which would push the level of aggregate demand to a level consistent with full employment (or any other desirable level of employment or output). There is a fourth way (which Kalecki, 1944, did not actually explore), namely the promotion of net exports through, for example, exchange rate policies or in the longer-term industrial and regional policies designed to increase international competitiveness. But, of course, promotion of net exports has elements of a 'beggar my neighbour' policy, and is not a policy, which the majority of countries can successfully pursue.

The effects of a shift in the distribution of income as between wages and profits would depend on whether the economy was in a wage-led or a profit-led regime (Bhaduri and Marglin, 1990).[5] The stimulation of investment may tend to raise the capital–output ratio, leading to a decline in the rate of profit. In both cases, we would suggest that a demand policy has to take into account the prevailing distribution of income and propensity to invest, and in terms of the coarse tuning approach outlined above the required budget deficit depends on the distribution of income (via its effects on savings and investment behaviour) and on the propensity to invest. However, we would argue that income distribution policies and encouragement or otherwise of investment should not be undertaken for reasons of their effects on aggregate demand but rather assessed in their own terms. For example, there are strong reasons to advocate a less egalitarian distribution of income in social and ethical terms, rather than because such a policy would stimulate demand.

Turning to the promotion of investment, it should be recognised that there are limits to this way of stimulating demand. The basis of the argument is that a higher investment to GDP ratio would lead to the capital stock rising relative to the output, and as such the rate of profit would tend to fall (since with a constant degree of monopoly, m, profits are equal to m.Y, so that the ratio P/K becomes m.Y/K; as K increases m would fall). The second part of the argument relates to savings. The paradox of thrift and the sense in which more savings may well be in the interests of an individual but not in the collective interest, and that intentions to save more will be frustrated unless matched by investment or budget deficit. One major route by which the average propensity to save could be reduced would be through the redistribution of income – from profits to wages, from high earners to low earners. Leading up the financial crisis and the 'great recession', the average propensity to save by households fell considerably in many countries (and, in particular, in the UK, the USA and Europe).

Although any precise calculations will always be rather difficult, the essence of the argument here is that savings, investment, net exports and budget deficit should be considered together with the aim of their relationship being consistent with full employment. In the above discussion on fiscal policy, the propensities to save and to investment and the net export position were rather taken as given with the focus on the use of fiscal policy to ensure a high level of economic activity. We have now argued to set this in a broader context, and to think about the other policy measures.[6]

3.3   Interest rate policy and financial stability

3.3.1   *Interest rate policy considerations*

Inflation has been relatively low in most industrialised countries and on a global scale for much of the past two decades, and proponents of inflation targeting have claimed the credit for that low inflation. We have argued elsewhere that inflation targeting itself has not been responsible for this low inflation (see, for example, Angeriz and Arestis, 2007a, 2007b, 2008; Arestis and Sawyer, 2008). Inflation targeting has, in effect, sought to return to a crude demand reduction approach to the control of inflation, albeit that the instrument chosen (interest rate) was not the most effective one (that is fiscal policy would have been more potent). The cloud on the horizon is to find an alternative and effective way of maintaining low inflation, without having to resort to demand deflation and the associated losses of employment and output.

There is, thus, a need to develop policy instruments to address the issue of inflation, which do not rely on demand deflation and which are effective (as doubt has been cast on the effectiveness of monetary policy as a tool for the control of inflation). There is also a need to recognise that interest rates set in pursuit of inflation targeting have an impact on a range of other significant variables, notably the exchange rate and asset prices. In part, the manner in which interest rates are seen to influence inflation is through the exchange rate and asset prices: higher interest rates are viewed as tending to raise the value of the exchange rate (having downward impact on domestic inflation) and to depress asset prices (thereby generating a wealth effect which tends to lower demand). But those economic variables are clearly important in their own right (rather than merely as a route to inflation) and, more significantly, interest rates and other changes may feed into price bubbles, whether of the exchange rate or asset prices. It is not a matter of incorporating (or not) asset prices into the targeted measure of inflation for that does not adequately reflect the possible implications of asset price bubbles (and in any event would be limited to assets such as housing). For example, Goodhart (2005a) argues that a focus on domestic variables only in interest rate determination may provide 'a combination of internal price stability and exchange rate instability' (p. 301; see, also, Goodhart, 2005b). In recent times, an important aspect of this can be the influence of low interest rates on asset prices, and whether the stimulus to asset price rises coming from low interest rates can be the spark setting off a price bubble. The argument of Wicksell (1898), and others, could be seen as one that suggests interest rate policy has an effect on asset price inflation – or at least some subset of asset prices. Asset prices develop a speculative element (meaning here purchase of asset to benefit from expected rise in price, rather than for income stream from asset). It is obvious to say that asset price bubbles have developed – dot.com, house prices, and so on. Current arrangements are powerless to deal with those bubbles.

The setting of the interest rate has some clear and obvious implications for the operation of fiscal policy. As indicated above, a total budget deficit relative to GDP of d would lead to a debt ratio of d/g. Let us write $d = d' + rb$ where d' is the primary deficit (that is, excluding interest payments), then $b = d/g = (d' + rb)/g$ and hence $d' = (g - r)b$. When growth rate is greater than (post-tax) rate of interest then there would be a primary deficit, and this would not lead to an unsustainable rise in the debt ratio. When growth rate is below the rate of interest, then a primary surplus would result. The case where $g = r$ is of particular interest, particularly as this would appear a good approximation to the relationship between growth rate and government's cost of borrowing. Pasinetti (1997, p. 163) remarks that this case

> represents the 'golden rule' of capital accumulation. ... In this case, the public budget can be permanently in deficit and the public debt

can thereby increase indefinitely, but national income increases at the same rate (g) so that the D/Y ratio remains constant. Another way of looking at this case is to say that the government budget has a deficit, which is wholly due to interest payments. (p. 163)

In Arestis and Sawyer (2010c) we put the case for a stable real rate of interest as an appropriate target for the policy interest rate of the Central Bank, and suggested that a real rate of interest aligned with the rate of growth had some attractive features. The simplest way to implement such a policy would be to set the nominal policy interest rate at the beginning of the year, taking into account the expected rate of inflation for the coming year (with perhaps some adjustment based on the difference between the actual and expected inflation in the preceding year). Outside of crisis (and perhaps even then) the nominal policy interest rate would be maintained for the year, with avoidance of costs of further decision-making and implementation of interest rate changes. In some respects this could be seen as equivalent to the monetarist constant growth of money supply rule to avoid problems of fine-tuning, but applied to the rate of interest!

There are some unresolved issues relating to such a policy approach. The arguments for a constant real rate equal to the rate of growth relate to some market rate of interest, which is not equal to the policy rate, and which may bear a varying relationship with the policy rate. There can be international complications in so far as domestic interest rate relative to interest rates elsewhere can have implications for the exchange rate. This is neither to suggest some simple uncovered interest rate parity idea nor to suggest that the effects of interest rate differentials on exchange rate are firm and predictable.

In effect we wish to put forward two lines of argument here. First, to argue that the view against fine-tuning apply to the setting of interest rates, and that such fine-tuning should be foregone and rather the nominal rate of interest should be set to achieve a constant target real rate of interest. Second, there are a number of arguments to support the view that the target real rate of interest be the underlying rate of growth of the economy.

3.3.2 *The financial stability dimension*

It is true that financial stability has not been at the forefront of monetary policy to say the least. The belief in the efficiency of financial markets prevented a realistic and necessary approach to financial stability (IMF, 2009, 2010). As a result, both the supporters of the New Consensus

Macroeconomics framework and policy makers have ignored 'the implications for systemic stability of financial market imperfections, including those stemming from international frictions, moral hazard and other distortions to incentives, such as externalities and herding' (IMF, 2010, p. 7). As a result potential systemic risk was ignored and financial regulation and supervision 'were increasingly light-touch and reliant on self-correcting market forces' (IMF, 2010, p. 7); and, indeed, in the case of the 'shadow banking' it was completely absent.

The focus of financial stability should be on the proper control of the financial sector so that it becomes socially and economically useful to the economy as a whole and to the productive economy in particular. Banks should serve the needs of their customers rather than providing short-term gains for shareholders and huge profits for themselves. In order to achieve these objectives a number of prerequisites should be in place. To begin with, the core function of banking should be re-stated. This should be to facilitate the allocation and deployment of economic resources over time and place to socially useful purposes. It should also be to maximise long-term financial and social returns under conditions of uncertainty. In order to achieve these objectives a number of reforms should be undertaken. The most important, perhaps, is the separation of commercial banking from investment banking. Commercial banking sits at the moment uncomfortably with the risky activities of the investment banking; and most commercial banks have moved into investment banking in search of quick profits. Separation then should allow investment banks to go bust, if necessary, thereby instilling greater discipline and avoiding moral hazard.

A second reform should be the break up of banks that are 'too big to fail'. Allowing banks that are big to fail creates moral hazard: banks pursuing high-risk activities confident that the public will have to bail them if and when things go wrong. Also banks need to be broken up both to reduce costs and risks to the taxpayer, and also to improve the quality and range of services. A further reform is to tax the financial sector and also to introduce a financial transactions tax. These would need to take place on a worldwide basis and be used to slow financial speculation, one of the principal causes of the credit crunch. Better regulation should be introduced. Banks should hold more capital, in the form of leverage and liquidity requirements, particularly in booms when the risks they face are much greater. This proposed requirement, which forces banks to hold more capital, could push the countries concerned into depression. This can come about since stringent capital requirements may leave the banks with insufficient funds for lending purposes. Due care and attention are, therefore, vital when constructing the relevant new rules.

The argument made here is that financial stability should become the central objective of the Central Bank. Buiter (2008) indicates that 'financial stability means (1) the absence of asset price bubbles; (2) the absence of illiquidity of financial institutions and financial markets that may threaten systemic stability; (3) the absence of insolvency of financial institutions that may threaten systemic stability' (p. 10). It can be noted that the recent Banking Act 2009 in the UK establishes that 'an objective of the Bank (of England) shall be to contribute to protecting and enhancing the stability of the financial systems of the United Kingdom (the "Financial Stability Objective")'.[7] The Bank will work with other bodies such as the Treasury and the Financial Services Authority (FSA) and will establish a Financial Stability Committee. At present this is placed alongside the monetary stability objective under the heading of inflation targeting. This could be seen as a significant step away from the operational independence of the Bank of England and from the single inflationary objective. Our argument here is that the financial stability objective should be the prime objective and there should be an end to the operational independence of the Bank of England.

Current events and the general record on financial crises (see, Laeven and Valencia, 2008, for details of crises over past three decades and their costs) indicate the substantial costs associated with financial crisis and financial instability (which would far outweigh any costs associated with inflation). In terms of the general multiple instruments–multiple objectives framework it may be impossible to uniquely assign each instrument to a specific objective. Nevertheless, it may be possible to link an instrument mainly with a specific objective, recognising that coordination in the use of instruments can be advantageous. In this context, the argument is that the main link should be monetary policy – monetary and financial stability. However, we have argued above for the policy of seeking to target a specified real rate of interest and to seek to maintain a constant rate of interest. Such a policy may have some beneficial effects on financial stability in that lowering interest rates can be seen to inflate asset prices with the possibility of setting off an asset price bubble which will burst at some point. Further, as recent experience suggests, asset price inflation may be inimical to financial stability given the interrelationships between asset price inflation and credit expansion.

Greenspan (2002) put forward one approach to financial stability when considering how to respond to asset price bubbles. He argued that 'the degree of monetary tightening that would be required to contain or offset a bubble of any substantial dimension appears to be so great as to risk an unacceptable amount of collateral damage to the wider economy' (p. 4). But further his general attitude was that policy should be directed towards cleaning up after a crisis rather than seeking to prevent a crisis. He had already argued on another occasion that 'Faced with this uncertainty, the Federal Reserve has focused on policies that would, as I testified before the Congress in 1999, ... mitigate the fallout [of an asset bubble] when it occurs and, hopefully, ease the transition to the next expansion.'[8] The costs (in terms of lost output, unemployment and fiscal costs) as well as the sheer difficulties of propping up the financial system following the financial collapse indicate that this approach should not be applied in the future. An interesting distinction in this context and on the policy score is made by Blinder (2010). It is suggested that there are two types of bubbles. Those associated with relatively little debt finance, where the typical example is 'equity-like bubbles'. Under this type of bubble the recommended policy is to react after the bubble has burst. The second type is the debt-financed bubbles, where early intervention to contain the bubble is proposed. In this context 'supervisory weapons' are recommended rather than monetary policy. The rationale for this recommendation is based on the fact that 'the central bank *does* have weapons to target straight at the bubble – *provided it is also a bank supervisor*' (Blinder, 2010, p. 2).

The argument here is made more relevant by Goodhart (2007), who in fact suggests that

> [i]n so far, therefore, as the central bank has a prime concern for systemic financial stability, it should want to promote a program of counter-cyclical prudential regulations, where these latter become restrictive during asset price bubbles and relax during asset price downturns. Unfortunately the system of financial regulation is developing in a manner, which will have exactly the reverse proclivity. Under the Basel II accord for financial regulation, this will become more pro-cyclical. (p. 68)

Goodhart goes on to point out problems with national adoption of standards different from Basel II.

There are already in place a variety of regulatory policies, which are intended to develop financial stability, but it could be said that these are often focused on the stability and viability (or otherwise) of individual banking institutions rather than on systemic factors. As D'Arista (2009) argues, in the context of the use of capital requirement,

> As a strategy for ensuring that market forces rather than regulations and quantity controls would determine the volume of bank lending, capital requirements became the rationale for – and poster child of – deregulation. But they have subsequently been seen as its Achilles' heel because of their focus on the individual institution rather than the system as a whole. William R. White describes this 'fallacy of composition' as one that can exacerbate a system-wide problem when recommendations for a sale of assets by one institution in a stressful situation could reduce prices and the value of remaining assets, leaving other institutions weaker (White 2007, p. 83). (p. 10)

The argument here is: (i) monetary and financial stability should be adopted as an objective of macroeconomic policy. This is argued in part on the basis of the relative frequency of financial instability and the significant costs associated with financial crisis; (ii) the objective relates to the whole of the financial system, and not as has generally been the case to the banking system. It is now generally recognised that the financial system has evolved and changed such that the banking system has become a (relatively) smaller part of the overall financial system. The key point here is to bring to the forefront a form of monetary and financial policy, which is focused on financial stability. The key elements of such a policy would be tools to influence and control the activities of financial firms as they bear on the issue of financial stability. This firstly suggests that such a policy, financial regulation, has to be comprehensive in its coverage, and this applies to the range of financial institutions, which are covered and also to its international coverage. It may further suggest that the policy would need to act in a countercyclical manner and to be potentially differentiated. This points away from the capital adequacy ratios of the Basle II system in light of its pro-cyclical nature of operation and the way in which the required capital depends on risk assessment. In contrast an asset-based reserve requirement (see, for example, D'Arista, 2009, Palley, 2004, for proposals) system has countercyclical features and can apply differential reserve requirements against different classes of assets.

There is an element here of the end of monetary policy, and its replacement by (or incorporation into) financial stability policy. With an objective of financial stability, the Central Bank would become more like a Central Financial Agency (CFA). It would be responsible for policies which seek to influence the credit and lending policies of the full range of financial institutions by, for example, assets-based reserve requirements. Our approach suggests that interest rate policy should be set so that the real rate of interest is as low as possible, but in line with the trend rate of growth (see also, Arestis and Saywer, 2010b). In this sense, a real rate of interest in line with the perceived trend rate of growth could be targeted so that the nominal rate is set by the central bank equal to the target rate plus the expected rate of inflation; the operations of the central bank should ultimately be directed towards financial stability. This, of course, may be constrained by world levels of interest rates. Most important, though, the operation of the central bank should ultimately be directed towards financial stability and this objective of financial stability should be placed as the most significant one for the Central Bank. This requires the development of alternative policy instruments alongside the downgrading of interest rate policy and of any notion of inflation targeting.

Financial stability should entail a new toolkit, incorporating both macroprudential and microprudential instruments. Both instruments should be under the banner of the policy makers avoiding rules and employing judgement and thus discretion. The macroprudential toolkit should account for the failures of the system: low levels of liquid assets; inadequate levels of capital with which to absorb losses; too big a financial sector; too leveraged a sector with high risks to the taxpayer and the economy. Thus, macroprudential financial instruments should be able to control the size, leverage, fragility and risk of the financial system. Microprudential instruments relate to the structure and regulation of individual banks. Banks that are 'too big to fail' should be cut down in size; guarantees to retail depositors should be limited to banks with a narrower range of investments; risky banks to taxpayers and economy should face higher capital requirements; large and complex financial institutions can be wound down in an orderly manner; and large banks should not be allowed to combine retail banking with risky investment business. Possibly, combining all the elements just suggested.

Addressing issues of financial stability (or what may be termed the pursuit of macroprudential regulation) clearly requires the development of a range of policy instruments. There are, however, two other important ingredients in this idea of financial stability as the key objective of the monetary authorities. First, many of the arguments for an independent Central Bank, based on the 'conservative' (inflation-averse) central banker with credibility, weaken substantially. Further with multiple objectives pursued by multiple instruments there is a need for co-ordination between the macroeconomic authorities (such as the Ministry of Finance or the Central Bank), which is precluded by independence strictly interpreted. Second (and related), monetary policy under inflation targeting was intended to not only target inflation but also to reduce the volatility of output and guide output to its 'natural' level. This was summarised in Taylor's rule (Taylor, 1993), where the interest rate was intended to be set based on deviations of inflation from target and output from 'natural' level. The idea of the Phillips curve melds those together – in that constant inflation rate is said to be consistent with zero output gap and a positive output gap would be associated with rising inflation both of which would point towards a higher rate of interest. All of these arguments are weakened substantially under the financial stability objective.

3.4   International relations and exchange rate policy

The level, rate of change and the volatility of the exchange rate have significant effects on the domestic economy in terms of both the level of demand (and hence economic activity) and the rate of inflation. The exchange rate has significant implications for the real standard of living and to some degree the distribution of income, and can be seen as an intermediate rather than final target for economic policy. With regard to the exchange rate, policy concerns would involve the volatility of the exchange rate (in both nominal and real terms) and general level of the real exchange rate. In terms of policy objectives we would argue for the benefits of a stable (real) exchange rate set at a level which is most conducive for the level of demand. But in an era of market-determined exchange rates and high capital mobility what are the possibilities of achieving a stable exchange rate? Or is it a matter of letting the exchange rate roam where the market determines, and seeking to deal with the consequences?

Changes in the exchange rate affect the domestic economy primarily in terms of the level of demand, and hence economic activity, and of prices. Interest rate could be varied for exchange rate purposes. The effects of exchange rate variations will depend on the extent of pass through. There are several approaches to modelling the exchange rate, but notoriously movements in the exchange rate are difficult (impossible) to predict. It can be readily observed that there is considerable volatility in exchange rates with consequent effects on the current account position. What we can argue, however, is that there are serious difficulties with a floating market-determined exchange rate system.

A high real exchange rate contributes to 'imbalances' in the economy through its impact on the domestic composition of output: declines in manufacturing and exports, and increases in services and current account deficit, occur. As argued above, the pass-through effect of a change in the exchange rate first on import prices and subsequently on the generality of prices, both goods and services, has weakened since the late 1980s. Consequently, the stronger real exchange rate has had less offsetting effect on domestic prices than in earlier periods.

It follows, then, that the argument normally used to justify appreciation in the exchange rate that such a move slows inflation is no longer valid under such circumstances. Also, and as argued above, the impact of interest rate changes may have become more ambiguous. It would appear to be the case that capital movements are based more on equities than on other assets. A change in interest rates then may have the opposite effect on capital movements than otherwise. In any case, the argument sketched above points in the direction of setting a real interest rate broadly in line with the rate of growth. In view of this argument, the interest rate could not be varied for exchange rate purposes. It should be recognised, though, that the general global level of interest rates may constrain the domestic rates. Despite the lack of evidence supporting uncovered interest rate parity, it would be difficult for a country's real interest rate to diverge persistently from real interest rates around the world. Consequently, it becomes difficult for any single country to secure a stable exchange rate without tightly controlling it. The use of the domestic interest rate does not appear to be an effective instrument, and in any event depends on some cooperation from others since it is the relative interest rate which would be relevant. This suggests that securing a stable exchange rate requires significant intervention along with international cooperation and agreement. Indeed, this is particularly relevant in relation to stability between the major currencies.

These nominal exchange rate fluctuations have also been real exchange rate fluctuations. In a world where exchange rates are set by 'fundamentals' on the trade side, it would be anticipated that exchange rates were rather stable, only evolving as there were changes in the underlying 'fundamentals' (including the relative demand for imports and exports). The era of flexible exchange rates has also been associated with large current account imbalances. Under a floating exchange rate, the balance of payments of a country must balance (that is a change in official reserves of zero), there have been major and often persistent imbalances of current accounts and of capital accounts. The capital account positions can be interpreted as permitting capital flows between countries and the reallocation of capital between countries allowing its more effective use in so far as it flows from low-profit to high-profit areas. Capital inflows leaves a country vulnerable to rapid reversals – a combination of refusal of further capital inflows and the reversal of previous inflows. China, and other countries, has at least for the past decade, run a large and growing current account surplus and hence associated capital outflow and accumulation of dollar-denominated assets. The Euro area (as other currency unions) has established a fixed exchange rate regime amongst its member countries but has developed current account imbalances between member countries within an overall setting where the euro area is broadly in current account balance.

It can also be observed that the volume of transactions across the foreign exchanges has grown rapidly in recent years. The recent rises are also remarkable in that the creation of the euro has reduced the need for foreign exchange transactions between the former currencies of the members of the Economic and Monetary Union. These transactions far exceed (by an order of 50) the volume of international trade, and even making allowance for net capital flows, the volume of transactions looks massive and raises the issue of whether the resources devoted to those transactions are being used in a social useful manner. There have been many debates as to whether the volumes of transactions are generating the observed volatility of exchange rates. The global economy is dominated by three or four currencies – the dollar, the euro, the yen and (to a less degree) sterling. But of course much trade and many commodity prices are expressed in dollars. The currencies of many other countries are pegged in one form or another with one of the major currencies. Can there be agreement between major currencies over appropriate exchange rates and agreed intervention? There is the further question of the distribution of deficits and surpluses between countries. If the world were in a position where each country has a current account position which moved around zero there would not be a severe problem. In a similar vein, the countries had a mixture of deficits and surpluses, and the corresponding capital account surpluses and deficits were sustainable and not subject to sudden reversals (that is, through capital flight) there again would be little problem. But the situation which is faced is one in which there are severe imbalances in which capital is flowing from countries such as China, Germany and Japan to countries such as the USA, the UK and Spain.

Capital inflows can be viewed to address the twin gaps issue; namely, the shortage of domestic savings relative to investment needs and current account deficit. At what level a current account deficit becomes unsustainable is an interesting question. Also, to what degree do capital inflows create credit booms and asset price bubbles? Would it be possible to define an upper limit on current account deficits? This may be a principle rather than a numerical value, recognising the difficulties of determining whether a principle held in practice. Let us suppose for a few minutes that some rules could be enunciated on the size of current account deficits (and that may also require some corresponding rules on current account surpluses). The question then is whether there is any way in which such rules could be implemented. The Stability and Growth Pact drew up rules on budget deficits; why should there not be corresponding rules in relation to current account deficits? Indeed, and noting the national accounts identity, a budget deficit rule implies half a current account deficit rule in the sense that for a given difference between savings and investment, budget deficit implies current account deficit. The operation of rules requires cooperation of all countries – if there were limits on deficits there would have to be limits on surpluses (at least the collective surplus). But a country running a current account deficit generally sees advantages in being able to do so in the short run – it enables its citizens to import more than they export and to consume more than they otherwise would be able to do, and it also provides additional capital. A country with a current account deficit, which appears to be readily financed (even through portfolio investment which can be readily reversed), would not take kindly to instructions to curb its deficit. Further there is the difficult question of what policy instruments are available. Perhaps limits on capital inflows, which then enforce a limit on current account deficit, might be appropriate; but still there is the question of how the exchange rate would respond to it.

The ability of policy to influence the (nominal) exchange rate may, thus, be doubted. Interest rate policy can be viewed as one way in which the exchange rate could be influenced. The uncovered interest rate parity notion suggests that the rate of change of the nominal exchange rate is equal to the interest rate differential between the rest of the world and the country concerned. Casual observation suggests that large movements in an exchange rate (say of the order of 10 per cent per annum or more changes) go alongside relatively small interest rate differentials (say of the order of 1 or 2 percentage points). As the Bank of England (2006) states on its website,

> changes in interest rates can also affect the exchange rate. An unexpected rise in the rate of interest in the UK relative to overseas would

give investors a higher return on UK assets relative to their foreign-currency equivalents, tending to make sterling assets more attractive. That should raise the value of sterling, reduce the price of imports, and reduce demand for UK goods and services abroad. However, the impact of interest rates on the exchange rate is, unfortunately, seldom that predictable.

The argument sketched above points in the direction of setting a real interest rate broadly in line with the rate of growth. If that is accepted, then the interest rate could not also be varied for exchange rate purposes. It would, however, need to be recognised that the general global level of interest rates may constrain the domestic rates. Despite the lack of evidence supporting uncovered interest rate parity, the degree to which a country's real interest rate could diverge persistently from real interest rates around the world can be doubted. It seems rather unlikely that any single country can secure a stable exchange rate without having tight control over it. The use of the domestic interest rate does not appear to be an effective instrument, and in any event depends on some cooperation from others since it is the relative interest rate which would be relevant. This suggests that securing a stable exchange rate requires international cooperation and agreement, and this is particularly relevant for stability between the major currencies (dollar, euro, yen and, perhaps, sterling and yuan).

4   Summary and conclusions

The theoretical framework proposed in this contribution entails a number of economic policies, which can be summarised succinctly. Use fiscal policy in the short term and in the long term to address demand issues. Interest rate policy should be such that the real rate of interest is in line with trend rate of growth in the economy. The central bank role should be financial stability. Major central bank cooperation and intervention in the foreign exchange market is necessary to control the exchange rate. Employ regional and industrial policies to create the required capacity. Our analysis has implications for inflation. Given its uncertain relationship to growth, it implies that inflationary pressures should only worry economic policy makers when they are substantial. When inflation reaches such high rates a relevant economic policy suggestion is to develop incomes policy to contain such serious inflationary pressures.

Notes

1. The model described in this section draws on and develops further a similar model initiated in Arestis (2010). See, also, Arestis (2007, 2009a, 2009b) and Arestis and Sawyer (2008, 2010a, 2010c) and Sawyer (2009a).
2. An early attempt to construct and estimate a model along similar lines as described in the text was undertaken in Arestis (1989). For a more recent attempt along similar focus see Arestis and Sawyer (2010b) and also Arestis (2010).
3. Further references include Angeriz and Arestis (2007a, 2007b, 2008), as well as Arestis and Sawyer (2004).
4. It should be noted, though, that automatic stabilisers can change. Creel and Saraceno (2009) argue that the automatic stabilisers in the EU countries have diminished recently.
5. For some empirical work on this issue see Stockhammer, Onaran and Ederer (2009).
6. It is interesting to note that recent empirical evidence (Eggertson, 2006) suggests that under fiscal and monetary policy coordination, fiscal multipliers are higher than when no policy coordination prevails (even bigger than the Keynesian ones). This is possible so long as the fiscal and monetary authority have a common objective, for example maximisation of social welfare. Eggertsson (2006) utilising a calibrated model, not dissimilar in substance to the NCM type of macroeconomic model (see, for example, Arestis, 2007), concludes that under fiscal and monetary policy coordination fiscal multipliers are higher than when no policy coordination prevails. Indeed, they are bigger than those found in the traditional Keynesian literature.
7. See http://www.opsi.gov.uk/acts/acts2009/ukpga_20090001_en_1.
8. Committee on Banking and Financial Services, U.S. House of Representatives, 22 July 1999.

References

Angeriz, A. and Arestis, P. (2007a) 'Monetary Policy in the UK', *Cambridge Journal of Economics*, 31(6), pp. 863–84.

Angeriz, A. and Arestis, P. (2007b) 'Assessing the Performance of Inflation Targeting Lite Countries', *World Economy*, 30(11), pp. 1–25.

Angeriz, A. and Arestis, P. (2008) 'Assessing Inflation Targeting Through Intervention Analysis', *Oxford Economic Papers*, 60(2), pp. 293–317.

Angeriz, A. and Arestis, P. (2009) 'The Consensus View on Interest Rates and Fiscal Policy: Reality or Innocent Fraud?', *Journal of Post Keynesian Economics*, 31(4), pp. 567–86.

Arestis, P. (1986) 'Wages and Prices in the UK: The Post Keynesian View', *Journal of Post Keynesian Economics*, 8(3), 339–58. Reprinted in M.C. Sawyer (ed.), *Post-Keynesian Economics*. Aldershot: Edward Elgar Publishing Limited, 1989.

Arestis, P. (1987–8) 'The Credit Segment of a UK Post Keynesian Model', *Journal of Post Keynesian Economics*, 10(2), pp. 250–69.

Arestis, P. (1989) 'On the Post Keynesian Challenge to Neo-Classical Economics: A Complete Quantitative Macro-Model for the UK Economy', *Journal of Post Keynesian Economics*, 11(4), pp. 611–29.

Arestis, P. (2007) 'What is the New Consensus in Macroeconomics?', chapter 2 in P. Arestis (ed.), *Is There a New Consensus in Macroeconomics?* Basingstoke: Palgrave Macmillan.

Arestis, P. (2009a) 'Fiscal Policy within the NCM Framework', in J. Creel and M. Sawyer (eds), *Current Thinking on Fiscal Policy*. Basingstoke: Palgrave Macmillan.

Arestis, P. (2009b) 'New Consensus Macroeconomics: A Critical Appraisal', in E. Hein, T. Niechoj and E. Stockhammer (eds), *Macroeconomic Policies on Shaky Foundations – Whither Mainstream Economics?* Marburg: Metropolis, pp. 165–86.

Arestis, P. (2010) 'Economic Policies after the New Consensus Macroeconomics', in S. Dullien, E. Hein, A. Truger and T. van Treeck (eds), *The World Economy in Crisis – The Return of Keynesianism?* Marburg: Metropolis, pp. 271–94.

Arestis, P., Driver, C. and Rooney, J. (1985–6) 'The Real Segment of a UK Post Keynesian Model', *Journal of Post Keynesian Economics*, 8(2), pp. 163–81.

Arestis, P. and Sawyer, M. (2003) 'On the Effectiveness of Monetary and Fiscal Policy', *Review of Social Economics*, 62(4), pp. 441–63.

Arestis, P. and Sawyer, M. (2004) 'Can Monetary Policy Affect the Real Economy?', *European Review of Economics and Finance*, 3(3), pp. 9–32.

Arestis, P. and Sawyer, M. (2006) 'Fiscal Policy Matters', *Public Finance*, 54(1), pp. 133–53.

Arestis, P. and Sawyer, M. (2008) 'New Consensus Macroeconomics and Inflation Targeting: Keynesian Critique', *Economia & Sociedade*, 17 (Special Issue), pp. 631–56.

Arestis, P. and Sawyer, M. (2009) 'Path Dependency and Demand–Supply Interactions in Macroeconomic Analysis', in P. Arestis and M. Sawyer (eds), *Path Dependency and Macroeconomics*, Annual edition of International Papers in Political Economy. Basingstoke: Palgrave Macmillan, pp. 1–36.

Arestis, P. and Sawyer, M. (2010a) '21st Keynesian Economic Policy', in P. Arestis and M. Sawyer (eds), *21st Century Keynesian Economics*, Annual edition of International Papers in Political Economy. Basingstoke: Palgrave Macmillan, pp. 81–119.

Arestis, P. and Sawyer, M. (2010b) 'The Return of Fiscal Policy', *Journal of Post Keynesian Economics*, 32(3), pp. 327–46.

Arestis, P. and Sawyer, M. (2010c) 'What Monetary Policy After the Crisis?', *Review of Political Economy*, 22(4), pp. 499–515.

Bank of England (2006) 'From Interest Rates to Inflation'. Available at: http://www.bankofengland.co.uk/monetarypolicy/how.htm.

Baunsgaard, T. and Symansky, S. (2009) 'Automatic Fiscal Stabilizers', IMF Staff Position Note SPN/09/23. Washington, DC: International Monetary Fund.

Bhaduri, A. and Marglin, S. (1990) 'Unemployment and the Real Wage: The Economic Basis for Contesting Political Ideologies', *Cambridge Journal of Economics*, 14(3), pp. 375–93.

Blinder, A.S. (2010) 'Commentary: Rethinking Moneatry Policy in Light of the Crisis', *Federal Reserve Bank of Kansas City Annual Conference*, 28 August, Jackson Hole, Wyoming.

Bruno, M. and Easterly, W. (1996) 'Inflation and Growth: In Search of a Justifiable Relationship', *Federal Reserve Bank of St. Louis Review*, 78(3), pp. 139–46.

Buiter, W.H. (2008) 'Central Banks and Financial Crises'. Paper presented at the Federal Reserve Bank of Kansas City's Symposium on *Maintaining Stability in a Changing Financial System*, August, Jackson Hole, Wyoming.

Creel, J. and Saraceno, F. (2009) 'Automatic Stabilisation, Discretionary Policy and the Stability Pact', in J. Creel and M. Sawyer (eds), *Current Thinking on Fiscal Policy*. Basingstoke: Palgrave Macmillan.

D'Arista, Jane (2009) 'Setting an Agenda for Monetary Reform', Political Economy Research Institute, University of Massachusetts, Amherst, *Working Paper Series*, No. 190.

Eggerston, G. B. (2006) 'Fiscal Multipliers and Policy Coordination', *Federal Reserve Bank of New York Staff Reports*, No. 241, New York: Federal Reserve Bank of New York.

Ferguson, R. (2005) 'Monetary Credibility, Inflation, and Economic Growth'. Speech at the Cato Institute 23rd Annual Monetary Conference on *Monetary Institutions and Economic Development*, Washington, DC, 3 November.

Fischer, S. (1993) 'The Role of Macroeconomic Factors in Growth', *Journal of Monetary Economics*, 32(3), pp. 458–512.

Ghosh, A. and Phillips, S. (1998) 'Warning: Inflation May be Harmful to Your Growth', IMF Staff Papers, 45(4), pp. 672–710.

Goodhart, C.A.E. (2005a) 'Safeguarding Good Policy Practice', in *Reflections on Monetary Policy 25 Years after October 1979*, Federal Reserve Bank of St Louis Review, March/April, 87(2, Part 2), pp. 298–302.

Goodhart, C.A.E. (2005b) 'The Experience of Inflation Targeting since 1993', in P. Arestis, M. Baddeley and J. McCombie (eds), *The New Monetary Policy*. Cheltenham: Edward Elgar.

Goodhart, C.A.E. (2007) 'The Future of Central Banking', in P. Arestis (ed.), *Is There a New Consensus in Macroeconomics?* Basingstoke: Palgrave Macmillan, pp. 61–81.

Greenspan, A. (2002) 'Opening Remarks', in *Rethinking Stabilization Policy*, Kansas: Federal Reserve Bank of Kansas City, pp. 1–10.

Hein, E. and Stockhammer, E (2007) 'Macroeconomic Policy Mix, Employment and Inflation in a Post-Keynesian Alternative to the New Consensus Model', mimeo.

IMF (2009) *World Economic Outlook*, October. Washington, DC: International Monetary Fund.

IMF (2010) 'Central Banking Lessons from the Crisis', Monetary and Capital Markets Department, 27 May. Washington, DC: International Monetary Fund.

Kalecki, M. (1937) 'The Principle of Increasing Risk', *Economica*, 4(4), pp. 440–7.

Kalecki, M. (1944) 'Three Ways to Full Employment', in *The Economics of Full Employment*. Oxford: Blackwell for Oxford University Institute of Statistics.

Khan, M.S. and Senhadji, A.S. (2001) 'Threshold Effects in the Relationship between Inflation and Growth', *IMF Staff Papers*, 48(1), pp. 1–21.

Laeven, L. and Valencia, F. (2008) 'Systemic Banking Crises: A New Database', *IMF Working Paper WP/2008/0224*. Washington, DC: International Monetary Fund.

Layard, R., Nickell, S. and Jackman. R (1991) *Unemployment: Macroeconomic Performance and the Labour Market*. Oxford: Oxford University Press; second edition 2005.

Lerner, A. (1943) 'Functional Finance and the Federal Debt', *Social Research*, 10, pp. 8–51. Reprinted in M.G. Mueller (ed.), *Readings in Macroeconomics*. New York: Holt, Rinehart and Winston, 1966, pp. 353–60.

Levine, R. and Renelt, D. (1992) 'A Sensitivity Analysis of Cross-Country Growth Regressions', *American Economic Review*, 82(3), pp. 942–63.

Palley, T.I. (2004) 'Asset-based Reserve Requirements: Reasserting Domestic Monetary Control in an Era of Financial Innovation and Instability', *Review of Political Economy*, 16(1), pp. 43–58.

Pasinetti, L. (1997) 'The Social "Burden" of High Interest Rates', in P. Arestis, G. Palma and M. Sawyer (eds), *Capital Controversy, Post-Keynesian Economics and the History of Economics: Essays in Honour of Geoff Harcourt*. London: Routledge.

Sawyer, M. (2002) 'The NAIRU, Aggregate Demand and Investment', *Metroeconomica*, 53(1), pp. 66–94.

Sawyer, M. (2009a) 'Fiscal and Interest Rate Policies in the "New Consensus Framework": A Different Perspective', *Journal of Post Keynesian Economics*, 31(4), pp. 549–65.

Sawyer, M. (2009b) 'The Continuing Relevance of Fiscal Policy', in J. Creel and M. Sawyer (eds), *Current Thinking on Fiscal Policy*. Basingstoke: Palgrave Macmillan.

Stockhammer, E., Onaran, O. and Ederer, S. (2009) 'Functional Income Distribution and Aggregate Demand in the Euro Area', *Cambridge Journal of Economics*, 33(1), pp. 139–59.

Taylor, J.B. (1993) 'Discretion Versus Policy Rules in Practice', *Carnegie-Rochester Conference Series on Public Policy*, December, 195–214.

White, W. R. (2007) 'The Need for a Larger Policy Horizon: A Less Orthodox Approach', in J.J. Teunisson and A.A. Akkerman (eds), *Global Imbalances and Developing Countries: Remedies for a Failing International Financial System*. The Hague: Forum on Debt and Development (FONDA).

Wicksell, K. (1898) *Geldzins und Güterpreise*. Frankfurt: Gustav Fischer Verlag. English translation in R.F. Kahn (1965) *Interest and Prices*. New York: Kelley.

2
Towards a 'New Economics': Values, Resources, Money, Markets, Growth and Policy

Terry Barker
University of Cambridge

Abstract

'New economics', as outlined in this chapter, is developed from the Post Keynesian approach to macroeconomics to allow for intrinsic values, institutional change and diverse consumers and producers. The chapter presents a self-evident set of assumptions on which to base the theory and then develops an analysis of demand-driven markets within a historical process of globalisation. The asymmetry between consumption and production is emphasised, with production being concentrated and preceding consumption, but consumption being more generalised and causing production. A theory of economic growth through endogenous technological change and increasing trade is presented. Fiscal policies and regulation, with incomes policies, are required to manage the system to achieve full employment, with monetary policies accommodating demand for money. The chapter concludes with a discussion of the quantitative modelling at the global level to represent the economic system in accordance with the theory.

Keywords: New Economics; Post Keynesian economics; endogenous technological change; demand-led growth

JEL Classifications: A13, B52, E02

1 Introduction[1]

The climate and financial crises have shown the inadequacies of traditional thinking in economics and encouraged new approaches to understanding economic behaviour. New thinking in economics is an interdisciplinary approach to economic problems that acknowledges and respects the insights and analysis from other disciplines, especially those from ethics, history and engineering as well as institutional, complexity and evolutionary theory. The economic system embedded in human society is nonlinear and complex.

This chapter proposes some theoretical foundations for such a new economics, drawing on and developing the Post Keynesian approach to macroeconomics and including strands of institutional, evolutionary and ecological economics. It starts with a discussion of the antecedents in the literature and proposes some defining features of new economics. The chapter continues with a consideration of ethics and an assertion that intrinsic values are distinct from monetary values and should not generally be converted to them. It then introduces resources, including people and institutions. The role of money as a critical economic resource is discussed. It sets out some assumptions to provide the theoretical basis for the understanding of the economic system. Markets and growth in trade and output are treated as emergent properties of a complex economic system in which money allows the specialisation of production and the generalisation of consumption across regional and national boundaries over time. Technological change is intrinsic to the process. Policy is required to manage externalities and impose social values.

The theory has been developed in parallel with the construction and application of large-scale computable models of the economy. The representation of the system is limited by the data, but it follows the theory in that it is structural, path-dependent and allows for different responses by institutional categories. The modelling of the system is intended to be forward-looking, projecting the outcomes evident in the past into the future. The models are policy-oriented, designed to assess how portfolios of national and international policies, for example those for mitigating climate change, can achieve their objectives efficiently, effectively and equitably. Models have been developed to simulate behaviour of industries and consumers at different spatial scales (the UK, Europe, and the world) over the period since 1970, using computing algorithms to solve the systems of equations.

2　Antecedents of new economics[2]

New economics is generally associated with Keynesian economics, the 'new'[3] being in contrast to the neoclassical, traditional economics, with its emphasis on equilibrium, mathematical formalisation and deterministic solutions. Here the term 'new' is being used to cover several approaches that oppose this traditional economics, including Post Keynesian, institutional and evolutionary economics and allowing for complexity theory. Holt (2007) characterises Post Keynesian economics by four features: (1) a commitment to understanding how actual market economies function in historical time, providing explanations of observed economic behaviour; (2) a recognition of the irreversibility of events in historical time or 'path dependence', which makes equilibrium problematic as an organising concept; (3) a crucial role for uncertainty and expectations in the theory, with deep uncertainty and outcomes that cannot be predicted; and (4) an emphasis on the role of institutions in shaping and channelling economic behaviour. These features are also those, with a different emphasis on each, of institutionalist and evolutionary economics.

This new economics is in contrast with what might be called traditional economics, based on the neoclassical mathematical synthesis promoted by Samuelson (1947) that came to dominate mainstream economics thinking in the late twentieth century. Traditional economics has been defined as 'the set of concepts and theories articulated in ... textbooks. It also includes concepts and theories that peer-reviewed surveys claim, or assume, that the field generally agrees on' (Beinhocker, 2006, p. 24). This traditional economics is characterised by an emphasis on rationality, via the use of utility maximisation in conditions of equilibrium, and by neglect of strong kinds of uncertainty, particularly of fundamental uncertainty (Dequech, 2007, p. 290). The approach adopts a version of expected utility theory with human welfare usually translating into private market consumption per head in the applied models. The theory is applied to utility across countries with huge differences in consumption and to utility gained many years into the future, when consumption can rise perhaps many times over.

This traditional approach to economics has largely ignored other disciplines tackling the same problems of justifying assumptions and understanding human behaviour. In particular, the study of ethics considers utility theory and social justice, exploring the limitations and contradictions in utility maximisation (see Ackerman and Nadal, 2004) and providing alternatives. Engineering and architecture give insights into how the equipment and buildings can be designed to save energy. Economic geography and history provides understanding as to how economies grow and how technologies diffuse and evolve. Political science considers how societies make decisions regarding public policy. Furthermore, economics is not confined to the study of equilibrium in various guises, assuming groups of identical representative agents, with entirely self-interested consumers and known, quantifiable social welfare functions.

The weakening of the neoclassical paradigm has been accompanied by a more general undermining of the ideology and prescriptions of traditional economics through deconstruction of the origins of the theory in physics and cybernetics (Mirowski, 1989, 2002). Behavioural economics going back to Kahneman and Tversky (1989) has revealed key relevant empirical findings for risk aversion and utility maximisation that are inconsistent with traditional treatments. Complexity theory and agent-based modelling has developed a theory of economic evolution (Arthur, 1994; Beinhocker, 2006). The new economics is more pluralistic and respectful of other disciplines. Cost–benefit analysis is formally replaced by a Multi-Criteria Analysis developed in management science and applied to sustainable development (Munda, 2005) in which socio-economic, ecological, and ethical perspectives are taken into account.

In the debate as to what has become mainstream economics, it seems agreed that the traditional neoclassical approach has become less influential, but it is not clear what has taken its place (Colander et al., 2004; Dequech, 2007). Hodgson (2007) speculates whether institutional and evolutionary economics has become the new mainstream. In climate change economics, the Stern Review appears to have shifted the mainstream away from the traditional neoclassical approach to a more pluralist, risk-based approach (Stern, 2007).

One aspect of the shift in the mainstream is a debate on the ethics underlying traditional prescriptions, particularly in climate policy. Utility maximisation as a method rests on the idea that individual preferences are fixed and utilities can be aggregated and converted into well-behaved mathematical equations in a 'social welfare function', and differentiated to give stable marginal properties, as the basis for policy. In climate policy, this approach leads to utilities being aggregated and discounted over generations, and social choices involving irreversible and substantial losses of ecosystems and human lives. Such implications raise ethical problems that have led to a questioning of the underlying value system in the traditional approach (Maréchal, 2007; Barker, 2008). The next section reviews the values that should underlie economics.

3   Values in new economics

Many issues of economic policy (traditionally called 'welfare economics') are primarily ethical in nature, and should be informed by moral philosophy rather than economics in isolation. Intrinsic values are distinct from monetary values and should not generally be converted to them. Traditional economic models adopt an extreme form of utilitarianism, with a questionable choice and use of discount rates, ignoring the philosophical literature and the concept of justice.

Moral philosophers have long debated the relative weighting to be given in utility theory between social groups. Broome (2006) insists that economics is not ethics-free, that basing economics on the ethics of individuals assumed to be entirely self-interested can go badly wrong, and that 'willingness to pay' is invalid as a means of valuation (Broome, 2005). In economic analysis, justice as a theory of ethics (Rawls, 1971) deserves serious attention as an alternative to utilitarianism. Rawlsian ethics would focus social policy on preventing the harm and damage to the most vulnerable in society and on caring for the subsistence minority of developing countries, unlike the traditional policies, which have focused on averages and set aside problems of inequality.

Traditional economists assume the fungibility of natural and human-made assets – that is, they all have monetary values and can be exchanged. This is economics as a religion (Nelson, 2001), in which society is composed of self-interested individuals, whose behaviour is to be assumed rational, then interpreted and described by economics as a mathematical science, for example. in finding and using the pure rate of time preference, or the value of human life. The underlying fallacy is that market forces lead by themselves to intrinsically good outcomes (Foley, 2006).

A new economics approach is to acknowledge that there are ethical, aesthetic and other values, and that resources seen to have intrinsic value should not routinely be converted into money, with the exchangeability that money permits (Ackerman and Heinzerling, 2004; Gowdy, 2005). The use of the discount rate to account for time preference and risk should be re-thought to allow for subjective time preference and a risk analysis independent of the return (Price, 2005). The distribution of rights consistent with sustainable development should be considered (Padilla, 2004). These considerations suggest that it is necessary to go back to the treatment of resource allocation by institutions, to allow for the evolution of diverse social valuations of resources. The next section bridges the divide between micro- and macroeconomics in the treatment of resources and establishes a basis for macroeconomic analysis that does not involve the aggregation of representative agents.

4   Resources, including institutions, in space and time

Economic activity requires resources, including people, institutions, knowledge as well as things, and takes place in specific locations at particular times. Space and time are fundamental categories in any attempt to explain the world: first, they are universal; second, they are essential features of physical and economic laws; and third, they are required for causation. People and objects must be in contact or communication with each other across space if they are to interact; and the arrow of time requires that causation goes one way only, from the past to the future. The treatment of space and time is therefore fundamental in economics and the social sciences.[4]

4.1   Institutions and evolution

People live and interact in social groups each with their characteristic institutional rules and behaviours. These social groups or organisations, with a life of their own, provide a context which shapes and guides economic life. They play an essential role in providing the framework that governs economic behaviour. Each group or organisation has its own places and its own history, each has its own birth and death, each has its own institutional habits, procedures, ways of being, objectives, motivations and, in the case of companies, corporations, schools, and many other groups, laws imposing duties and responsibilities. In modelling these groups, a balance has to be struck between the integrity of the group, the differences between groups and the multiplication of groups making the analysis unmanageable.

Institutions are fundamental to economic life and human society (Veblen, 1899; Commons, 1934; Sowell, 1967; Coase, 1988; Samuels, 1989; Williamson and Winter, 1991; Hodgson, 1999). Several institutional social groups would appear to go back through all human history since they exist in other, closely related, animal societies (for example, all primates have the family, and the tribe or the village). Such institutionalisation, therefore, goes back into human evolutionary past. The rules and procedures associated with social groups are embedded deep within human conceptualisation of the world and are associated with instinctive behaviours with regard to individual and group behaviour for everyday living and long-term survival. Understanding economic behaviour involves understanding these instinctive responses and reactions in social and institutional contexts.

4.2   The economic characteristics of products

Characteristics of products can be distinguished from the products themselves. A *product* is a collection of goods and services, normally goods *or* services, having similar combinations of characteristics. *Characteristics* can be defined, following Lancaster's work (1971), as 'properties of people, institutions and resources, (such as products) that are relevant to the economic activities of people and social groups'.[5] Examples of characteristics of goods are volume, calories, availability, colour and many other properties that enter the choice made between alternative goods. Two important and obvious characteristics of goods are where they are located (space) and when they are available to buy or sell or use or enjoy (time). A *good* is defined as a material object with the property that two equal quantities of it are completely equivalent with respect to all characteristics for each seller and each buyer. Thus the quantity of a good bought and sold in a transaction will consist of a number of 'replicated units' of the good. In some markets there is, strictly speaking, only one such unit on offer, for example in the housing market each house is unique with respect to its location; in other markets there are large numbers of such units, as in the case of manufactured foods.

A *unit-service* is non-material with otherwise the same definition as a good. A replicated service is distinct from a replicated good because it must last for a period of time (material goods obviously have the property of persisting over time) and it is more liable to change through space and time (the good comes into existence at an instant of time and usually remains invariant through space and time). Goods are one type of 'particle' in economics; the unit-service in the form, for example, of the availability of a telephone connection or an attractive park might be seen as another type. Markets are locations in economic space-time where products are exchanged. The definitions of a product and a market are necessarily rather fuzzy because they are intended to match definitions in official statistics. Products can be identified with groups by conventional classifications.

The price of a good has a singular and identifiable meaning only at the level of the replicated unit. A breakdown of the price of such a unit in terms of the characteristics of the good may be possible by hedonic functions or regression analysis (see Griliches, 1971). However, it is critical to the theory below that the characteristics are not obtainable independently, but only in a finite number of fixed combinations.

4.3   Externalities and institutions

Externalities are defined by boundaries, so economic externalities are those external to the economic system, although most become 'internalities' if we consider the whole system of the interacting planetary ecosystems, climate and human economy. Externalities are extensive and pervasive, and affect virtually every area of economic life. The fact that this may not be very apparent is simply because institutions, laws and rules have evolved to restrict most of these externalities, turn them into internalities, and contain them within respectable limits (Ostrom, 1990). Mechanisms are brought to bear that will cut down the externality, either by reducing the originating activity ('passive abatement'), or by introducing a new activity ('active abatement' such as end-of-pipe equipment to remove a polluting emission). If the latter, the same originating activity takes place, but the new activity of abatement lessens the effect outside the space-time region in which it originates, and insofar as any costs of the abatement are borne by the polluter, this might at least be an equitable solution, if not an efficient one.

A problematic form of externality is that in which the damage may be so small or its cause so uncertain that it is expensive or difficult to establish the property rights of those who are damaged. In these cases it is difficult to institutionalise the externality leaving it unclear who manages it, and who is responsible for it.

4.4 Technology and economies of specialisation

Technology is the application of knowledge to the making of products. The existence and growth of technical knowledge provides growing opportunities for consumers to discover new products and new varieties of old ones and firms to supply them. It allows firms to develop and exploit new or improved process technologies and economies of specialisation and scale in reducing costs. To the extent that technology responds to economic signals, for example, higher real prices of carbon leading to lower-carbon intensities in production processes, it is an intrinsic aspect of economic growth.[6]

Economies of specialisation relate to social groups, usually firms, specialising in a particular niche market in order to exploit technologies and the economies of scale (discussed below) applicable to that niche. They involve specialisation in particular skills, expertise, knowledge and information on special places, products and markets. Young (1928) ascribes great importance to these economies of specialisation, which he calls 'roundabout methods of production and the division of labour among industries' (p. 529). He distinguishes these economies from those discussed by Adam Smith, when arguing that the division of labour leads to invention because workers involved in specialised production see better ways of doing things. (Smith's workers could be seeing new techniques, new management, and larger economies of specialisation or economies of scale of all sorts.) Young argues that with the division of labour and the use of machinery 'a group of complex processes is transformed into a succession of simpler processes' (p. 530). This phenomenon is associated with 'large' production – and hence the extent of the market is to be distinguished from that of 'large-scale' production, i.e. economies of *scale* (p. 531).

4.5   Integralities and evolution

The concept of 'integrality' or indivisibility is inherent in a human understanding of the world, since as far as each of us is concerned our bodies are indivisible. And since the human body and many of the tools and other objects around us are integral (if they were divided they would lose their function) it seems reasonable to speculate that human conceptualisation and 'views of the world' are deeply influenced by this property. The combination of integralities and increasing returns has led to a uniformity in the buildings, vehicles and other objects designed and built for human use: door height, chair size, the shape of a spoon have all 'evolved' for human beings as if we were a homogeneous group.

It also seems likely that we have evolved to work together in the face of integralities and to develop institutions to share out the resources. Money is a resource, which is divisible in order to allow exchange with integral goods and services of any value. This relates to the question of equity between members of a social group – a basic feature of an institutional group is how benefits and costs are shared between members of the group. Money is also essential in the process of separating production from consumption that is at the heart of economic growth because it allows economies of specialisation and scale to be realised. One social group, namely the banking community, has as its main function the creation and management of money in the economy. The next section considers the importance of money in more depth.

5   Usefulness of money[7]

Money can be defined as a 'resource with a set of characteristics that are embodied in different combinations in monetary assets'; examples of such assets are notes and coin, bank deposits, credit and debit cards, bank loans and various government-backed, short-term bills of exchange. The important distinction between the characteristics of money or its 'essence' on the one hand, and the forms of money or monetary assets on the other, was clearly set out by Simmel in 1900 (1978 translation, pp. 119–20), who also emphasised the innumerable errors that arise if this basic distinction is not made.[8]

The characteristics that form the set that describe 'perfect money' include the following seven distinct items:

1. complete trustworthiness
2. perfect divisibility
3. complete invariance over space and time
4. complete limitation of supply
5. complete acceptance as a unit of account or *numeraire*
6. perfect convenience as a means of exchange
7. attractiveness as a physical object, or as an immaterial form of money, e.g. credit cards.

Although we think of money in physical terms – gold, silver, notes and coins – it is the services that monetary assets offer that are important, not their physical form. Most of these services are yielded when money is exchanged, but one of these services (money as a unit of account) is a general service yielded through time, allowing the valuation of all goods and all other services in an economy. There is no single asset that embodies all the characteristics of money. The implication is that the money supply is endogenous and uncertain. Money demand is derived from the desire of holders of money in all its forms for liquidity. Banks provide liquidity in exchange for returns from bank lending for financial or real investment, or speculation, so the desire for loans then leads to the banks supplying loans. The loans thereby create money as a systemic property in that social groups taking out bank loans then deposit the money in banks, so that the banks can lend it out again, all subject to reserve requirements.

6   Proposed theoretical foundations for a new economics

Several self-evident assumptions are proposed to form the theoretical basis of understanding economic behaviour and the economic system. The first five of these assumptions are quite different from those that have been adopted in traditional economic analysis, but they are fundamental and it is asserted that they are obviously true. The last two assumptions concern motivation and rationality and the approach is more general than usual.

6.1 All individuals are different
Each of us occupies a different position in space-time; we are endowed with different physical characteristics at birth, and, through experience,

using our various skills and intelligence, the individuality of each of us becomes more and more marked.[9] Individuals *can* be grouped by common characteristics such as gender, place of dwelling, nationality or social group but this does not mean that they are the same. In evolutionary theory, the random or contrived differences within species are essential for selection to work; they are biological imperatives. That people are different in their characteristics and behaviour is also true of institutional groups. All social groups occupy different and precise niches in economic space-time with different human members, different names and different objectives. These differences are a crucial to the economic success of the groups and their interaction within the economic system.

6.2 All *economic activities take place in a particular location at a specific time.* The study of human beings within social groups located in space and time is at the core of all social sciences, including economics.

6.3 *Externalities are pervasive in economic life.* Economic externalities are effects resulting from activity within the boundaries of a specific location in economic space-time, but affecting other locations later in time. Potential externalities are assumed to be present in all economic activity.

6.4 *Nonlinearities in the form of indivisibilities and boundaries in economic space, and discontinuities in economic time, are intrinsic and normal.* Baumol (1987) defines an indivisible (or integral) good as one that has 'a minimum size below which it is unavailable, at least without significant qualitative change'. All vehicles – such as the motor car, the railway carriage, the oil tanker, the Jumbo jet – are readily reducible to integral units. Fixed assets, such as dwellings, factories, offices, infrastructure such as the Channel Tunnel, are almost all entirely integral in the sense that if they were to be divided they would normally lose economic value. At the macro scale, whole technological systems (such as modern road transport with substantial network economies) have an integral quality in that they depend for their viability on a particular scale and coverage. The dispersion of markets across space-time, and the tendency to mould the integral good to suit the single purchase, both ensure that understanding the implications of indivisibilities is central to understanding the economic system itself.

6.5 *Human beings have evolved within this economic space-time as social animals* in such a way that there is no 'beginning'; there is no 'desert island'; there is no start without a complex set of interacting, evolving social groups such as households, families or villages. There are many economic activities in animal behaviour that correspond closely to those in human behaviour, for example, the exchange of gifts, group organisation as a means to an end, sharing of economic goods and services within the group, and storage of goods for later use.

6.6 *The economic motivation of most individuals and groups in a monetary economy can be summarised as 'more money is better than less' within a context of institutional inertia.* Given the monetary motivation, two sets of problems arise both for the individual and the group. The first is how to behave to secure more money, faced with the availability and costs of information and the costs of decision making; and the second is how to allocate the extra resources over time and between the members of the group. Social groups face the extra problem that allocation of resources within the group will affect the group's motivation and behaviour. The individual or group may then behave, in ways of increasing complexity, following the principles of

1 the simple rule of more is better than less, without satisficing or maximising, or
2 'satisficing', in that a want or objective is perceived and on its attainment the individual or group is satisfied, or
3 'maximising' in that the individual or social group reviews all the information available and acts so as to maximise some objective criterion, such as the profits of a firm or the real wage rates of trade union members.

Complexity here is measured by the amount of information needed to allow the motivation to be realised in economic life. Because of the more general complexities involved in predicting the future and the cost of obtaining information, the motive of maximising is the most complex of the three. Occam's Razor suggests that a less complex behaviour is to be preferred to a more complex one, other things being equal.

6.7 *The behaviour of individuals and social groups is assumed to be rational* in the sense that the means adopted to satisfy wants or objectives are those of lowest perceived costs, including the transaction costs of obtaining more information. These costs can be economic, social, aesthetic, environmental, religious or ethical; in general, it is impossible to reduce all costs to the purely economic. In addition, the assessment of minimum costs is itself a decision by the individual or group that will depend on specific circumstances and may not be predictable. However, once habits, rules, procedures and laws have been established to achieve wants and objectives, it becomes rational to follow such habits and rules to avoid spending time recalculating the best strategy to fulfil those wants and meeting those objectives. Such habits are most likely to change at particular times (for example, during economic and political crises and revolutions, or on certain critical dates and events) – these are discontinuities in individual and social behaviour.

With these concepts and the behavioural and technical assumptions listed above, we have the basis (in the next section) for considering the relationship between demand and supply, both by product market and in aggregate.

7   Demand-driven markets

The approach is Post Keynesian and intended to be the basis for large-scale quantitative modelling. The theory can be seen as complementing the insights of the theory of transformational growth (Nell, 1998; Argyrous, 1996, 2002) in as much as it applies to modern capitalist economies. The theory emphasises the role of money and finance in allowing the separation of supply and demand. The growth of markets can be seen in a historical perspective as a relationship between households becoming ever more separated from the complex large-scale production of goods and services, so that employment is increasingly separated from domestic work and subsistence farming. Nell explains growth as a historical rather than an equilibrium phenomenon, explaining how different systems have evolved into the modern advanced capitalist economy. Here the additional features of location and timing are discussed in the context of the modern global economy with the emergence of China, India and other developing economies as fast-growing economies, increasingly linked to the world economy through trade and investment, and a transformation of the global economy as never seen before.

Markets are areas of economic activity in which goods and services grouped into products are exchanged. (Products are collections of goods and services with combinations of economic characteristics in common.) Markets are characterised by institutional regularities, taking place at the same venue, or arranged at customary or advertised venues; they may take place each day, each week, each year or at other known times; or they may be continuous – for example, the world equity market or the telecommunications market. The markets transmit effects mainly through those activities creating demand for inputs of materials, fuels and labour, through wages and prices affecting incomes, and through incomes, in turn leading to further demands for goods and services. Note that there are crucial differences between the markets for labour services and those for products. Mixing them up is an example of Boulding's 'taxonomy as a source of error' (1992, chapter 9). People are consumers as well as workers, derive welfare for working with others, learn by doing and training and can actively affect production.[10]

Those who demand and supply, consumers and producers, buyers and sellers, shoppers and shopkeepers are dependent on one another but, in some sense, asymmetrical in location or timing. Each of the two partners in the exchange is engaged in an *asymmetrical* dialectic, the asymmetry in location being very different from that in time; each requires the other and their motivations, behaviour and activities can most easily be understood in the light of the asymmetrical dependency.

7.1   Demand and supply asymmetries in location

The principal asymmetry in location is in spatial distribution; on the demand side, households, consumers, buyers and shoppers are generally scattered, and are therefore less concentrated in economic space than their suppliers. There are many reasons for this. First, there are many more consuming than producing economic and social organisations (there are more people and households than firms and producers). Second, each final consumer (individual person or household) generally purchases a small number of each good or service, while the producers take advantage of economies of scale to produce a huge number of goods and services rapidly and in long production runs. Third, the consumers' wants and tastes are very diverse, with a vast range of requirements and desires while the producers specialise in niche markets, producing a small range of each unit, designed to be sold to large numbers of buyers. Fourth, households choose to locate for amenity and a variety of other non-economic reasons, whereas firms are motivated mainly by economic reasons, including economies of scale in transport and distribution.

Firms, therefore, tend to be located together, clustering near to transport networks and particular transport nodes in order that their own goods can be transported cheaply to their markets while, at the same time, the goods *they* require for production, including fuels, raw materials and other goods in various states of completion, can be brought to the factory; location near transport nodes also enables their workers to travel more easily between work and home.

7.2   Demand and supply asymmetries in timing

Economic behaviour is greatly affected by the 'arrow of time' (Coveney and Highfield, 1990): time is irreversible, flowing in one direction only so the past is closed and the future is open. Since production necessarily precedes – or, at most, accompanies – consumption, the two activities are fundamentally different: those consuming in the present can be certain of the activities of those producing in the past; but those producing *cannot* be certain of the factors affecting future consumption. It is paradoxical that the direction of economic causation usually runs opposite to that of time: the desire of consumers causes goods and services to be produced; the desire of purchasers causes goods and services to be sold; the desire of shoppers causes shopkeepers to advertise and sell particular goods and services. The exception is when producers innovate and seek to persuade potential consumers to buy their new products. Schumpeter argued that it is 'the producer who as a rule initiates economic change, and consumers are educated by him if necessary; they are, as it were, taught to want new things' (1934, p. 65). However, the process has to be managed carefully if the producers are to succeed, because desires cannot be manipulated completely.

Of course, the arrow of economic causation does not contradict the arrow of time. It can be reconciled with the arrow of time by making the assumption that producers behave *as if* they had perfect foresight regarding the desires of consumers. If this were the case, producers would make exactly what the consumers of their goods and services wanted and the direction of economic causation would be unambiguous – from consumers to producers, even though the consumption of goods, and services deriving from goods, necessarily takes place after the goods have been produced. In fact, successful producers envision consumption of their products and do their best to make the vision come true.

7.3   The interconnectedness of consumption and production

In modern economies the processes of consumption and production have reached extraordinary levels of complexity and sophistication. The basic distinction between consuming decision makers (consumers) and producing decision makers (producers) is that the consumers' vision largely ignores, or takes for granted, the producers' vision, but the producers' vision includes as an essential component a projected or imagined consumers' vision. When producers envisage the design of the product, the purchase of the materials, services of inputs required to produce it, the actual manufacture and then the sale, they must then envisage the use and consumption of the product; otherwise they are more likely to be caught out by changes in tastes, the different desires of new groups of consumers, or the loss of old groups, and so give opportunities to competitors to encroach upon their markets.

7.4 Market clearing

In the case of commodities (which are exchanged for money) the location and time of sale, defined in legal and institutional terms, is the defining place and moment in the related visions of the producer and consumer. Market clearing requires the matching of the purchasers' and sellers' visions of the goods or services being bought and sold. These visions derive largely, and sometimes exclusively (when the purchaser is identified with the consumer and the seller with the producer), from the visions of the original producers and of the final consumers. This matching may well require the purchaser to revise or compromise his or her vision at the point of sale if the actual goods or services available do not accord precisely with the expectations that brought the purchaser to the market in the first place.

Market clearing is occasionally achieved largely by price – as in the equity or forex financial markets – but more often in industrial markets the price is set by the producer or seller as part of the vision, and the consumer accepts or rejects the price on offer. Market clearing can be achieved in part by the adjustment by the seller of the characteristics of the goods and services in order to induce a sale or by the buyer in accepting what is on offer. Although adjustment in any or all of these variable characteristics, including price, can lead to market clearing, complete clearing of the market in the sense of all the products being sold is not the usual outcome, and normally surplus goods are left on the shelf or in the warehouse when the market closes, and 'surplus' capacity of the service provider is left partly unused. If no surplus goods or unused capacity for service are left, then purchasers are left unsatisfied and queues are likely to develop, with rationing of all types, and again the market does not clear.

Although adjustment through price is by its very nature obvious, advertised and emphasised, it is not nearly as important as it appears. For many goods and services the price, occasionally adjusted for general inflation, is kept constant by the seller for long periods in the expectation that demand for the good or service in question will change so as to help clear the market. For example, in the selling of houses there may be a persistence of high prices that do not clear the market because the seller still hopes that the demand will eventually rise sufficiently for the fixed price to be accepted.

7.5   Prices and wage rates

Prices and wage rates emerge from a resolution of conflicting interests; the expectations of prices and wage rates are in turn based on past experience. These valuations are social concepts, and depend, like the acceptance of money, on social agreement and custom. This is made obvious by comparing valuations or prices in different cultures and economic systems. For example, in the People's Republic of China, the relative values of goods and services are quite different from those in the USA. Values in a specific location at a specific time are influenced by values in adjacent locations and times (the recent past in the same location and in other regions in the same industry, and in other industries in the same region). The valuations are partly trial and error, since both producers and consumers, and both buyers and sellers, are uncertain as to what prices are acceptable. The process has to be like this because producers do not know the extent of the economies of specialisation and scale they can achieve at a particular set of prices (this demand may be years in the future at the time the production facilities are being designed). Market clearing, if it takes place at all, is by adjustment over a range of variables, including prices.

In this extremely relativistic view of valuation, it is worth distinguishing between three sets of valuations. *Market values* are the context-specific values that are manifested in the actual prices of the exchange of goods and services in the market, and the actual wage rates paid and received, that is, exactly what people, households and firms actually pay, allowing for all discounts, special offers and the like. Exchange values are actual or imputed market values. *Worth values* are purely subjective evaluations by consumers of goods and services or by employers of employees providing labour, although they are related to the market value. *Social values* are worth values at the social level, taking into account non-market externalities. These are the values that government wish to put on goods and services and employment using taxes, subsidies and regulation to abate or control the externalities, allowing for the overall effects on the level of production, consumption, employment, equity, the achievement of basic needs, the environment and future generations.

Worth values and market values are related as follows: consumers have a notion of intrinsic values that in the case of marketable goods are associated with, but not identical to, market values. People and economic organisations repeatedly assess worth values, which are seen as fair prices or 'just' wages, from their observations of market values. Worth values are consensus valuations, not specific to a location or time, repeatedly compared with other peoples' valuations and other group valuations, repeatedly updated and revised. Normally, in order to save time and effort and to make sense of the flow of information, assessments of worth values stay constant for long periods of time, especially when the overall rate of inflation is low. It is by comparing worth values with market values that purchasers decide whether to buy or not.

Worth values are measurable simply by asking people or organisations to provide valuations of particular items in contexts which are as non-locational and as non-time-specific as possible. There is a spectrum of valuations of such items as bread and milk, all the items that people purchase on a regular basis, as well as of those items that people dream about and imagine purchasing, such as cars and houses. These worth values allow people to say whether items are cheap or expensive. Some goods and services can be established as having worth values that are more or less identical to their market values, a feature of great advantage to the consumer and sometimes to the producer. For example, the fact that it costs the same price to send a letter to all parts of a country is normally an indication of this convergence of the market value and the worth value.

General inflation prevents prices being completely invariant over time, but the attractions of prices being invariant across space are such that for many replicated goods, efforts are made by the producer to standardise the price across a wide number of locations. This is in spite of the fact that there are different costs incurred in supplying, for example, replicated goods to the Highlands of Scotland when they are produced in London. And the same phenomenon accounts for the desire for prices to stay constant through time, and hence the dislike of inflation. Inflation spoils the information content of worth values and weakens the connection between the worth value and the market value. It means that consumers must take more time to learn new prices, and those who do not learn will find themselves at a disadvantage.

7.6 Asymmetrical information and uncertainty

This problem of asymmetrical information is very closely allied to the general problem of uncertainty in the minds of both the sellers and the buyers as to the value of the good or service. In addition to the obvious, known and verifiable characteristics of goods and services – the location of the sale, the time of the sale, the prices charged by the seller and offered by the buyer (if it is a double auction market), the physical characteristics – weight, shape, and so on – of the good and the quality characteristics of the service, there are a number of characteristics, unknown or guessed at the time of sale, that will emerge during the subsequent ownership and consumption of the good or service. Some of these could be classed as externalities, others as by-products of consumption – such as food that damages the consumer. It is clear that uncertainties are pervasive regarding the characteristics of the goods and services on sale and that there are extensive institutional procedures and regulations to protect against harmful effects of hidden characteristics and to put an obligation on the seller not to sell defective goods, especially those whose defects can be readily hidden.

This feature (asymmetrical information) explains a huge body of laws, regulations and procedures, and indeed institutions, surrounding the quality of goods and services on sale. It explains the trade-off in terms of the price of second-hand goods and that of new goods. It explains the creation and presence of brand names and replicated goods in terms of quality assurance that the characteristics are as advertised, and that any hidden negative characteristics have been minimised. It explains the use of guarantees to strengthen further and enhance the quality of the new good and the importance of guarantees ensuring that the purchaser has some recourse if he or she has indeed been misinformed. The uncertainty about quality means that following the purchase of certain goods and services, the subsequent location of the purchaser, and indeed the location of the consumer, is important in relation to the location of the sale. If something goes wrong, there are transport and other communication costs that will have to be borne if the purchaser is to return to the seller. It also explains why in many markets purchasers and consumers are one and the same, simply because it is necessary to form a legal contract between *consumer* and seller at the point of sale and, therefore, for the contract to be viable there must be this link, a close identification of purchase with consumption.

8   Economic growth and technological progress

8.1   Technology, economies of scale and economic growth

Economic historians have long argued that technological change and economic growth are intimately related (Maddison, 2001) and path dependent (David, 2001). Technological change, in turn, stems from the exploitation of scientific discoveries, given the availability of resources and an institutional structure that encourages innovation and investment. Nell (1998, pp. 144–8) outlines the evolutionary processes in what he calls transformational growth. A crucial feature of markets is that they select and spread innovation through financing expansion of investment in successful products. There is a population of firms, households, banks and other social groups and variation within each group that allows selection of successful organisational forms, products and characteristics through competition and emulation. The basic economic institutions change over time in response to new technologies, changes in tastes and in availability of resources.

The effects of technological change spread through the economy, creating new demands and saving resources in supply. In their historical account of how firms and industries innovate and change over time, Freeman and Soete (1997) emphasise the importance of heterogeneity in sectors and the role of niche markets. R&D and innovation is not spread evenly, but concentrated in successful firms and diffuses through an evolutionary and competitive process under uncertainty. Success comes from three important features of the innovation process (p. 202). First, there is a constant stream of potential innovations coming from scientific discoveries and those firms with high R&D and investment are in the best position to take advantage of them. Second, firms with close contact with their customers and markets are better able to recognise new opportunities for products. And third, successful firms are able to link the new products to the customers' needs. The implication is that economic growth should be modelled as a dynamic stochastic process with historical and country detail. Path dependence means that technological advantages persist over time and become locked into trading patterns. Technological change can be highly nonlinear, depending on the availability of markets, actual and expected changes in prices and the industrial organisation of the sectors concerned.

A critical feature of this process is increasing returns to scale. Oulton, in a study of increasing returns in UK manufacturing 1954–86, starts his paper as follows:

> No-one doubts that economies of scale exist and are important – generations of economists and engineers have established this ... Similarly, in a broad sense, no-one can doubt the existence and importance of externalities, of which the most obvious and economically relevant is the cumulative nature of scientific and technical knowledge. (1996, p. 99)

His study addresses the question of whether industrial growth is associated with increasing exploitation of economies of scale. The model is similar to models used by Caballero and Lyons (1990) and Bartelsman et al. (1991) for data on USA manufacturing and (1990) on European manufacturing, and he reaches similar conclusions for each. The assumptions are rather implausible, for example, assuming that the elasticity of scale and the effects of externalities are constant though time, but the conclusions are that economies of scale internal to each industry are unimportant for growth, but those *external* to the industry are significant. In addition, Oulton finds that increasing returns are a long-run feature of the system.

Studies using panel data on regional manufacturing have also assessed economics of scale and found increasing returns. In particular, Fingleton and McCombie (1998) found evidence of substantial returns to scale for EU manufacturing in estimating an equation based on Verdoorn's Law (1949). The estimates of were confirmed for later data 1986–2002 by Angeriz et al. (2008). The law asserts that labour productivity grows with output, through the growth in output, inducing technological change. The estimates confirm that there is a correlation between growth in labour productivity and growth in output, allowing for the fact that productivity is output per person employed. In employment equations explaining employment in terms of output, the law shows up as a coefficient on output less than one. Typically for cross-section data on manufacturing sectoral employement across countries, a statistically significant coefficient of 0.5 is estimated, providing strong evidence of economies of scale.

8.2   Demand-side growth

Economic growth involves technological change and the interaction between the increasing desire for variety or diversity in consumption on the demand side and increasing returns and specialisation in production on the supply side. The theoretical basis of the approach is developed in Post Keynesian theory where economic growth is demand-led and supply-constrained (for example, Setterfield, 2002) in both the short term and the long term. The demand for products is not necessarily matched by the supply, so that prices, waiting lists, stocks and the utilisation of capacity can all change to balance supply and demand. These changes provide signals to the markets and lead to adjustments of both demand and supply. Each industry has expectations of a normal rate of growth, which is affected by the actual rate both in the industry and across the economy. The ratio of the actual to normal output by industry will affect investment and employment, hence the long-run potential output. If expectations are shocked, as in the financial crisis of 2008 with the collapse of the banks, then governments can influence them by stimulating demand either directly through government spending or indirectly through tax cuts and investment incentives for the private sector.

Complexity economists (Arthur 1994; Beinhocker 2006) argue strongly for path dependency and increasing returns. In modelling effects of technological change on long-run economic growth, the history approach of cumulative causation fits with the emphasis on increasing returns (Kaldor, 1957, 1972, 1985). 'Cumulative causation' refers to a dynamic institutional process in which various factors combine to create a vicious or virtual circle to strengthen an initial effect (Berger, 2008). The specific cumulative causation as a feature of economic development is a feedback process depending on technological change and increasing returns. Through a shift in relative costs or prices or the discovery of a new product or process, growth of demand is encouraged. If the national market is open to trade, the growth may also be in export demand. As demand rises and trade expands, increasing returns lead to lower costs and prices, thereby further increasing the size of the market. New opportunities may arise for using the process or product. Particular regions and sectors develop differentially, as the growing markets lead to a diffusion of higher income and employment in the sectors supplying the original new product or process. The feedback is stronger the larger the national market and the more open it is to international trade.

8.3 Economic growth and diversity in consumption

Consider purchasers' choice when the goods and services are indivisible and each has a different combination of desired characteristics. The effects of increasing real per capita incomes are to increase the variety of goods and services purchased. Total expenditure allocated by each purchaser to the market will grow, since all the characteristics are positively desired, and an increasing proportion of the available goods become feasible for increasing numbers of purchasers. In other words, each purchaser is more able to buy his or her preferred combination of characteristics as incomes rise over time. The variety of goods available will increase and demand will be spread ever more thinly over the various goods on offer.

The theory is supported by cross-section evidence from the analysis of family budgets, mainly for the spending on food in developing countries. The first expectation from the theory is that, in any market, the average price of the goods bought will increase as real per capita incomes increase, even though the prices of individual goods remain constant. This positive 'quality elasticity' of expenditure with respect to income has been noted in many studies of consumer expenditure for various countries and products (Prais and Houthakker, 1955; Deaton, 1988, p. 428; Dong and Gould, 2007, p. 268; Gale and Huang, 2007, p. 18). A second expectation from the theory is that in any market the variance of prices paid for the goods on the market will increase as real per capita incomes increase (because purchases will spread over the available set). This has been noticed as a problem of heteroscedasticity in the regression of price on real income (Prais and Houthakker, 1955, pp. 55–7).

8.4 Growth and trade

The theory also has implications for trade, both domestic and international. Consider the availability of different varieties of a product on the international and the domestic markets. The varieties available on the international market are likely to be more numerous and more expensive (due to transport and other costs associated with distance) than those on the domestic market. The variety hypothesis (Barker, 1977, p. 161) states that, up to the point of market saturation, increases in real per capita income cause a greater increase in purchases of imported goods compared with domestically produced goods. If real output varies proportionally with real income per capita then the elasticity of total imports with respect to this income will be *greater* than unity. At the limit when incomes are high enough to buy all the available goods, this elasticity will fall towards unity.

In contrast to theories that emphasise supply determination of growth, the theory underlying the variety hypothesis emphasises the effects on trade of real income and its growth. Consider a product, noting now that some of the constituent homogeneous goods are imported; indeed, the fact that they are imported may be their only distinguishing feature. Imports tend to be more expensive because of transport and other costs, and also there are numerically more types of goods imported than home-produced, even although the quantity consumed of the imported goods may be much less than that of the home-produced goods. If the desire for quality, variety and distinction is linked with the quantity demanded of the commodity rather than real income in general, then the share of imports in the demand is positively related to the level of demand. The proportionate change in imports brought about by a proportionate unit change in the level of demand is defined as the 'demand elasticity' for imports of the commodity.

This theory, ceteris paribus, yields the following hypotheses about these elasticities:

(i)   Since in general one country is able to supply only a small proportion of the possible varieties of a commodity, then the demand elasticity will be greater than unity. This applies *a fortiori* to the total imports of a country.

(ii) The more varieties of a commodity there are available, the higher the demand elasticity for imports. Economies of mass production and standardisation militate against the production of an ever-increasing variety of goods within a commodity; the fact that a good more exactly meets the desires of its consumers is outweighed by the increased cost of its production. Trade, especially international trade, provides a means of extending the range of economically produced varieties of a commodity. In general, higher demand elasticities are expected for manufactured goods than for foodstuffs, raw materials or fuels; the elasticity would rise as the degree of manufacturing rises since the opportunities for product differentiation also tend to rise. Thus with a uniform world distribution of natural resources, labour and capital – but not of demands – most trade would be in highly sophisticated and differentiated manufactures such as computers and aircraft, and least trade would be in standardised products such as wheat or crude oil.

Technological progress in this view of the world economy would show up in higher growth in exports, since firms would be seeking the widest possible markets for their more technically advanced or innovative products. Studies of innovation and export performance using German microeconomic data come to unambiguous conclusions finding significant effects and that the direction of causation is from R&D innovation to export volumes (Lachenmaier and Wößmann, 2006).

In this open system, economic growth emerges through technological change and the increasing interdependence of markets. Full employment and an equitable distribution of income are not guaranteed. Instead, through inertia of expectations, the world economy will continue to grow (or contract) until changes are forced by social groups, such as governments or banks, responding to unacceptable or unfavourable outcomes, such as inequalities, inflation, unemployment or bankruptcies.

9 Economic policy

So far the chapter has been concerned mainly with the problem of how to abstract from the facts and theories about the economic system to achieve an understanding of the main features that underlie economic activity. This section addresses the issue of the role of economic policy in the new economics, which is essentially characterised by a Keynesian emphasis on the importance of intervention by governments through monetary, fiscal and regulatory policies to achieve socially and politically acceptable outcomes for the economy. Governments usually have a wide range of instruments at their disposal to achieve their targets for economic, social and environmental policy. Governments set the rules for the operation of the market economy, manage their own spending for the provision of public services and social transfers, raise taxes and provide information on the economy. The justification for governments for this intervention is that the market system without such management is subject to social, financial and environmental problems, such as inequality, unemployment, financial risk-taking, or global warming, i.e. market failures.

9.1 Inequalities

It is clear from international comparisons of inequalities in income and wealth that great inequalities can exist in market economies. Inequalities tend to be persistent and to be associated with many social problems, such as long-term unemployment and drug abuse. It has long been accepted that fiscal policy can be progressive, raising proportionally more taxes from those with more income and wealth and directing public spending so that it is targeted on those who are most vulnerable in society. Typically income taxes are progressive and exemptions and lower rates are included in Value Added Tax (VAT) systems to benefit lower-income groups. Fiscal policy can be complemented by incomes policies, including minimum wage legislation, to reduce inequalities.

9.2 Market externalities and system risks

There are two other classes of market failure – the first, largely uncontested across schools of economic thought, is that relating to externalities such as those relating to the natural environment. The market system relies on the environment to provide vital services without cost. If these services are limited in supply, they can be overused and damaged. This market failure can be addressed by regulation, or by imposing a price on the use of the service, for example, a carbon price to discourage the emissions of CO_2 from combustion of fossil fuels. Another generally agreed market failure relates to the beneficial externality associated with innovation. An innovating firm can take out patents and copyright, develop a brand, and impose other barriers to entry into the market, but it is very difficult to prevent rivals from taking some benefit from the innovation. The consequence is that the operation of the market will lead to a lower level of innovation than is justified by the social benefit, so providing a case for special treatment of innovation spending, either a direct subsidy or privileged access to funding or allowances against tax liabilities. An additional externality is the systemic risk in the financial markets associated with long-term speculation on the direction of asset prices. The risk is that of banking insolvencies – as in the 2008 crisis – leading to a massive increase in public debt and volatility in prices and demand.

These externalities justify a portfolio of public policies, with the mix of regulation, fiscal and monetary policies depending on the specific conditions and the political stance of the government. Some of them are intrinsically global issues, such as climate change and systemic banking risk, and justify global taxation and regulation, such as international emission trading schemes and standards for low-carbon equipment. Among the policies used to reduce the banking risks are regulation and taxation. At the G20 meeting in June 2010 the IMF (2010) proposed a Financial Stability Contribution (FSC) and Financial Activities Tax (FAT). The FSC is intended to provide governments with funding to help resolve future crises when a bank or other financial group is deemed to be too big to fail. It is a form of insurance payment so that when a bank failure is threatened, the financial authorities can provide some value to unsecured creditors and maintain vital services when equity becomes worthless and management is replaced. The FAT is a tax, like VAT, on wages and profits, designed to reduce the size of the financial sector, which is largely VAT-exempt, in relation to other sectors of the economy that pay VAT. Other externalities also justify specific taxes and subsidies, such as tax allowances for business spending on innovation.

The second class of market failure is macroeconomic. Here there is the likelihood that inconsistencies between desired investment and saving will lead to excess demand and inflation, or involuntary unemployment. There is a strong case, widely accepted, for automatic stabilisers in the fiscal system. The stabilisers, for example the progressive tax and benefit systems, allow government expenditures to be maintained when government revenues fall because of a collapse in incomes or spending from an unanticipated shock. There is also a case, less accepted in the literature but central to the response by governments to the financial crisis of 2008, for interventionist fiscal policy even without the rise in involuntary unemployment seen in many economies after the crisis (Arestis and Sawyer, 2003, 2004; Heise, 2009; Fontana, 2009). The traditional view is that of the 'New Consensus Macroeconomics' in which the role for interventionist fiscal policy is negligible, because it is seen as ineffective though the response of the private sector, namely that public spending 'crowds out' private spending. Arestis and Sawyer (2003) comprehensively address the theoretical arguments for crowding out, including the Ricardian Equivalence Theorem, and conclude that unless the economy is at full employment and generating wage inflation there is a role for fiscal policy. They provide a brief review of the estimates of crowding out in the literature and conclude that 'Fiscal multipliers and other tests tend to provide favorable evidence for fiscal policy' (p. 23).

Spilimbergo et al. (2009) provide a more recent review of empirical estimates of fiscal multipliers and the implicit crowding out of government-induced increases in investment. They confirm a repeated finding of substantial differences in estimates of the fiscal multiplier both across countries, over time. It is particularly noticeable that different researchers for the same country and time period can estimate substantially different multipliers. The main reason for the substantial difference in long-run multipliers seems to be in the theoretical approach: New Keynesians and others assuming rational expectations in the modelling assume no long-run effect, that is, full crowding out; those assuming adaptive expectation in a Keynesian framework, find multipliers above 1. In general, the multipliers reviewed increase with the economic size of the region and are largest for globally coordinated policies, they increase over time and they vary according to the source of the fiscal stimulus.

Official economic policy making since the 2008 financial crisis in many large economies was initially dominated by Keynesian thinking, given the widespread adoption of stimulus packages. There are two aspects of the procedures that appear to be particularly important. First, the policies are usually concentrated on macroeconomic variables such as total private consumption or total investment, almost to the exclusion of their components; and second, the objectives of the policies and the consideration of their effects have been confined mainly to the short-term future – that is, over the following 12 to 18 months. The emphasis on macroeconomic variables has its counterpart in the use of hypothetical concepts such as the 'non-accelerating inflation rate of unemployment' (NAIRU for short). These concepts are used as a guide to the required changes in policy, but if the changes have important structural effects then the analyses and policies may result in departures from the targets in the form of higher unemployment or extra inflation. The problem is that actual changes in policy to pursue macroeconomic objectives often provoke structural effects, thus undermining the very basis of the policy. Another weakness has been the use of changes in tax rates and levels of expenditures to meet short-term needs, with the consequence that policy objectives, which can be reached only by a medium-term or long-term strategy, come to be seen as unrealistic and unattainable.

9.3 Aggregation in economic modelling

The problem of aggregation arises because all people and social groups are different, and the explanation of behaviour at the level of the individual person or group cannot simply be aggregated to give an explanation of behaviour of the aggregate of all social groups. If consistent aggregation, in the sense of mathematically valid aggregation of known behaviour at the micro level, is not possible, the issue is the choice of the *appropriate* level of aggregation. The following factors influence the choice of the level of aggregation in economic modelling: the purpose of the model, the specification errors likely to be involved, the data available, and the required simplicity and parsimony. If the purpose is pedagogical, aggregation becomes a simplifying technique permitting a clearer understanding of the nature of the forces at work. If the purpose is policy formulation, for example the appropriate structure of the tax system to promote greenhouse gas abatement, then disaggregation of policy instruments is essential and disaggregation of the revenue base into its major components is advisable. If the purpose is forecasting, then the decisions that rely on the forecast will determine the minimum level of disaggregation required. Aggregate macro variables such as GDP are sufficient for the overall management of the economy unless the economy is close to full employment and management of the structure of demand is required. And scenarios relating to global warming will require much greater detail of the energy and industrial structure, and of the implications for greenhouse gas emissions.

9.4 Policy scenarios

Social choice regarding the future of the economy involves social groups such as government, parliament and political parties. But it also involves information. A real choice requires the equal and simultaneous presentation of feasible alternatives, and this can only be done properly by using a quantitative, computable model of the system. In this way changes in the levels of the policy instruments can be simulated to explore how they might affect economic behaviour. This exercise serves two purposes. First, it shows the effects of the instruments on the targets, giving us some indication of their ability to achieve a target without adversely affecting other targets of policy. The second purpose of the exercise is that it keeps a check on the plausibility of the model as a means of simulating economic policy. When several targets are achieved simultaneously, it is difficult to disentangle the effects of the several instruments: the problem is made easier if we have an idea of how each acts in isolation.

10 Representing the energy–environment–economy systems in models

10.1 The challenge of representing the system

The problem is how to represent the economic system for the purpose of economic policy. If understanding social behaviour is context-specific in space and time, then economic models intended for economic policy making must take account of economic geography and history; moreover, the roles and operating procedures, that is, the institutions, governing social and economic behaviour are fundamental. Any representation in an economic model must assume the continuity of the roles and the procedures of these institutions being modelled. The implication is that the models should simulate the historical development of the system and include specific policy instruments for managing the system. This in turn implies the construction and use of large-scale computable models, either of the whole system or in part.

10.2 Criteria of good economic models

It is worth listing the criteria of a good economic model for economic policy making.

1. *Consistent* – The treatment of the different parts of the represented system should be internally consistent. It is a great advantage to base a model on a system of accounts because this enforces statistical conventions and accounting identities – for example, the relation between stocks and flows.

2. *Understandable* – The model should be divided into modules, and into different levels of scale, so that the interconnections between economic variables can be readily seen. If we are to understand the

world, we must understand the model. It should not be a 'black box', opaque to the observer; instead, the relationships between the different variables should be made quite clear, and a good model structure should help to keep these clear. Models of complex systems are not themselves necessarily difficult to understand. Good models are, however, coherent. It should be possible to turn the results of models into words to give a clear verbal explanation of economic behaviour, thus giving insight into that behaviour.

3. *Comprehensive* – A good model should cover comprehensively the relevant variables of those parts of the economic system being modelled over space and time, otherwise some of the essential connections will be missing, and the understanding flawed. The detail may help to identify those small effects that would otherwise be hidden in the aggregate responses.

4. *Spatial and temporal* – Any economic model should be absolutely clear about the way in which it represents both location and time; Adequate representation will acknowledge the regional interactions and the path dependence of the economy.

5. *Able to recognise uncertainty* – Models of the economy miss out a crucial feature if they do not recognise the uncertainty in the values of their parameters, the projections of their exogenous variables and their general representation of the economy.

6. *Documented and reproducible* – Models should be well documented and reproducible.

7. *At the appropriate scale* – Models are built to a scale appropriate to the objectives or requirements set by the model builder in the use of the model. Good models simplify and show the main features relevant to the understanding of the systems.

10.3 Large-scale energy–environment–economy models

These ideas have been brought together in models at different spatial scales, with the latest being a global model, E3MG (Barker and Scrieciu, 2010). E3MG is an annual econometric simulation model with 20 regional economies and substantial sectoral detail including 42 industrial sectors. There is no presumption that the economies are operating at some optimal level in their allocation of resources or their growth rates. Instead the assumption is that they are interacting over time in a constrained complex system with various negative and positive feedback loops such that behaviours become self-reinforcing until they provoke a change in the institutional rules.

These changes can be political, such as the break-up of the Soviet Union, or due to the inherent tendency of some social groups to exploit their economic power until the behaviour causes a break in the system, as in the banking crisis. By 2007 the banks had reached such levels of leverage that very small reductions in the values of the underlying assets were enough to bring about a collapse of the system, only prevented by a change in the rules so that the major banks avoided bankruptcy. The state, through the policies of finance departments and central banks, reduced interest rates for central bank lending, provided loans to troubled banks and took on the risks of default. The most convincing account of the processes leading up to the crisis is that by Minsky (1986, chapter 8). He argues that during periods of expansion, the financial sector, encouraged by success, gradually downplays risks and uncertainties, and engages in financial innovation to create new forms of money, leading to more and more financial instability. The financial expansion feeds on itself through the capital gains of the collateral real assets until the point is reached at which it becomes clear that the real returns on the underlying assets cannot support the loans. The system then collapses with bankruptcies and defaults.

The generality of the approach lies in leaving the explanations of consumption, investment and trade to be consistent with the data without the constraints imposed by traditional theory based on assuming representative agents (Kirman, 1992), but assuming some coherence, that is, demand for products fall when their relative price rises. Accounting balances should also be imposed, such as GDP components adding up to GDP and global exports being equal to imports, allowing for measurement errors and differences in valuation. Other constraints can be imposed on stockbuilding and supplies of labour and natural resources. However, unemployment, balance of payments deficits and public sector deficits can all easily persist for some countries, depending on the tolerance of the population for unemployment and the markets for debt. So the models are open with respect to the markets for labour, foreign exchange and government debt, allowing imbalances to persist, with an increasing risk of institutional breaks as the unemployment and deficits increase. Different assumptions on the resolution of the imbalances lead to sets of scenarios, which can be developed to illustrate the uncertainties in projections.

The financial and banking sector is represented in these models as one of some 40 sectors of the economy, with annual data on its output, employment, investment, trade and purchases of goods and services from other sectors. The models calculate the financial surpluses and deficits for the main instructional groups in the economy and the aggregate balances for the foreign sector. These deficits and surpluses can lead to increasing imbalances in the underlying debt and credit positions of the groups. However, there are also the uncertainties associated with changes in valuations in the asset markets, especially in dwellings. These are included as a variable affecting the change in private consumers' expenditure, along with changes in disposable incomes and relative prices. One aspect of the 2008 banking crisis was the slowing of investment by the financial sector in general, and this exogenous shock can be imposed directly on the projections.

If we consider the theoretical properties of the global model in the long run and at a macro level, the crucial features determining the effects of fiscal policies can be identified. Fiscal policies affect prices, incomes and expenditures in the model. The wage–price interaction is affected by the level of unemployment, changes in global prices, such as the oil price, and productivity, with real wage rates rising according to labour productivity. Employment and investment are derived demands relating to real output by sector allowing for effects of unit costs relative to the prices of output. Total demand and supply come from industrial demand (the model uses input–output tables), private and public consumption, and investment. At a regional level, for example, in the case of the UK, exports are added into the demand for and imports into the supply of products.

The critical relationship affecting the global multiplier is that of the consumption function, that is, how long-run consumption responds to changes in real disposable income. Fiscal policy can affect real disposable income through the price level, with carbon taxes and permit schemes affecting prices, through transfers such as income tax, affecting income, and through employment affecting total wages, the main component of income in most regions. Government expenditure directly on investment or incentives for private investment will increase output and employment; and the extra employment will lead to extra consumption in the Keynesian multiplier process. At a regional level the size of the multiplier will also be affected by the extent to which the region is open to world trade. The more open an economy is to international trade, the more any stimulus in domestic demand will go into imports rather than domestic production, so the regional multiplier will be smaller.

10.4   Features of large-scale 'new economics' models

The demand-led long-run growth in this approach is dependent on Kondratiev waves of investment as a macroeconomic phenomenon arising out of increasing returns, which leads to technological change and diffusion. Other features of the empirical modelling of growth, not limited to Post Keynesian theory, include: varying returns to scale across industries (which are derived from estimation), no assumption of full employment, varying degrees of competition, the feature that industries act as social groups and not as a group of individual firms (that is, bounded rationality is implied), and the grouping of countries and regions based on political criteria. Since technological change is embodied in gross investment (Scott, 1989), accumulated investment can be used as an indicator of technological progress by industry and country. Quantitative relationships can be found between technological progress as measured and the growth in demands and/or the saving of resources to meet these demands. These provide a basis for representing the effects of technological progress on long-term macroeconomic growth in large-scale models. The approach allows for long-term unemployed resources and a simplified form of the consumption function for long-term analysis. It assumes adaptive expectations and a demand-side and technological determination of long-run economic growth. Uncertainty is treated through sets of scenarios, and fiscal imbalances can be maintained or removed through variations in government spending and tax or other revenues.

11 Conclusions

This paper has set out the basis for a new approach to understanding economic behaviour based on intrinsic as well as monetary values and allowing for diversity instead of assuming representative agents. The argument is that an approach that allows for the diverse experience in different sectors and world regions can be developed to give theoretical and empirical relationships explaining economic variables such as output, trade, employment and prices. Moreover, technological change can be included so that it is affected by investment and it in turn affects demand and hence economic growth. Regional economic growth is path dependent and essentially derived from global demand growth, but it is constrained by the available resources, including capital and labour. Economic policy is required to manage demand; otherwise the system will be unsustainable in terms of unemployment and/or inflation. Since money is endogenous, inflation has to be managed by incomes policies and fiscal policy. These features have been embodied in quantitative economic models at different special scales, estimated assuming that the time-series data show sufficient inertia to allow the measurement of averaged responses at an industrial level.

Notes

1. Thanks to contributors to the 2010 Bilbao conference of Post Keynesian Economics, as well as David Taylor, Serban Scrieciu and Richard Lewney for comments. Thanks are also due to The Three Guineas Trust, one of the Sainsbury Family Trusts, and to the Cambridge Trust for New Thinking in Economics for financial support.
2. Barker (2008) develops many of the ideas summarised in this and the next section, but in the context of climate change economics.
3. The term 'New Economics' has been used since the 1920s to refer to Keynes' approach to economics and later to the Keynesian approach, for example, in the title of Harris's edited book originally published in 1947. The book provides a comprehensive review and critique of Keynes's work (Harris, 2005). Then, as now, 'new' is to be contrasted with 'traditional', but now traditional economics has incorporated a synthesis of Keynesian and neo-classical theory (for example, in New Keynesian macroeconomics).
4. See Barker (1996) for more details. Faden (1977, pp. 10–11) starts from this point. Isard and Liossatos (1979, chapter 2) discuss perceptively the various intuitive notions of time and its interrelation with space, but without any emphasis on the role of institutions.
5. Lancaster's own definition is more restricted in that he defines character-istics as 'those objective properties of things that are relevant to choice by people' (1971, p. 6). He considers a model of final consumer demand where a *continuous* range of alternative combinations of characteristics is available (he needs continuity for his mathematics); in what follows, mar-kets are defined for purchasers in general in which only limited numbers of alternative combinations are available.
6. Computable general equilibrium models have traditionally treated techno-logical change as autonomous.
7. This discussion is drawn from Barker (2010).
8. The neoclassical approach to money, based on the quantity theory of money, does not make this distinction.
9. The assumption that everyone is different does not mean that we are not equal under the law, or that we do not have equal rights.
10. In neoclassical economic analysis people are treated as if they are the services they can perform in the production function. Labour services are disem-bodied from the people that produce them and are available in continuous amounts.

References

Ackerman, F. and Heinzerling, L. (2004) *Priceless: On Knowing the Price of Every-thing and the Value of Nothing*. New York: The New Press.

Ackerman, F. and Nadal, A. (2004) *The Flawed Foundations of General Equilibrium: Critical Essays on Economic Theory*. London: Routledge.

Angeriz, A., McCombie, J. and Roberts, M. (2008) 'New Estimates of Returns to Scale for EU Regional Manufacturing, 1986–2002', *International Review of Regional Science*, 31, pp. 62–87.

Argyrous, G. (1996) 'Cumulative Causation and Industrial Evolution: Kaldor's Four Stages of Industrialization as an Evolutionary Model', *Journal of Economic Issues*, 30, pp. 97–119.

Argyrous, G. (2002) 'Endogenous Demand in the Theory of Transformational Growth', in M. Setterfield (ed.), *The Economics of Demand-Led Growth – Challenging the Supply-side Vision of the Long Run*. Cheltenham, UK: Edward Elgar, pp. 237–50.

Arestis, P. and Sawyer, M. (2003) 'Reinventing Fiscal Policy', *Journal of Post Keynesian Economics*, 26(1), pp. 3–25.

Arestis, P. and Sawyer, M. (2004) 'Fiscal Policy: A Potent Instrument', *New School Economic Review*, 1(1), pp. 21–32.

Arthur, W.B. (1994) *Increasing Returns and Path Dependence in the Economy*. Ann Arbor, MI: University of Michigan Press.

Barker, T. (1977) 'International Trade and Economic Growth: An Alternative to the Neoclassical Approach', *Cambridge Journal of Economics*, 1, pp. 153–72.

Barker, T. (1996) *Space-Time Economics*. Cambridge: Cambridge Econometrics.

Barker, T. (2008) 'The Economics of Avoiding Dangerous Climate Change. An Editorial Essay on The Stern Review', *Climatic Change*, 89:173–94. doi: 10.1007/s10584-008-9433-x.

Barker, T. (2010) 'Endogenous Money in 21st Century Keynesian Economics', in P. Arestis and M. Sawyer (eds), *21st Century Keynesian Economics*. Basingstoke: Palgrave Macmillan.

Barker, T. and Scrieciu, S. (2010) 'Modeling Low Stabilization with E3MG: Towards a "New Economics" Approach to Simulating Energy–Environment–Economy System Dynamics', *Energy Journal* Special Issue on 'The Economics of Low Stabilisation', January, pp. 137–64

Bartelsman, E.J., Caballero, R.J. and Lyons, R.K. (1991) 'Short and Long Run Externalities', NBER Working Paper No. 3810, August. Cambridge, MA: NBER.

Baumol, W. (1987) 'Indivisibilities', in J. Eatwell, M. Milgate and P. Newman (eds), *The New Palgrave: A Dictionary of Economics*. Basingstoke: Palgrave Macmillan.

Beinhocker, E. (2006) *The Origin of Wealth: Evolution, Complexity and the Radical Remaking of Economics*. London: Random House Business Books.

Berger, S. (2008) 'Circular Cumulative Causation (CCC) à la Myrdal and Kapp – Political Institutionalism for Minimizing Social Costs', *Journal of Economic Issues*, 42(2), pp. 357–65.

Boulding, K. (1992) *Towards A New Economics*. Cheltenham: Edward Elgar Publishing.

Broome, J. (2005) 'Why Economics Needs Ethical Theory', *Pelican Record*, 42, 80–8; reprinted in J. Broome (2008) 'Why Economics Needs Ethical Theory', in K. Basu and R. Kanbur (eds), *Welfare, Development, Philosophy and Social Science: Essays for Amartya Sen's 75th Birthday*, vol. 3. Oxford: Oxford University Press.

Broome, J. (2006) 'Valuing Policies in Response to Climate Change: Some Ethical Issues', contribution to the work of the Stern Review of the Economics of Climate Change. See http://philpapers.org/browse/climate-change.

Caballero, R.J. and Lyons, R.K. (1990) 'Internal Versus External Economies in European Industry', *European Economic Review*, 34, pp. 805–30.

Coase, R. (1988) *The Firm, The Market, and The Law*. Chicago: University of Chicago Press.

Colander, D., Holt, R. and Rosser Jr, J.B. (2004) 'The Changing Face of Mainstream Economics', *Review of Political Economy*, 6(4), pp. 485–99.

Commons, J.R. (1934) *Institutional Economics*. New York: Macmillan.

Coveney, P. and Highfield, R. (1990) *The Arrow of Time*. New York: HarperCollins edition 1991.

David, P. (2001) 'Path Dependence, Its Critics, and the Quest for "Historical Economics"', in P. Garrouste and S. Ioannides (eds), *Evolution and Path Dependence in Economic Ideas: Past and Present*. London: Edward Elgar.

Deaton, A. (1988) 'Quality, Quantity, and Spatial Variation of Price', *American Economic Review*, 78(3), pp. 418–30.

Dequech, D. (2007) 'Neoclassical, Mainstream, Orthodox, and Heterodox Economics', *Journal of Post Keynesian Economics*, 30(2), pp. 279–302.

Dong, D. and Gould, B. (2007) 'Product Quality and the Demand for Food: The Case of Urban China', Chapter 12 in I. Seldon (ed.), *China's Agricultural Trade: Issues and Prospects*, Papers presented at an IATRC International Symposium, Beijing, China, July.

Faden, A.M. (1977) *Economics of Space and Time: The Measure-Theoretic Foundations of Social Science*. Ames, IA: Iowa State University Press.

Fingleton, B. and McCombie, J.S.L. (1998) 'Increasing Returns and Economic Growth: Some Evidence for Manufacturing from the European Union Regions', *Oxford Economic Papers*, 50, pp. 89–105.

Foley, D. (2006) *Adam's Fallacy: A Guide to Economic Theology*. Cambridge, MA: Harvard University Press.

Fontana, G. (2009) 'The Transmission Mechanism of Fiscal Policy: A Critical Assessment of Current Theories and Empirical Methodologies', *Journal of Post Keynesian Economics*, 31(4), pp. 587–604. doi:10.2753/PKE0160-3477310404.

Freeman, C. and Soete, L. (1997) *The Economics of Industrial Innovation*, 3rd edn. London: Pinter.

Gale, F. and Huang, K. (2007) 'Demand for Food Quantity and Quality in China', Economic Research Report No. 32, US Department of Agriculture, January.

Gowdy, J. (2005) 'Towards a New Welfare Economics for Sustainability', *Ecological Economics*, 53, pp. 211–22.

Griliches, Z. (ed.) (1971) *Prices Indices and Quality Change*. Cambridge, MA: Harvard University Press.

Harris, S.E. (ed.) (2005) *New Economics: Keynes' Influence on Theory And Public Policy*. Montana, USA: Kessinger Publishing (original edition 1947).

Heise, A. (2009) 'A Post Keynesian Theory of Economic Policy – Filling a Void', *Journal of Post Keynesian Economics*, 31(3), pp. 383–401.

Hodgson, G.M. (1999) *Evolution and Institutions: On Evolutionary Economics and the Evolution of Economics*. Cheltenham: Edward Elgar.

Hodgson, G.M. (2007) 'Evolutionary and Institutional Economics as the New Mainstream?', *Evolutionary and Institutional Economics Review*, 4(1), pp. 7–25.

Holt, R. (2007) 'What is Post *Keynesian* Economics?', in M. Forstater, G. Mongiovi and S. Pressman (eds), *Post* Keynesian *Macroeconomics*. New York and London: Routledge Press.

Isard, W. and Liossatos, P. (1979) *Spatial Dynamics and Optimal Space-Time Development*. Amsterdam: North-Holland Publishing Company.

Kahneman, D. and Tversky, A. (1989) 'Prospect Theory: An Analysis of Decisions Under Risk', *Econometrica*, 47(2), pp. 263–91.

Kaldor, N. (1957) 'A Model of Economic Growth', *The Economic Journal*, 67(268), pp. 591–624.

Kaldor, N. (1972) 'The Irrelevance of Equilibrium Economics', *The Economic Journal*, 52, pp. 1237–55.

Kaldor, N. (1985) *Economics without Equilibrium*. Cardiff: University College of Cardiff Press.

Kirman, A.P. (1992) 'Whom or What Does the Representative Individual Represent?', *Journal of Economic Perspectives*, 6(2), pp. 117–36.

Lachenmaier, S. and Wößmann, L. (2006) 'Does Innovation Cause Exports? Evidence from Exogenous Innovation Impulses and Obstacles Using German Micro Data', *Oxford Economic Papers*, 58(2), pp. 317–50.

Lancaster, K. (1971) *Consumer Demand: A New Approach*. New York: Columbia University Press.

Maddison, A. (2001) *The World Economy. A Millennial Perspective*. Paris: OECD.

Maréchal, K. (2007) 'The Economics of Climate Change and the Change of Climate in Economics', *Energy Policy*, 35, pp. 5181–94.

Minsky, H. (1986) *Stabilizing an Unstable Economy*. New York: McGraw Hill.

Mirowski, P. (1989) *More Heat Than Light Economics as Social Physics: Physics as Nature's Economics*. Cambridge: Cambridge University Press.

Mirowski, P. (2002) *Machine Dreams: Economics Becomes a Cyborg Science*. Cambridge: Cambridge University Press.

Munda, G. (2005) 'Multiple Criteria Decision Analysis and Sustainable Development', in J. Figueira, S. Greco and M. Ehrogott (eds), *Multiple Criteria Decision Analysis: State of the Art Surveys. International Series in Operations Research & Management Science*, vol. 78. Berlin, Heidelberg and New York: Springer, pp. 953–86.

Nell, E.J. (1998) *The General Theory of Transformational Growth: Keynes After Sraffa*. Cambridge: Cambridge University Press.

Nelson, R.H. (2001) *Economics as Religion from Samuelson to Chicago and Beyond*. Philadelphia, PA: Pennsylvania State University Press.

Oulton, N. (1996) 'Increasing Returns and Externalities in UK Manufacturing: Myth or Reality?', *The Journal of Industrial Economics*, 44, March, pp. 99–113.

Ostrom, E. (1990) *Governing the Commons: The Evolution of Institutions for Collective Action*. Cambridge: Cambridge University Press.

Padilla, E. (2004) 'Climate Change, Economic Analysis and Sustainable Development', *Environmental Values*, 13, pp. 523–44.

Prais, S.J. and Houthakker, H.S. (1955) *The Analysis of Family Budgets*. Cambridge: Cambridge University Press.

Price, C. (2005) 'An Intergenerational Perspective on Effects of Environmental Changes: Discounting the Future's Viewpoint', in J.L. Innes, G.M. Hickey and H.F. Hoen (eds), *Forestry and Environmental Change: Socioeconomic and Political Dimensions*. Report 5 IUFRO Task Force on Environmental Change.

Rawls, J. (1971) *A Theory of Justice*. Cambridge, MA: Harvard University Press

Samuels, W.J. (1989) *Fundamentals of the Economic Role of Government*. Westport, CT: Greenwood Press.

Samuelson, P.A. (1947) *Foundations of Economic Analysis*. Cambridge, MA: Harvard University Press.

Schumpeter, J. (1934) *The Theory of Economic Development*. Cambridge, MA: Harvard University Press.

Scott, M. (1989) *A New View of Economic Growth*. Oxford: Clarendon Press.

Setterfield, M. (2002) *The Economics of Demand-Led Growth – Challenging the Supply-side Vision of the Long Run*. Cheltenham, UK: Edward Elgar.

Simmel, G. (1900, 7. second edition 1907). *The Philosophy of Money*, translation by Tom Bottomore and David Frisby (1978). London: Routledge and Kegan Paul.

Sowell, T. (1967) 'The "Evolutionary" Economics of Thorstein Veblen', *Oxford Economic Papers*, 19, pp. 177–98.

Spilimbergo, A., Symansky, S. and Schindler, M. (2009) 'Fiscal Multipliers', *IMF Staff Position Note* SPN/09/11.

Stern, N. (2007) *The Economics of Climate Change: The Stern Review*. Cambridge, UK: Cambridge University Press.

Veblen, T. (1899) *The Theory of the Leisure Class*. New York: Macmillan.

Verdoorn, P.J. (1949) 'Fattori che regolano lo sviluppo della produttivita del lavoro', *L'Industria*, 1, p. 310.

Williamson, O.E and Winter, S.G. (1991) *The Nature of the Firm, Origins, Evolution, and Development*. Oxford: Oxford University Press.

Young, A. (1928) 'Increasing Returns and Economic Progress', *The Economic Journal*, 38, pp. 527–42.

3

On the Possible Replacement of the Efficient-Market Hypothesis: Social Efficiency as a 'Thick' Approach to Financial Policy

Gary A. Dymski
University of California, Riverside

Abstract

So long as the efficient-market hypothesis remains the unchallenged arbiter of financial market outcomes, efforts to rethink the financial system – at either a policy or conceptual level – will be thwarted. The efficient-market hypothesis, which translates the idea of Walrasian general equilibrium into financial markets, has a profound hold on economists' thinking; it represents an intellectual sink that leads to ideas about financial policy reform which protect established interests and disregard any reform's broader economic consequences. This reference point is problematic because it refers to a world that does not exist except in the realms of pure theory. It is imperative to find an alternative frame of reference for evaluating financial-regulatory policy, one which takes into account whether financial market institutions are meeting the needs of society. This is done here by introducing 'social efficiency' as an alternative to the 'economic efficiency' derived from the Walrasian system. This social efficiency criterion focuses on whether financial policy changes are likely to reduce or widen inequality, and to reduce or increase a society's ability to guarantee the attainment of basic capabilities for all.

Keywords: Social efficiency; efficient-market hypothesis; financial regulation; heterodox economic theory; neoclassical economic theory; capabilities; equality

JEL Classifications: B52, D61, D62, G20, G28

1 Introduction

This paper contributes to the dialogue about the reshaping of economics after the global financial-economic crisis of 2007–10 by reflecting on the role of the efficient-market hypothesis (hereafter, EMH) both in orthodox economics and in the recent debate over reshaping US financial regulation. The EMH occupies a privileged place in economic thinking based on orthodox theory because it transports the core ideas of Walrasian general equilibrium (hereafter, WGE) into the realm of finance. Like the WGE, the EMH requires underlying conditions so rigorous that they are unlikely ever to be observed, yet it remains a core reference point not only for finance theory but also for policy analysis. Nonetheless, for the past 30 years, the EMH has been a central benchmark for financial regulation in the USA.

The 2007–08 financial crisis and the subsequent 2009–10 US financial reforms illustrated the dire consequences of this privileging of market efficiency. These reforms maintained financial stability and preserved large banks' operational freedom and solvency in the name of market efficiency, with no serious evaluation of the economic role or social impacts of the institutions that were bailed out.

Financial policy debate should centre on, rather than avoiding, the question of whether the banking and financial system is economically functional. But so long as the EMH remains the unchallenged arbiter of financial market outcomes, efforts to rethink the financial system will be thwarted. The intellectual hold of the EMH on economists' thinking about the functionality of the financial system must be broken. This can be done by introducing a notion of 'social efficiency' as an alternative to the 'economic' or 'market' efficiency' that has, until now, both constituted a core tenet of economic theory and guided analyses of financial regulatory policy options. A social efficiency criterion will render visible social justice dimensions of financial processes that are removed as irrelevant by assumption in orthodox analyses.

We proceed as follows. Section 2 shows how neoclassical economics explains the real economy's dynamics in the context of a timeless economic equilibrium. Section 3 describes the role of the EMH, which is one version of this timeless equilibrium, in understanding financial processes and reform proposals. Section 4 shows how the EMH informed neoclassical economists' reactions to the 2007–08 financial meltdown. Sections 5–7 propose a social efficiency concept as an alternative benchmark for evaluating financial policy alternatives. Section 8 considers the implications of the ideas developed here for the future of heterodox economics, and proposes a 'new economics'.

2   The Walrasian general equilibrium as an intellectual sink

What exactly is the 'neoclassical model', which makes neoclassical economists so reluctant to include financial instability as a centrepiece of financial economics? Here we define neoclassical economics as the set of approaches that understand the economy primarily by focusing on supply and demand forces, which are driven, in turn, by utility-maximising behaviour and by the distribution of wealth. This is clear enough. But in what does the practice of neoclassical economics consist? Here is where problems arise. The term 'neoclassical' is generic, not specific. If we turn to the subject list of doctoral 'microeconomics' and 'macroeconomics' courses, we find a daunting list of subfields: game theory, welfare economics, real-business cycle theory, the Ramsay–Solow growth model, information theory, and so on.

The analytical conventions within these subfields vary widely; the list of elements held in common by all these subfields would be quite small. But what these subfields share is an analytical ground zero: the 'Walrasian' model of a competitive economic equilibrium. This is not immediately obvious. The WGE is well known as that unique set of prices that equate demand and supply in every market, thus demonstrating that a decentralised, market-coordinated allocation of goods and services is feasible. The WGE requires such strong assumptions about the preferences of the agents participating in the equilibrium, market structure, and information that it can only be held up as an imaginary construction.

But this is precisely a feature that accentuates the role of the WGE as a unified point of reference, an intellectual centre, for mainstream theorists. It constitutes an empty centre for mainstream economics, and also serves as a convenient 'straw man'.

Much, if not most of contemporary mainstream theory has been built up precisely through theorists' calculated use of deviations from the Walrasian assumption set. For example, game theory begins by challenging the assumption that every agent is sufficiently 'small' that she can treat prices as given; information theory emerges only when the assumption of complete information is relaxed, and so on. As Arnsperger and Varoufakis (2006) point out, neoclassical theorists depart regularly from the strict assumption set of WGE, even while working well within the conceptual confines of neoclassicism.

The need to deviate from the strict conditions under which WGE is generated was recognised as long ago as 1968 by Friedman (1968), whose presidential address to the American Economic Association included this passage:

> The 'natural rate of unemployment,' in other words, is the level that would be ground out by the Walrasian system of general equilibrium equations, provided there is embedded in them the actual structural characteristics of the labor and commodity markets, including market imperfections, stochastic variability in demands and supplies, the cost of gathering information about job vacancies and labor availabilities, the costs of mobility, and so on. (p. 8)

Friedman's 'provided' is rich indeed. He apparently affirms the centrality of the Walrasian equilibrium, only to undercut it as unrealistic insofar as it does not represent 'actual structural characteristics of the labor and commodity markets'. Each of the items on his suggested list of 'actual structural characteristics' has generated an entire literature within economics. In effect, Friedman is aware of the limitations of the core model around which he has framed his ideas. Friedman's subtle move here is to both recognise the centrality of the WGE for his approach, while also absolving it of responsibility for carrying analytical weight.

Eighteen years later, Friedman's successor at Chicago, Lucas, Jr. (1986), wrote an essay that summarised the policy implications of the then-maturing 'New Classical' approach to macroeconomics. He made an analytical distinction similar in form to that drawn by Friedman (1968) but with an important twist. He wrote:

> My objective in this lecture will be to spell out in a unified way all of the neoclassical welfare-economic principles that bear on the efficient conduct of national, or aggregative, monetary and fiscal policy. ... But it would not be useful for me simply to run through the various writings of [Friedman, Phelps, Barro, and Kydland and Prescott], taking one principle here and another one there... Instead, I will begin by considering the dynamics of policy in the context of a specific, necessarily very simple, general equilibrium model. This will occupy most of my time, and when I am finished, we will have arrived at a fully understood consensus as to how monetary and fiscal policy ought to be conducted in this artificial society. (p. 117)

This analysis uses Friedman's approach, with an important shift. For while Friedman pays attention to the 'actual structural conditions' that are needed to move from the WGE to the real world, Lucas takes analytical shortcuts that push his model further in the direction of an 'artificial society'. Like Friedman, he undercuts the intellectual status of the model he chooses as his principal reference point – it only describes an 'artificial' world. But that world is a real reference point nonetheless – and one that is all the more powerful because it is absolved of any need to be realistic. This frees the modeller to introduce whatever features he wishes; that some such features will be added specifically to generate more powerful analytical conclusions is regarded as unobjectionable, even laudatory, by fellow neoclassical economists.

Lucas's move linked macroeconomics irrevocably (in the eyes of neoclassical theorists) into the matrix of agent-based equilibrium theory. Seven years later, Farmer (1993) famously affirmed this shift when he wrote: 'the future of macroeconomics is as a branch of applied general equilibrium theory' (p. 1). This statement is worthy of contemplation. It is certainly an oath of fealty. But it is not more than that. It cannot be accepted at face value as an analytical deduction because economic theory is an 'empty center': it is incomplete.

As Ingrao and Israel (1990), among others, have demonstrated, the grand effort to demonstrate the sufficiency of general equilibrium theory as the capstone of economics fails: for while existence and uniqueness can be demonstrated, temporal stability cannot be. This result devastates any notion that at the centre of neoclassical economics is a theory of markets that, albeit under rarified conditions, offers a complete depiction of economic motion. The pure theory itself cannot explain the attainment of equilibrium, only the characteristics of an equilibrium once attained. And among these characteristics, of course, is the Pareto efficiency at the core of the EMH. Neoclassical welfare theory does not encompass cases wherein markets begin outside of equilibrium and then attain it via a self-adjusting process that preserves the wealth positions every agent enjoyed at the outset. The concept of equilibrium only coheres if it is timeless. You cannot define a process of movement towards equilibrium without undercutting the premises of the very notion of equilibrium. An equilibrium that meets the theory's high expectations for itself can only be guaranteed by starting in equilibrium and forbidding out-of-equilibrium trading.

In effect, there *is* no *there* there, at the core of neoclassical theory: Walrasian general equilibrium is not identical to Nash equilibrium, nor to subgame perfection, nor to mixed-strategy equilibrium, nor to dynamic stability. To say, as Nash equilibrium does, that once a particular (possibly non-unique) equilibrium is attained, no participating agent has an incentive to be elsewhere, is not the same as saying that the equilibrium achieved represents a global optimum given participants' initial conditions (especially their wealth levels). But it is this latter assertion that forms the basis of the EMH, not the weaker Nash equilibrium assertion.

This is taken as a quibble by economists for whose work the WGE is an important reference point.[1] They might respond, vis-à-vis the relationship between the pure theory of an economy and applied work describing that economy, that the labour theory of value is similarly limited; and so, for that matter, is Keynesian uncertainty or aggregate demand. So no school of thought within the broad terrain of economic theory can make a claim to having a complete, internally consistent account of system dynamics and system equilibrium.

But it goes to the heart of the nature of theoretical inquiry in economics. If theory does not offer a complete mapping of system movement and system stasis, then it provides at best a metaphor – a reference point – for our thinking. We can argue for the relevance of whatever reference points we favour, based on empirical evidence and logic and historical sequences; but we cannot assert that the gains promised to us by following any particular approach to allocating economic resources are real, or even realisable.

This argument, then, asserts that all economists hoping to make statements about real-world economies using models, no matter their methods or favoured structures, stand outside the gates of whatever heaven that any pure theory might try to describe. For those who use model-building as one tool in their analytics, then, what good are the ideal states or pathways traced out by pure theory? The answer is this: models and modelling traditions are ways of establishing and maintaining intellectual identity. There are instances where a thinker invents something completely new; but, as Kuhn (1962) taught us, these are rare, since most intellectual enterprise unfolds within paradigms.

So the methods and substance of one's choice of a model convey meaning and are understood primarily in short-hand mathematical languages associated with one or another intellectual tradition. A scholar hoping to make an innovative point with a model is simultaneously declaring intellectual fealty. This fealty exists among those who call themselves Keynesians or Sraffians, and among those for whom the neo-classical vision of optimality through decentralised choice by utility-maximising agents is understood as the only coherent model of the economy. The Walrasian equilibrium and the economic (Pareto) efficiency criterion thus organises many economists' conceptual and empirical thinking, even about worlds whose characteristics differ sharply from its assumption set. And this makes neoclassical theory into a sink. Theorists committed to this enterprise – which is to say, theorists who have not committed to any alternative offered up by Keynesian or Marxian or other frameworks – recognise their commonality through their shared commitment to the animating idea of a market equilibrium.

This is why so many economists continually refer back to economic efficiency and measure their distance from Walrasian equilibrium. This is why New Keynesian models of the credit market contain such 'thin' descriptions of risk, and why economists' efforts to engage in interdisciplinary cooperation are so often tentative and non-committal. Ingrao and Israel point out the unresolvable tension for economic theorists between conceptual simplicity and elegance, on the one hand, and descriptive realism, on the other. Given the choice, the former always wins out; for this is what defines the common identity of the practitioners of this craft.

There are two notable benefits of this approach. First, it permits everyone to participate in and continually refer back to one shared core set of concepts. What makes us economists is that we all know *this theory and its implications*. Second, appeals to authority are built into the knowledge-creation process, and indeed hierarchies of authority arise, are acknowledged or challenged, and reproduce. It takes an act of conceptual rebellion to establish a different reference point.

In this context, it is not important that the WGE, as a fully realised version of the market equilibrium that neoclassical theory strives for, is an unachievable ideal. Nor does it matter that theorems built on the WGE break down even in simple laboratory experiments testing the consistency of preferences. The WGE as positioned by these skilled practitioners nonetheless provides the key impetus for a cluster of interrelated models and lines of research.

3   The efficient-market hypothesis and its role in financial economics

The privileged place assigned to market efficiency is especially pronounced in the analysis of finance. The efficient-market hypothesis (EMH) transports the idea of Walrasian general equilibrium to a financial market setting. But whereas agents in a WGE can be absolutely certain that what they have bought or sold will be delivered as contracted, the equilibria reached in financial markets settings are approximate. The agents achieve optimal ex ante positions subject to well-defined stochastic processes. Then, when market prices are competitive, trades can be made instantaneously at any scale, and agents are rational, then assets traded in financial markets will be efficiently priced. So as McKenzie (2006) puts it, financial markets are understood as a mirror of real-sector opportunities and processes, not as an engine that has its own autonomous momentum within the wider economy.

As the core concept for neoclassical understandings of financial markets, the EMH actually plays three intertwined roles:

(1) The EMH provides a *criterion for evaluating market outcomes*. It is linked to the notion of Pareto efficiency, and to the first welfare theorem – no one can be made better off without making someone else worse off, there are no $500 bills lying unclaimed on the street.

Further, allocative efficiency assures fair distribution. Each individual has the right to use her initial wealth endowment to maximise her utility; wealth redistribution must be voluntary, as market outcomes must respect and not override private property rights in the assets they own.

(2) The EMH makes strong assertions about *the relationship of the financial and 'real' sectors*:

1. Financing structure is irrelevant, because prices in efficient financial markets adjust perfectly for enterprise risk. This is the Modigliani–Miller theorem, which is readily paired with Fama (1980)'s result that banks can have no impact on the economy's financing choices.
2. Competitively set prices summarise all relevant information about all given assets, including the asset prices of the financial firms that bid on, securitise, and take off-balance sheet positions on those assets.
3. Competitively set asset-market prices and rates reflect the underlying risks and returns they fund. Uncertainty is eliminated. Familiar examples here are in the use of probability theory to convert uncertainty into certainty-equivalence in the capital asset pricing and the Black–Scholes models.

These assertions have very strong implications. Respectively, they suggest that the financial fragility hypothesis of Minsky (1986) is wrong; they deny the possibility that the financial sector could be disproportionately large, and instead view the financial sector as a source of competitive advantage; and they deny the possibility that financial exploitation and exclusion could exist in competitive markets.

(3) The EMH provides a *guideline for the construction and application of regulations to financial markets.* Specifically, the entry of government into financial-market processes is implicitly understood as *ex post.* Governmental action can disturb equilibria that would otherwise be achieved, and can squelch innovation. And, if foreseen perfectly, governmental action can be perfectly offset.

Again, this role of EMH has strong implications. First, it implies that market competitiveness must be protected in designing market regulations. If a market is malfunctioning, it is imperative to look at how its competitive equilibrium can be re-established. It suggests, further, that the proper offset for market power is competition. And competition depends on free market entry. Finally, any notion that regulators should consider how freedom of action in the financial sector might constrain opportunity or encourage exploitation in the 'real sector' is ruled out of bounds by assertion (2) – the markets *are* right.

Fox (2009) and Cassidy (2009) have shown that in the three decades prior to the 2007–08 subprime crisis, a number of factors gradually erased the line between the implications of the purely theoretical model of efficient markets and understandings of how real-world financial markets and financial regulations can and should function. So whereas Milton Friedman warned in 1968 that rigidities prevented the purely theoretical construct of WGE from operating in the real world, and in 1986 Lucas described his conclusions as pertaining to an artificial economy, proponents of efficient markets were reluctant to recognise limits in applying EMH insights to real markets. In retrospect, this can be seen as due to a combination of theorists' hubris and of financial firms' desire to profit by getting untested innovations to the marketplace. Confusing matters was the fact that these various innovations – default swaps, derivatives, and so on – could be readily understood as eliminating gaps in the set of feasible financial contracts. That is, innovations that presumed the existence of EFM were bringing financial markets ever closer to the ideal proclaimed in EFM theory.

Consider the declaration by Fama (1980) that banks have no impact on the economy's financial structure. This conclusion, of course, flies in the face of Bernanke's (1983) demonstration that bank lending matters in cyclical fluctuations. Fama's assertion presumes that financial markets are virtually complete. So when banks moved – as they did in the 1980s and 1990s – to widen markets for the securitisation of loans, and to participate ever more actively in portfolio-insurance and derivatives position-taking, it was easy to interpret these actions as simply permitting more optimal matches between 'investor preferences' and the distribution of risk. The idea that banks could be generating new sources of enterprise risk because of the fragility or incompleteness of these new markets was not considered; for the powerful analytical apparatus of EMH had already been used to pass judgement on banks – and found them largely inconsequential.

A crucial aspect of the increasingly important role of the EMH in shaping the evolution and regulation of financial markets was the assurance provided by this theoretical approach that increasing the scope for the largely unchecked operation of autonomous markets in finance would have benign effects. These arguments took their lead from Friedman's (1953) reassurance that exchange rates should be made flexible because speculative behaviour in foreign exchange markets would play the role of arbitrage and eliminate inefficient prices. EMH frameworks were used to draw conclusions about the real world. All relevant information about assets is incorporated into their market prices; the only information a perfectly informed investor requires is market prices; if an asset exists and has an equilibrium price, it must represent an efficient risk/return combination.[2] Such benign assertions had consequences. The notion, for example, that risk can be made certainty-equivalent through repeated investments – a feature of the capital-asset pricing model that represents one embodiment of the EMH – leads directly to the Black–Scholes arbitrage model.

In sum, the EMH does a huge amount of work in the neoclassical approach. As a criterion for evaluating market processes and outcomes, it suggests that free entry into markets and no limits on leverage are optimal, as these will maximise the use of arbitrage to discipline prices. The EMH also makes strong assertions about the relationship of the financial and 'real' sectors. It asserts that the financial sector passively reflects real-sector opportunities and risks. If inefficient financial instruments were introduced, no one would buy them. Finally, the EMH provides a simple guideline for regulating financial markets: let the markets police themselves; if abusive practices or exploitative contracts are proposed, self-interest will lead consumers to steer clear.

4   EMH and 'New Chicago' responses to the 2007–10 financial crises

Once these three roles of the EMH are accepted, there is no alternative to the conclusion that markets allocate most efficiently when they are freest, so that regulation must simply prevent fraud, not risk-taking. So why then did an extended episode of financial crisis arise in 2007 after almost three decades of financial deregulation legislation designed precisely to make financial markets freer? Before answering this question, we briefly review the relationship between the EMH and subprime lending, whose failures triggered the extended crisis.

The landscape of structured finance – subprime lending, the securitisation of mortgages and other loans and receivables, credit default hedging via swaps contracts, and so on – was built up in the 'originate and distribute' phase of banking, starting in the 1980s. The first question is why this entire institutional apparatus was established in the first place. If information were complete, transactions costless, assets infinitely scaleable, and a complete set of contingent markets existed, then no structured finance could arise. Any agent seeking a particular combination of risk–return characteristics available through a given set of securities could efficiently acquire them him/herself – no intermediary (that is, no seller of a structured investment vehicle) would be necessary. Fama (1985) himself provided the answer to this question: these intermediaries can exist only in the presence of transaction and/or information costs that are subject to increasing returns to scale. The structured investment vehicle (SIV) can efficiently exist only if it embodies a set of contingent and underlying claims that a wealthowner cannot access directly. Oldfield (2000, p. 445) provides the clue when he writes, 'Briefly, an underwriter must defeat arbitrage between pass-throughs and derivatives.' The efficiency of the SIV can thus be due either to transaction costs, or to the imperfect scaleability of assets, or to both. So in the EMH approach, as Partnoy and Skeel (2007) also point out, structured finance vehicles help to make markets more complete.

This said, per Fama (1980), if markets are otherwise efficient, these securitisation activities should have no net effect on capital or credit flows. So if these market institutions, taken together, were indeed passively carrying out the collective mandate of the markets, then the blame for the crisis must lie elsewhere: neither with banks, nor with non-bank lenders, nor with the securitisation process. There are three possibilities: borrower or lender irrationality or fraud, an unanticipated shock that affected all market participants, or distortions in the structure of incentives.

The first set of factors has attracted its share of attention. The blogosphere has resonated with intimations that many subprime borrowers acquired unpayable debt burdens due to either naïveté or their willingness to make very risky gambles on self-enrichment. Black (2010), in turn, has posited institutional fraud by financial fims as a fundamental cause of the crisis. But economists are generally reluctant to attribute crisis to irrationality or fraud, as both are ruled out in their baseline behavioural models.

The second approach, in turn, is quite plausible if the 'shock' in question was the revelation that the rising housing prices justifying much subprime lending represented a bubble, not a secular trend. In this case, no one could have foreseen the mistakes that were made – for if they had, this foresight would have permitted them to extract income from other market participants. There would, in turn, be nothing to blame but the fates or, perhaps, the absence of an early-warning mechanism such as a market in future housing prices. Shiller (2009) proposes precisely such a mechanism.

Attention among neoclassical economists has centred on the third possibility, which has a long history. Arguments about the ways in which government laws and regulations in the realm of finance distort incentives and generate crises were developed by a set of self-appointed experts termed the 'Shadow Financial Regulatory Committee' (Benston et al. 1986) in response to the US savings-and-loan crisis of the 1980s. The members of this 'Committee' attributed the thrift crisis to moral hazard in lending (Kane 1989; and Kaufman 1995). As described in detail in Dymski (2010), this Committee continues to function today under the sponsorship of the American Enterprise Institute; and its members have again pointed to deposit insurance as among the key distortions that led to the subprime crisis.

With the subprime crisis, three new elements have been added to the list of government-sponsored distortions. According to Wallison (2009) and others, banks were forced to take on overly risky loans due to the imposition of social criteria into lending decisions by legislation (the Community Reinvestment Act of 1977) and by poorly managed government-sponsored enterprises (Fannie Mae and Freddie Mac).[3] The third distortion is 'too big to fail' protection for very large banking firms (Kane, 2009).

In sum, from an EFM perspective, the banking and housing-finance market has too much rather than too little government interference. The crisis arose because of distortions in the market mechanism, which produced excessively risky credit contracts. As at the end of the savings-and-loan crisis, the solution is to get government out of the housing-mortgage market and to improve the regulation of mortgage and securitisation markets. Regarding financial intermediaries per se, there is little to be done. Kane (2010) warns that reversing the 1999 Gramm–Leach–Bliley Act would constitute an overreaction to the 'too big to fail' threat. Instead, he makes some proposals that are similar in kind to Shiller's proposed market-based 'early warning mechanism', so that adjustments can be made in advance when of bubbles in asset markets begin to emerge.

4.1   A 'New Chicago' approach?

Proponents of EMH are, of course, not the only participants in new research and policy investigations regarding the origins and mechanisms of the crises in financial markets. Among neoclassical theorists, models showing how financial markets fail have been given new prominence. Here, we briefly summarise several such models. The reason for so doing is to demonstrate that this new work remains centred on the presumed existence and optimality of a pure market equilibrium equivalent to the optimum envisioned in the efficient-markets hypothesis. So even in positing models that are unthinkable in EMH terms – because these models operate by violating key efficient-markets postulates – these models end up focusing anew on a hypothesised free-market equilibrium. As in Friedman's 1968 article, it is denied that the Walrasian general equilibrium exists in real life, but it remains a basic reference point, a conceptual 'sink'.

Nobel laureate Krugman (2009) wrote a long *New York Times* article in which he analysed why the economics profession had so badly missed the 2007–08 crisis. First, he blamed EMH proponents for ignoring the significance of the increasingly frequent financial market crashes of recent years because of both the 'force of a beautiful idea' and flawed empirical tests. The EMH 'blinded' economists to asset bubbles and helped to inflate the bubble itself. Second, he blamed the takeover of macroeconomic theory by 'neoclassical purists' – that is, those who 'believe that all worthwhile economic analysis starts from the premise that people are rational and markets work', and for whom 'overall failures of demand can't happen'. They rule out the possibility of system collapse. The New Keynesians, in turn, 'tried to keep their deviations from neoclassical orthodoxy as limited as possible. ... [so] there was no room in the prevailing models for such things as bubbles and banking-system collapse' Krugman (2009), pp. 36 *et seq.*

Krugman then asks where economics goes from here. He focuses specifically on approaches that allow for bubbles and asset-market-driven cyclicality: Shleifer and Vishny (1997), who show how irrational market prices, once they arise, can force agents who don't react to them into insolvency; Kiyotaki and Moore (1997), who show how credit cycles can arise, due to interactions between collateral and asset prices; and Bernanke and Gertler (1990), who demonstrate how variations in the value of borrower collateral can trigger output variability. Krugman's list could easily be extended. In Gorton and He (2005), bank credit cycles arise because of tension between public and private information about borrower firms' creditworthiness. Geanakoplos (2009) shows how irrational beliefs can lead to leverage cycles in which bubbles can arise.[4] Brunnermeier and Pedersen (2009), in turn, show how market speculation can prolong bubbles; their empirical evidence demonstrates how hedge funds 'rode' the IT and CDO bubbles.

These various models all derive their results by starting with one or another deviation from the assumption set required to obtain Walrasian general equilibrium: in one case, agents' beliefs about asset values are autonomous and not conditioned by the model's own outcomes; in another case, some agents have more information than others about when divergences between current and efficient prices will be eliminated; in a third case, banks' lending depends on fluctuating collateral value because of asymmetric information about borrowers. But while this puts us at an analytical distance from the WGE, we remain well within the orbit of influence of the WGE – which is to say, of the EMH. Consequently, the policy proposals that follow from these authors' work focus on improving market outcomes per se. For Geanakoplos, for example, maintaining viable markets means paying attention to structural limits of markets as well as incentives for the players in the markets. Solutions considered in his work include exchange-traded derivatives and capital requirements on off-balance sheet items. Brunnemeier, in turn, suggests restrictions on hedge funds' activities, and/or cyclically adjusted capital requirements. The work of Kiyotaki and Moore, and Gorton and He, in turn, suggests that pro-cyclical capital requirements or leverage limits be instituted.

This might be called a 'New Chicago' approach: the market can work if there are proper micro incentives and respect for macro limits. The idea of regulation is to permit the gap between the functioning of real-world markets and of the idealised market of WGE to be reduced as much as possible. The problem is then that the locus of thinking – the intellectual sink – remains in place.

An example of why this matters is readily provided: the debate in early 2010 over whether size limits and the 'Volcker rule' should be included in the US financial reform package then under consideration in Congress. Size limits on banks, as proposed by UK Prime Minister Gordon Brown and others, would have limited all banks to a fixed percentage of gross domestic product, as a means of guarding against 'too big to fail' dilemmas in future financial crises. The Volcker rule (Masters and Belton, 2010) would have forbidden financial firms with insured deposits from trading on their own account, again to limit risk-taking and excessive leverage by megabanks. President Obama supported the inclusion of both proposals, in general terms, in his 21 January statement on financial reform.

This notion flies in the face of thirty years of regulatory thinking. Zach Carter pointed out in the 4 January 2010 issue of *The Nation* magazine that the 1991 Treasury study, *Modernizing the Financial System: Recommendations for Safer, More Competitive Banks* – popularly known as the 'Green Book' – remains the reference point for financial reform in the USA. Its author, John Dugan, a former lobbyist for the American Bankers Association, remained until July 2010 the head of the Office of the Comptroller of the Currency (OCC), which oversees many of the very largest banks and non-bank banks. The Green Book contains this assertion:

> Laws must be adapted to permit banks to reclaim the profit opportunities they have lost to changing markets. Where banking organisations have natural expertise in other lines of business, they should be allowed to provide it. Adapting to market innovation is crucial.

Over the next several weeks, both of these proposals were diluted. Debate was confused. Paul Krugman (2010), whose advocacy of strong macroeconomic stimuli put him solidly in the Keynesian camp on macroeconomic policy, wrote in opposition to the size-limit proposal; meanwhile, Richard Fisher (2010), president of the Federal Reserve Bank of Dallas and a self-professed 'free-market advocate', spoke in favour of it before the Council on Foreign Relations. The point of this contrast is that there was no firm alternative to counter the utter dominance of EMH thinking regarding financial regulation and banking policy. Even Paul Krugman, who had discovered his inner Keynesian during the several years of the crisis, opposed a measure that was supported by many economists – including Simon Johnson, the former chief economist of the IMF (Johnson and Kwak, 2010).

5 'Thick' versus 'thin' approaches to economic theory and policy debate

To move out of the intellectual sink anchored by the EMH, what is needed is an alternative way of thinking about financial markets. But given the close linkage of the EMH to the WGE, this means developing an alternative way of thinking about economics more generally. The alternative favoured here is to understand the economy as a social construction, rather than as a compendium of individual choices. In this re-conceptualisation, then, fixing markets will not ensure that they more accurately represent demand–supply decisions made by individuals who are pursuing their own welfare as their pre-social right. These individuals' preferences, endowments and available technologies derive from complex social histories. Any one person's moment of choosing under constraints may embody her freedom of action; but it is preceded by untold thousands of prior actions that include force, repression, domination, invasion and threat. Each person has her own trail of precedent actions, and these individual trails cannot be untangled. They blur together, into inherited histories whose meaning we can debate, but whose importance in shaping all that we are and want and can afford cannot be.

What is being argued here is that the only coherent way to understand the economy, without denying history's force, is as a social construction. But for this way forward, the Pareto criterion, which privileges individuals' choices given one-step-back-in-time allocations of wealth, is readily seen as an inappropriate benchmark. To move from the individual-centred to a social approach to evaluating economic outcomes and policy proposals requires, first of all, that we opt for a *thick*, not a *thin*, alternative. A proposed alternative is 'thin' if it deviates as little as possible from the assumption set commonly used in equilibrium theory (that is, from the assumptions required for WGE); it becomes 'thicker' as it deviates from more WGE assumptions. The approaches of Geanakoplos and Bernanke and Gertler that were summarised above are thin. Especially notable is the latter, which builds on the notion of asymmetric information (ASI). ASI has become a standard device in many branches of economics, including research on credit markets.

Moral hazard has been a favoured design flaw in analyses of the 2007–08 financial crisis, as one hallmark of this extended episode has been the generation and then disposition of excessively risky loan contracts. It is readily argued that loan applicants with lower incomes and smaller down-payments available would be more likely to take on excessively risky mortgage loans. Similarly, a megabank employee who bundles and sells securities in the belief that they are insured by a third party will tend to generate excessively risky securities. And a bank which believes that a government will assume its bad debts – and that, in the extreme case, its solvency will be guaranteed by that government – will similarly take excessive risks in loan-making and securitisation.

ASI models of the credit market thus have many redeeming features, and represent a firm step away from the EMH. But at the same time, this approach represents an awkward half-way house for those seeking an alternative to the EMH. Its point of reference remains the EMH. It is located on the surface of the theoretical sink whose center is the Walrasian general equilibrium.

As such, it leads more towards debates with EMH practitioners than towards serious discussions among proponents of alternatives. For you only need one deviation from complete information to generate the imperfection. One side can claim racial discrimination in credit markets; the other, moral hazard due to the presence of deposit insurance, or the improper incentivisation of financial firms' managers or brokers. We quickly get lost in the technical details of *which* mechanism within the existing edifice of financial institutions and regulations is broken, rather than seeing our way through to a different set of operational principles.

In sum, asymmetric information as a thin approach makes clear to devoted followers of the EMH how that malfunction(s) may have occurred. But it is too narrow a reed to sustain an alternative that sees the economy as a social construction and not as a compendium of individual choices. We know we are at a second-best equilibrium. But we want to know, in effect, how to choose the first-best second-best. For example, we might want to ask whether it would be feasible to have banks – state-controlled or not – that provided more credit to small businesses than before; whether these banks could treat women on equal grounds with men; whether they could avoid discriminating by race; and so on. Each one of these concerns takes us further from the benchmarks for market performance associated with the WGE. Further, each involves a separate dimension of economic performance or social inequality. To accommodate these in a real alternative measure of banking performance, then, requires an alternative index that recognises the lived structure of social interaction, one that is thick, not thin.

5.1 A 'thick' approach to US financial reform

The debate over US financial reform that unfolded in 2009 and 2010 illustrated very clearly the need for a thick alternative to a neoclassical-economics-based, EMH-centred view of financial policy. On one side of the neoclassical spectrum were the free-market idealists, allied with the megabanks' lobbyists. These advocates reasserted the relevance of the EMH as a pure, apolitical standard capable of guiding the construction of efficient, non-politicised policies and regulations. The idea was to keep governmental regulatory oversight to a minimum so that megabank customers could sort out which financial instruments and contracts best met their needs; non-competitive products would fall into disuse, and non-competitive firms would fade from sight. These advocates were, of course, backed by the massive financial clout and political power amassed by Wall Street and the City of London. On the other side of the neoclassical spectrum were proponents of what was termed above the 'New Chicago' approach; these analysts were seeking technical fixes which could limit systemically risky behaviour either by incentivising firms or by imposing restrictions on financial firms' behaviour. Both regarded the debate over financial reform as an 'inside the Beltway/Wall Street corridor' matter: that is, getting banking and financial markets to work smoothly again was a matter for those with inside-industry knowledge to sort out; populist anger would just confuse the issues.

This explains the strangely passionless character of most public discussion of the financial reform legislation. The policy insiders, elected officials, and industry members who dominated debate expected to resolve their differences of opinion quietly; they might modify, but would not transform, existing practices. Neither those defending financial markets' unaccountability and their freedoms (EMH), nor those developing models of how financial institutions generate and profit from bubbles ('New Chicago'), addressed any of the broader open questions that explained the urgency of the reform process: the impacts of banking practices on economic and social inequality; the availability of bank credit for small/medium-sized enterprises, especially in lower-income and underserved markets; the relationship between macroeconomic imbalances and financial market leverage. These larger questions were largely kept off the agenda.

Fighting to broaden that agenda was a coalition of consumer and reinvestment advocates, largely organised by the poorly financed but intrepid Americans for Financial Reform (hereafter, AFR; see http:// ourfinancialsecurity.org). Headed by veteran organiser Heather Booth, the AFR operated with a 'thick' political agenda. Its staff consulted with members of different grassroots struggles, local government officials, and non-governmental organisation personnel and volunteers. It was effective precisely because of its breadth: its participants included those interested in racial and gender justice, consumer rights, family farming, economic sustainability, affordable housing, reinvestment, and so on. Thus, no master narrative supplied in advance by any one leader guided its strategy. Instead, the coalition was built and sustained through democratic participation. So the coalition moved adaptively from broad-based goals – such as social equality, 'bottom-up' development, and an end to exploitative financial practices and speculation – towards specific engagements with members of Congress who could be persuaded only to take smaller incremental steps toward a more consistently regulated and less exploitative financial system.[5]

During the intensive law-shaping months of January to June 2010, the AFR interacted with a number of economists, in different ways. Some of these economists – for example, Paul Krugman, Jamie Galbraith, Joseph Stiglitz, and Simon Johnson – wrote op-ed pieces and gave interviews that the AFR could use to lend support for particular amendments as the finance reform bill moved through Congress. Some other economists – for example, Jane D'Arista, Dean Baker, and Gerald Epstein – worked more directly with AFR coalition members, providing just-in-time expertise to assist in the sculpting of legislation. Several different networks provided mechanisms for communication and exchange among the economists involved. Most of the participants in these networks – certainly the most active members – are heterodox in orientation. Indeed, these networks provided the impetus for heterodox economists who had previously felt excluded from serious policy debate to become engaged.

There are some crucial lessons in this experience for the shaping of a New Economics. First, heterodox economists found ways to develop and express their own views, in partnership with their opposite numbers occupying largely parallel positions in the arena of legislative advocacy. Second, when opportunities arose for heterodox economists to exchange ideas with mainstream economists about the issues at hand, they were taken. Third, the theoretical commitments of the economists who became deeply immersed in advocating progressive financial reform are diverse: some are identified as mainstream, others as heterodox. And those heterodox economists who engaged these issues themselves held very different theoretical positions. So the 'left' did not 'own' the progressive financial agenda; instead, progressive economists contributed what they could. Nor was there a struggle over which left perspective was more correct.

Fourth, mainstream/heterodox differences caused no tensions among those advocating for a less speculative, less exploitative financial system. The questions on which expertise was needed did not probe the depths of theoretical models, but were instead pragmatic, involving questions about consumer protection in credit markets, 'too-big-to-fail' alternatives, permitting or reducing 'connectedness' among financial markets and instruments, and so on. What mix of policy changes could bring about a less crisis-prone, less exploitative, and more functional banking system?

6 An alternative to the efficient-markets hypothesis

This section proposes a 'social efficiency' criterion, which can replace the EMH-based 'market efficiency' measure that has been used to evaluate policy alternatives regarding financial regulations and institutional changes until now.[6]

How can an index for evaluating financial market outcomes and proposals, one which is both thick and rooted in a social-relations view of the economy, be constructed? This section makes two suggestions. The first step is to differentiate the concerns that heterodox critics of neoclassical economics have about the operational characteristics of capitalist financial markets and economies from the outcomes that are achieved by these economies. The second step is to propose an approach to measuring 'well-offness' in a social-efficiency benchmark. We then suggest an illustrative algorithm based on these two steps.

6.1 Separating operational characteristics from outcomes in a policy index

Critics of unchecked market processes do not focus on only one dimension of social reality. They propose changes in what market processes produce, pointing out variously the need for more sustainable technologies, more equal global or national income and wealth distributions, the reduction of racial, gender and regional inequality, the universal attainment of minimum levels of human capability, and so on. And they criticise the operations of capitalism as a system: its financial instability and cyclical swings, its occasional collapses or bouts of stagnation, its waste in displacing production from one site to another, its protection of profit making and disregard of the rights of workers, its inability to establish and maintain viable regulations in key sectors such as banking and finance.

To use the language suggested in Section 5, this is a very thick list of critiques and concerns. Any proposed policy alternative at the national or international level will almost invariably not satisfy this entire list of concerns. A given alternative might impact gender inequality in one way, racial inequality in another, regional injustice in a third way. It might simultaneously improve environmental sustainability, while increasing the risks of financial instability and collapse, or vice versa. These concerns are different and not reducible to one or two controlling dimensions. This means that no dimension of market outcomes will dominate all other evaluative dimensions on a point-by-point basis. Further, one set of concerns can pull in a different direction than another.

To see the problems in structuring an alternative based broadly on heterodox critiques of neoclassical theory, we use an example from the immediate pre-history of the 2007–10 crisis. Subprime mortgage lending in the early 2000s was provided disproportionately to borrowers who were racial minorities in predominantly minority neighbourhoods. Ex ante, these loans promised to expand homeownership and thus reduce racial wealth inequalities, even while containing exploitative terms that disproportionately affected minorities. At the same time, the growing weight of securitised subprime loans in financial portfolios added to the economy's financial fragility; and this episode clearly embodied the growing grip of financial speculation and of financialisation on the economy as a whole. So after subprime lending has blossomed into the extended financial crisis of 2008 and subsequent years, what principles should be emphasised in policy alternatives? Clearly, measures that reduce financial risk-taking are crucially important; but what if these close the door to a homeownership surge for racial minorities in the USA, or, more broadly, for reduced racial inequality in economic outcomes there? Would a New Economics then choose to prioritise 'Keynesian' criteria over 'racial justice' criteria? But what does 'Keynesian' mean in this context? Does it encompass solely attention to the consequences of real time and uncertainty on market processes, or does it also include the importance of autonomous aggregate demand in the level of economic output?

This example illustrates that an alternative to EMH-based 'market efficiency' can readily divide against itself. This is not surprising, since the EMH entails such a restricted view both of economic dynamics and of allocative efficiency. There are indeed two dimensions of disagreement to be sorted. We suggest, first, that only outcomes that pertain directly to the 'well-offness' of the individuals and of groups of individuals (members of the same gender, residents of the same regions, and so on) be included in a 'social efficiency' measure that can replace the Pareto criterion. That is, outcome measures that pertain to operational characteristics of capitalist financial markets and economies – for example, 'less volatility' or 'more stability due to reduced financial fragility' – should be excluded from any 'social efficiency' criterion.

This distinction attempts to draw a line between 'how capitalist economies function or malfunction' and 'how people are served by the economies they participate in'.

This distinction does not imply that the heterodox theories of the economy have no role in the construction of an alternative to the EMH. This cannot be done, for the same reason that the EMH is intertwined with the competitive model that generates WGE. Heterodox approaches to understanding how economies work provide the foundation for thinking differently in evaluating economic outcomes. This topic will be further discussed in Section 8.

6.2   Risk and 'well-offness'

Even for those who accept the broad goals of less inequality and more sustainability in economic outcomes, differences of view – conflicts – over how different economic outcomes should be rank-ordered are inevitable; and this means that conflicts over policy alternatives are inevitable as well. To take an obvious example, putting more or less weight on the availability of non-renewable resources for those not yet born will lead to different conclusions about levels of resource usage (and of material comfort) in the current period. The key is not to deny these conflicts, but to find a means of managing them.

We proceed here by reinterpreting risk in light of this paper's broad ambition of replacing an individualistic with a social approach to evaluating economic (especially financial) outcomes. We choose risk because 'risk' and 'return' are the two basic components that have defined the terrain of much finance (and especially EMH) theory in the past fifty years.

In the EMH, risk – the variability of return on a given investment – is asocial. Human agents are not subject to risk unless they take on risky investment projects. In the EMH, the 'risk of failure' of a investment project or an enterprise is a move by nature, a random draw beyond human control. Things go wrong only when some agents artificially alter probabilistic outcomes by selecting projects riskier than agents contracting with them have agreed to (the 'moral hazard' problem).

If we reject the naturalised presentation of risk, we can see things quite differently. The likelihood of success or failure for a given project can be seen as depending on the behaviour of other economic agents in a complex, interactive environment. There is nothing natural about it; it is social. The 'odds' of success or failure (the likelihood that a borrower's home-price will rise 20 per cent in a year) depend on systematic forces set in motion by human societies, not on a draw from nature.

And, in any case, why should we be concerned only with the riskiness of the financial asset that agents take on? Why aren't agents' own risks taken into account? The answer in the neoclassical model, as Shakespeare put it, is that 'what's past is prologue'.[7] Agents in economic models, including the WGE, don't have risks of the sort that human beings experience. Their resources are pre-given, and their lifespans fixed in length (even if only probabilistically). The fates have already shaped them to their task of achieving what happiness they can through exchange. In a WGE, the question of why every human being can't expect to reach the same level of income or education or resources never arises. We can never ask why agents in the model cannot seek equality (unless every agent with above average income also values equality).

But suppose, quite simply, that we step outside of the naturalised presentation of risk and fate in neoclassical theory, and acknowledge the social and, indeed, political nature of risk. We can then ask a question such as 'What rights are associated with being human?' and use it to evaluate economic outcomes. Then the level of satisfaction generated by any set of market parameters or transactions would depend on the number of human agents that were able to reach those minimal levels of well-offness. This could represent, then, a social measure of efficiency.

How then to determine a threshold for well-offness? Sen (1999) offers one possibility: the notion of human capability as a 'minimum' threshold. One might imagine evaluating any given policy alternative based on the extent to which it enhanced the human capability of the members of a given society. Sen's work on this topic has led to some efforts to create a measure of human happiness, most notably in a recent report commissioned by the French government and chaired by Joseph Stiglitz.[8]

Another possibility emerges from Roemer's (2000) work on equality of opportunity. He considers a situation in which discrimination in markets can generate differences in individuals' degree of access to resources and in individuals' ability to make productive use of assets. Roemer suggests that the only way to ensure equal opportunity in this case is to redistribute income and assets so as to guarantee equality in outcomes. While Roemer provides no rationale for why people might want this, Rawls (1971) argues that we can determine what people regard as a just society by having every member define it without knowing what place s/he would occupy therein. Because people would be risk-averse once behind this 'veil of ignorance', this experiment would lead to a societal embrace of greater equality as a shared objective. We leave aside whether this argument is as plausible in 2010 as it was when proposed in 1971; in any event, we shall assume that 'levelling up' the standard for human capabilities and moving toward income and wealth equality are indeed embraced as social goals. Adapting these goals to the case of financial policy, this suggests that the relevant benchmark for policy would be the extent to which a given proposal would lead toward a more equal – and ultimately completely equal – distribution of wealth assets among individuals in the society in question.

The objectives set out by Sen and Roemer engage with the concepts of capacities and equality at a very high level of abstraction. Here we accept their broad criteria: an upwards-levelling of human capabilities and equalisation of income and wealth. However, we suggest the creation of a policy benchmark that is 'closer to the ground', one that breaks these broad aims into specific social categories: for example, male/female differences in capacitation and income/wealth inequality, ethnic differences, and so on. The logic of so doing is as follows. Absolute equality in human capabilities and resources is worth striving for, but must be regarded as an unattainable goal. The key problem is not simply to want this, but to mobilise people to work towards it. And indeed, some of the barriers to across-the-board equality involve aspects of social difference that have often become arenas of struggle against injustice and discrimination. Making these different arenas of inequality analytically visible in a 'social efficiency' measure will then connect the measurement of inequality with movements organised to reduce these inequalities.

In sum, total social equality can be acknowledged as a worthy final goal; but moves towards it occur via step-by-step advances in different specific fields of struggle against exclusion and discrimination. One advantage of this shift from an absolute goal (total equality) to a series of relative goals (racial, gender, regional equality) is that distinguishing the effects of a given change in market regulations or institutions on the degree of overall inequality can be especially difficult. Working with sub-categories of inequality permits the analyst to screen out some effects, and focus on others – thus making an overwhelming task more plausible. A second advantage is that there is frequently accumulated research on the sources of sub-categories of inequality (gender, race, and so on). So one can then take advantage of accumulated research in mapping from regulation/law change to likely outcomes.

A third advantage of this thick, multidimensional approach to social efficiency is this: it is transparently clear that there is no intention to silence or invisibilise the voices of any movement for greater equality. This is important, because no one dimension of social reality – poverty in the global South, gender inequality, and so on – can be uniquely privileged as *the* focus in building an alternative to the orthodox Pareto criterion.

6.3   A 'social efficiency' algorithm

Financial markets are social, so they should be subject to an implicit contract among participants, some of whom enter with different types and levels of resource deprivation. In constructing a social efficiency formula, it is useful to think of an imaginary scenario. Suppose it would be possible to ask each member of a society, or each participant (or group of participants) in an economic team, to identify what they most value in economic outcomes. Different participants will value different things, with different levels of intensity. One person might propose evaluating market outcomes based on whether they improve or worsen gender inequality; another based on whether they improve or worsen racial/ethnic resource gaps or regional disparities; a third, whether they deplete the carbon-based resources available to future generations. The same person might value all three goals. It is unlikely that every participant in a given analysis will rank-order the same policy options in the same way (deregulate/don't deregulate, tax/don't tax, and so on).

An algorithm for social efficiency, then, should provide a means for including the various interests and endpoints that might be sought. And since broad agreement on the importance of equality and capability as endpoints does not preclude disagreements, this algorithm should provide a vehicle for debating ends and means vis-à-vis particular policy proposals – and, finally, for weighing the various interests. That is, this algorithm should be both a decision mechanism and a means of communicating with one another about our analytics and the benchmarks we set for policy. In one country, greater gender equality may be the highest priority for the majority of participants in the economy; in another, reduced regional disparities; and so on. We need a flexible, ex ante criterion for social efficiency evaluations of market outcomes and policy proposals which can differ substantially over time and across space.

This social efficiency index can be constructed much like the loss function in estimations wherein the core generating distribution is unknown. The 'loss' to be approximated would then consist of the sum of the losses from the various types of inequality that exist and are of concern to analysts, residents and policy makers. Gains in equality would result in a smaller sum. How much a gain or loss in any one dimension of loss matters would be determined by the weight assigned that dimension in the initially calculated sum. The idea would then be to make policy shifts that reduce the value of this loss function.

Purely as a thought experiment, then, we can specify social efficiency for a state of affairs in which we value equality of income and capabilities, value between genders, equality between regions (or nations), and sustainability over time. So the idea would be to minimise the following sum of sums: the weighted sum of the differences between every individual's income and average income, plus the weighted sum of the differences between the capabilities of every individual (defined per Sen) and the average level of capabilities, plus the weighted sum of gender differences within every household, plus the weighted sums of the differences between the social resources available to any community (neighbourhood, region, or nation) and the average resources available to all communities, plus the weighted sum of differences between the average resource use now and sustainable resource use.

Let SE equal social efficiency. Then suppose X_i equals any individual's income for all N individuals in a given society, and $\overline{X}$ equals average income; C_i, any individual's capabilities (defined for simplicity as a singleton); suppose there are M households in which male and female members are present, and that X_j^M and X_j^W, respectively, equal the incomes of the male and female members of each male–female household (and similarly for C_j^M and C_j^W); suppose $\overline{X}_k$ represents average income in the Kth region in a community that has K regions, and suppose $\overline{X}_s$ represents a sustainable level of income for this community. Suppose the value of each sum of differences is weighted by a weight θ, wherein the sum of the weights equals 1. Then:

$$\left.\begin{array}{l} \theta_X \sum_{i=1}^{N}\left(X_i - \overline{X}\right) + \theta_C \sum_{i=1}^{N}\left(C_i - \overline{C}\right) + \theta_{GX} \sum_{j=1}^{M}\left(X_j^M - X_j^W\right) \\[2em] + \theta_{GC} \sum_{j=1}^{M}\left(C_j^M - C_j^W\right) + \theta_{XX} \sum_{k=1}^{K}\left(\overline{X}_k - \overline{X}\right) + \theta_S \sum_{k=1}^{K}\left(\overline{X}_k - \overline{X}_s\right) \end{array}\right\} \tag{1}$$

This equation is a measure of how well a given configuration of market possibilities (rules, and so on) meets the criteria established in this economy's social contract. This social efficiency equation does not replace prudential financial oversight. It instead provides a way of making visible the implicit social contract among participants in a market economy. It can be used, in particular, as a rough guide for evaluating possible institutional changes in financial market arrangements and practices. How will the various elements of the economy's social contract be affected? Consider the evolution of debate about the sub-prime industry. Government agencies made a decision to change home ownership. The law was passed that blocked predatory lending, but its implementation was given to the Federal Reserve, which did not implement its provisions. The Federal Reserve was not under any mandate to consider the social efficiency implications of its refusal to implement this law, and it indeed disregarded them.

The less the value of the weighted sums of differences, the more socially efficient the outcome or the intended policy intervention. We leave aside all the difficulties that would arise in calculating the quanta in equation (1). The emphasis on capabilities reflects what Fleurbaey (2009) would call a perfectionist impulse, the weights a liberalist impulse. This framework provides a way of assessing the impact of any decision on the distribution of income, wealth, and capabilities. It permits consideration of the concerns for equality of opportunity and resources that Rawls and Roemer, among others, have articulated.

We also acknowledge that there are many different ways to compute any one of these inequality measures; for example, gender could be calculated as the difference of mean or median male and female earnings, rather than on a household-by-household basis. How differences are computed – on the basis of gender, race, region, and so on – and how they are weighted is flexible, and can be adapted as analytics and social issues evolve. One advantage of this schema is that protagonists who are especially interested in one sub-category of inequality can have some autonomy in deciding how to measure it; social consensus is required only in the assignment of weights for each sub-category.

It is interesting to apply the logic of classical economic theory to equation (1). It is common in classical theory to imagine a linear production system in which input–output relationships are specified, along with labour requirements, for every commodity. Recall that a model of this sort is underspecified; to 'close' it requires the level of real wages (or of profit, which is to say surplus) in advance. This demonstrates clearly how distribution is prior to allocation in the classical system, in contrast to the simultaneous determination of both in the neoclassical system. In this context, equation (1) suggests the idea that a prior exercise might be feasible in which various values of wages and returns to productive factors of production are tested to determine their implications for the various forms of income (and other) inequality that equation (1) picks up. Then a socially optimal set of wages and returns – for example, for men and women, for different regions, and so on – could be determined and used either to determine wages or as a benchmark against a real-world economy's performance.

In effect, equation (1) represents one abstract approach to a set of justice criteria. 'Justice' here means the evaluation of the fairness of economic outcomes using evaluative criteria other than individuals' or families' initial levels of income and wealth. The idea is to have a rich, multidimensional, inclusive index. Ideas such equity, capability, and sustainability (natural, social, and human) can be incorporated as a way of countering the pervasive gravitational pull of the notion of 'economic efficiency' embedded in neoclassical thinking.

The index specified in equation (1), or something like it, should be linked to a decisional process. *Who* is at the table deciding which criteria to incorporate, what geographical unit, what weights to decide on? Determining precisely what might be included in a social efficiency index, how to measure it, and how its weights should be determined: all these are questions that will require specific solutions in real-world contexts. The point in building a 'social efficiency' measure is not to resolve timeless philosophical quandaries, but to work up specific indices as the need arises in policy debate. These indices should be broad enough to be inclusive, socially engaged, and historically informed. Deciding on their components and on who decides the components and weights is a question of contingency and of politics – of compromise and exchange.

In the US financial reform example in Section 5, something like equation (1) implicitly operated. The different concerns – a fairer and less exploitative financial system, a safer and less failure-prone system, and so on – constituted the components of this (imaginary) index; the weights assigned each depended on the interests of the members of the AFR coalition. The advantages of making an index like equation (1) explicit are these: it disciplines members of an alliance to recognise and respect one another's priorities; (2) it permits discussion in advance about which policy ends should be prioritised (instead of simply reacting to events as they happen); (3) it forces some consideration of the relative costs and benefits associated with different options. In effect, an effort at building an effective democratic coalition is, with equation (1), paralleled by an effort at building a democratic evaluation of policy options. And what is most crucial is that this 'social efficiency' equation, or something like it, provides a concrete alternative to the EMH.

7   Social efficiency and economic models

We argued on pragmatic grounds in Section 6 that the social efficiency benchmark for evaluating an economy's outcomes should include only well-offness criteria, not analyses of economic dynamics per se. This distinction is unnecessary in the neoclassical approach, in which distribution is settled only after prices are determined through the interaction of resource constraints and preferences. However, in heterodox analysis, this is a hard line to draw. In the linear system developed by Sraffa to depict Marx's ideas of capitalist reproduction, the distribution of income – the determination of real wages or of profit rates – has to be determined before prices are set. In Keynes' system, the level of income depends on commitments made to provide for social needs (via aggregate-demand commitments). The way in which gender roles are organised in a society determines how much labour is done by men and by women, what portions of their labour results in paid income, and thus the level of measured GDP – even leaving aside the challenge of whether a society has 'equal pay for equal work' (Folbre 1994). As van Staveren (2011) points out, gender is endogenous, not exogenous, in economic outcomes; and so, for that matter, is race and ethnicity.

This very interconnectedness of distribution and value, and of demand and supply, of gender roles and output, and of racial separation and output, is then a consequence of heterodox economists' theoretical commitments. The neoclassical view that people simply allocate available income and savings among capital assets based on preferences alone is replaced by the idea of feedback loops between capital allocations and the level and distribution of income and wealth.

But it is one thing to accommodate diverse goals in evaluations of policy options; it is another to require agreement on visions and models regarding how the economy works. The former should not be held hostage by the latter. Debates about what constitutes the analytical core of alternative approaches to economics have been ongoing among Keynesian, institutionalist, Marxian, feminist and other heterodox economists for years. These debates show no signs of abating. And indeed, just as different views about what forms of inequality are most onerous should not be rendered invisible, so too, neither should different views about economic dynamics be repressed.

How then to proceed, given the analytical interconnectedness of economic processes and outcomes in heterodox approaches? Here we suggest the following method of cutting this Gordian knot: participants in debate about which policy options maximise social efficiency should not eliminate the social/economic justice concerns of other participants by using models or analytical short cuts that eliminate those concerns in advance. If some participants in a debate assert that reducing racial inequality can have induced effects that raise overall productivity – so that reducing racial inequality does not involve zero-sum trade-offs – then this claim should be scrutinised carefully. How significant the productivity- or output-enhancing effects from focusing on any one dimension of inequality in any case will, of course, be subject to discussion and debate.

The key point is this: accepting a criterion for policy evaluation that identifies different dimensions of social inequality implies the need to create space for debating trade-offs along these various dimensions. An inclusive measure of well-offness needs an inclusive atmosphere for debate. The strong possibility of various forms of endogeneity between inputs and outputs only strengthens this conclusion.

The following approaches to substantive economic analysis will permit a full consideration of the connections among the various dimensions of social inequality incorporated into a social efficiency criterion, in considering any policy proposal:

- **A holistic micro–macro approach**. The first imperative is to evaluate any given proposal from different perspectives. It is important to be open to exploring interactions (and not just deterministic relationships) between micro-level and macro-level variables and processes, and to interdisciplinary exchange. This will avoid problems such as using a macro evaluative model for a policy whose impacts are felt primarily at the micro level.
- **Aggregate demand or supply impacts**. Evaluations of the economic outcomes of different policy shifts should always examine whether aggregate-demand multiplier effects or supply-constraints might be independently important.
- **Power**. Power can take on many forms in an economy. Relations of economic power – either expressed through the exercise of market power in exchange, or through the exercise of coercive power

in sustained relationships. Some economic agents have multiple exit options, while others have few or none. Some agents have private knowledge that can be used to exploit or defraud others; this was a particular problem in the subprime lending episode. Some agents are more powerfully interconnected with economically valuable external partners or activities than others. And some agents have a greater ability to suffer losses or to renew resources than do others. All these levels of differential power can be affected by policy shifts.[9]

- **Uncertainty**. Uncertainty breeds instability, as Keynes (1936) showed long ago. Depressed expectations can lead to collapsing financial and real markets; and euphoria grounded in hope or greed can generate asset bubbles and spread financial fragility. Changing institutional structures and regulatory guidelines can shift the locus and depth of uncertainty, and its impact on economic outcomes. Careful scrutiny for how any policy change will affect uncertainty, and what can be done about this, is thus always warranted.

The logic behind this list of elements is as follows. For any variable included in equation (1), the difference between the point-measure of that variable at present and under any envisioned policy shift is calculated by an analytical method of some kind. And there is no reason to assume that all analytical methods used by policy analysts are themselves fair or inclusive. To the contrary, the 'black box' estimation methods that Departments of Finance or Treasury deploy should be subject to scrutiny before they are allowed to wipe policy options off the board. It is common for quantitative policy analyses to utilise low or zero multipliers, to assume Say's Law, to ignore the implications of market power, and so on.

8 Conclusion: the future of heterodox economics and a 'New Economics'

While the 2007–10 financial-economic crisis has damaged the credibility of neoclassical economics, most analyses of what was broken and needed fixing in the financial system have used the same EMH criteria that guided policy choices and market innovation during the build-up to the crisis. This paper has argued that a new and independent criterion for evaluating financial market outcomes and financial policy alternatives is needed. The criterion developed here for illustrative purposes, termed 'social efficiency', focuses on whether any given change in financial regulations or institutions will reduce or widen inequality in wealth and in capabilities in a given society. Since there are several salient dimensions of inequality and capability – differences by gender, race and ethnicity, region, and so on – social efficiency is envisioned as a 'thick' concept. This sort of 'social efficiency' criterion, focusing on the reduction of multidimensional economic inequality and on sustainability, implicitly informed the recent debate in the USA over the passage of financial-reform legislation.

The remainder of this concluding section reflects on the implications of the argument developed here for the future of heterodox economics (Section 8.1) and for the creation of a distinctive approach to a 'new' economics (Section 8.2).

8.1 Social efficiency and the debate over the future of heterodox economics

The ideas discussed here are relevant for the ongoing debate about the future of heterodox economic theory. To make this link, we first sketch out some of the main positions. Davis (2006, 2008) has argued that since the 1980s, a number of 'competing research approaches which share relatively little in common with each other or with neoclassical economics' have emerged, supplanting the dominance of neoclassical economics as the dominant research programme in economics (Davis, 2006, p. 1). So 'neoclassical economics' no longer dominates a 'mainstream economics'. Davis argues that one or more of the following three principles, widely embraced in the heterodoxy, have been taken on board by 'non-neoclassical' portions of the mainstream: (1) individuals are socially embedded rather than atomistic; (2) processes are evolutionary rather than mechanical; (3) individuals and social-economic structures are mutually influencing. He admits that since 'non-neoclassical' mainstream economists generally do not embrace all three elements, dialogues between heterodox and mainstream economists will likely lead to a new economics orthodoxy that partially incorporates elements of the mainstream heterodoxy and of the heterodox heterodoxy.

Garnett has argued against this, in favour of 'an emerging pluralist view in which the principal goal of heterodox economics is to promote intellectual tolerance and exchange among academic economists at large' (Garnett, 2006, p. 521). Garnett suggests a vision of economics as not a process of inquiry within a restabilised master paradigm, but rather as 'civilized conversation among equals', to use McCloskey's phrase (McCloskey, 2001, p. 107), who have different substantive and methodological commitments.

One key question is whether a conversation is really feasible. Doubts have been raised on both sides. Arnsperger and Varoufakis (2006) argue that neoclassical economists are reluctant to engage. They argue that three fundamental, if typically unstated, meta-axioms define neoclassical economics: methodological individualism, methodological instrumentalism ('all behavior is ... a means for maximizing preference-satisfaction', p. 3), and methodological equilibration. Neoclassical theorists rely on 'the axiomatic imposition of equilibrium'; the actual existence of equilibrium, as the authors note, is a strictly secondary matter and of little interest (p. 5). The authors make the point that because these meta-axioms are largely undiscussed since, mainstream economists have an aversion to discussions of methodology. Further, heterodox economists are generally critical of one or more of these meta-axioms. Injecting criticism of these axioms into analytical work puts one's work out of discursive bounds for neoclassical economists. This empowers neoclassical economists and explains their 'silence' (p. 9) in the face of challenges from heterodox economists.

Lawson (2006, p. 499) has described reluctance on the heterodox side as follows:

> we can explain the heterodox resistance to the mainstream incor-poration of their key categories (uncertainty, evolutionary change, caring relations, etc.) only by recognising that the latter are really defended as manifestations of, and that heterodox economists carry commitments to, an underlying ontology of openness, process and internal-relationality. The latter is an ontology which mainstream economists simply cannot accommodate as long as they insist on employing only mathematical–deductivist methods.

Davis's view that significant shifts in mainstream theory are under-way receives some support in our suggestion that a 'New Chicago' approach to financial regulation may be emerging. But it is not clear that 'New Chicago' ideas will open the way to new dialogues with het-erodox economists about social efficiency in finance. As argued here, the intellectual sink of WGE remains in place. That said, the account of debate over US financial reform finds more mainstream/heterodox contact than Arnsperger and Varoufakis would have anticipated. It should be cautioned, however, that that these contacts were cautious and unfolded in the realm of policy, not in Ivy League seminar rooms.

The argument advanced here for a 'social efficiency' alternative to the EMH also has some implications for the other central question in this debate: whether one or another approach among the many favoured by heterodox economists should be selected as the most 'fit'. Clearly, the very structure of the proposed algorithm supports the notion of a 'pluralist' heterodox economics. This index can be used effectively only by a heterodox economics which addresses not just the logic of capitalism, but questions of equity between men and women, between global North and global South, between ethnic majorities and minorities, and questions about sustainability. The 'social efficiency' concept proposed here to evaluate financial policy options is structured as a weighted sum of indicators that ask precisely whether the policies in question will worsen, leave unaffected, or improve the social justice (and sustainability) performance of the financial system. The concern with 'social efficiency' is not, then, structured as the exclusive terrain of economists who define themselves as Keynesians or Marxians or institutionalists.

8.2   Towards a 'New Economics'

Vis-à-vis the debate about heterodox economics, this social efficiency criterion implies the need to democratise the economic discourse. Claims about scientific rigour are one thing; claims about the inherent superiority of one value (say, systemic stability) versus another (say, greater gender equality) are another. The former involve questions about epistemology and the nature of economic theory, and as such are subject to debate. The latter are incommensurable, and necessarily require politics – a means of choosing among competing ends for those with different values and desires. We propose that the term 'new economics' be adopted to indicate a conversational space which is open to the perspectives and voices of economists working in all the extant paradigms of economics. Such a space – a 'new economics' – can permit heterodox economists to articulate and debate policy alternatives, and indeed, can encompass dialogues with mainstream economists.

The central tenet of this 'new economics' is not to erase the various paradigms within heterodox economics, much less to seek a synthesis of selected elements of neoclassical and heterodox theory in some appropriately balanced 'mix'. Rather the idea is to create space for horizontal conversations between and among heterodox and neoclassical economists. This levelling of the discursive field, with the ultimate aim of democratising theoretical practices, will be facilitated by creating and using 'social efficiency' as a trans-paradigmatic device for debating financial policy alternatives.

As envisioned here, the 'new economics' would create a space for exploring patterns and interconnections between different economic policies and a set of social justice goals that can be determined by democratic processes. It would then feature exchanges of ideas grounded in different analytical centres. So 'new economics' is best conceptualised not as a unified theoretical enterprise with one centre, but rather as a meeting ground for theorists who are investigating the relevance of a variety of factors – class, nation, race, gender, and so on. So analytical tolerance must be a guiding principle. There is something to learn from the field of urban studies in the 1960s and 1970s, which viewed the city as a structured system, whose terrain of action was incomparably more complex, layered, and subtle than any one perspective could encompass. The first insight in comprehending the city was analytical humility – an acceptance of the inability of any one seer to completely see the phenomenon in view. 'New economics' also needs this humility and openness.

The vision of 'new economics' proposed here does not intend to simplify progressive discourse through subtraction. To the contrary; as Lawson (2006, p. 498) puts it, 'it is their particular substantive orientations, concerns and emphases, not answers or principles, that distinguishes the heterodox traditions from each other'. There is no one master narrative lurking behind these different traditions. Nor is there any intention here of eliminating the possibility of scientific discourse – that is, of principled exchanges of ideas based on conceptual and empirical relationships developed under rules by which participating members agree to be bound.

Rather, the intention here is to democratise economics and to renew the possibilities of economic science This can be done through an inversion of the commonly held view of the relationships of science and discourse within a disciplinary field. It is widely held that scientific findings define the limits of acceptable discourse within a field of inquiry; then discourse involves the sharing of ideas about what science has already found out. We propose here that the disciplinary field of economics should be understood as a broad terrain of discourse which encompasses findings, theories and competing principles of justice;

within this broad terrain exist pools of scientific inquiry, in which sub-sets of the members of 'new economics' use tools of formal inquiry to investigate propositions that can, in turn, be shared with members of the broader community.

Notes

1. In a recent paper, Smolin (2009) disagrees that the tension between equilibria and initial states constitutes a major limitation of neoclassical theory.
2. Cassidy (2009) provides references for these theoretical assertions.
3. Dymski (2010) summarises evidence suggesting these charges are not valid.
4. Farmer and Geanakoplos (2009) have written a critique of the EMH, though they assert that accumulating empirical evidence – not theoretical incoherence – should be used to either discard or revise it.
5. Kuttner (2010) provides insight into the political dynamics of, and issues involved in, the US financial reform process.
6. The idea of 'social efficiency' originated in work that Dorene Isenberg and I did on housing finance systems in several countries, including the USA; see Dymski and Isenberg (1998, 2001).
7. William Shakespeare, *The Tempest*, II.i., lines 253–4.
8. *Report by the Commission on the Measurement of Economic Performance and Social Progress.* Chair, Joseph Stiglitz, Amartya Sen, Chair Adviser, Jean-Paul Fitoussi, Coordinator of the Commission. Paris, 2009. Accessed at www.stiglitz-sen-fitoussi.fr/en/documents.htm. In a recent article exploring some of the terrain covered in this section, Marc Fleurbaey (2009) identified several alternatives to GDP as measures of well-being: sustainability; happiness; social choice and fair allocation; and capabilities. He distinguished three fundamental approaches, which he describes as welfarist (neoclassical), liberal (Rawls), and perfectionist (Sen); these approaches differ based on whether the individual is viewed as a resource owner, a participant in deciding a social contract, or an endpoint.
9. For elaboration on these points, see Dymski (2010).

References

Arnsperger, C. and Varoufakis, Y. (2006) 'What Is Neoclassical Economics? The Three Axioms Responsible for Its Theoretical Oeuvre, Practical Irrelevance and, Thus, Discursive Power', *Panoeconomicus*, 53(1), pp. 5–18.

Benston, G. J., Eisenbeis, R.A., Horvitz, P.M., Kane, E.J., and Kaufman, G.G. (1986) *Perspectives on Safe and Sound Banking: Past, Present, and Future.* Boston, MA: MIT Press.

Bernanke, B.S. (1983) 'Non-monetary Effects of the Financial Crisis in the Propagation of the Great Depression', *American Economic Review*, 73(3), pp. 257–76.

Bernanke, B. and Gertler, M. (1990) 'Financial Fragility and Economic Performance', *Quarterly Journal of Economics*, 105(1), pp. 87–114.

Black, W.K. (2010) 'Neo-Classical Economic Theories, Methodology and Praxis Optimize Criminogenic Environments and Produce Recurrent, Intensifying Crises', *Creighton Law Review*.

Brunnermeier, M.K., and Pedersen, L.H. (2009) 'Market Liquidity and Funding Liquidity', *Review of Financial Studies*, 22(6), pp. 2201–38.

Cassidy, J. (2009) *How Markets Fail: The Logic of Economic Calamities*. New York: Farrar, Straus, and Giroux.

Davis, J.B. (2006) 'The Turn in Economics: Neoclassical Dominance to Mainstream Pluralism?', *Journal of Institutional Economics*, 2(1), pp. 1–20.

Davis, J.B. (2008) 'The Turn in Recent Economics and Return of Orthodoxy', *Cambridge Journal of Economics*, 32, pp. 349–66.

Dymski, G.A. (2010) 'From Financial Exploitation to Global Banking Instability: Two Overlooked Roots of the Subprime Crisis', in M. Konings (ed.), *Beyond the Subprime Headlines: Critical Perspectives on the Financial Crisis*. London: Verso Press: pp. 72–102.

Dymski, G.A. and Isenberg, D. (1998) 'Housing Finance in the Age of Globalization: From Social Housing to Life-Cycle Risk', in D. Baker, G. Epstein and R. Pollin (eds), *Globalization and Progressive Economic Policy*. Cambridge: Cambridge University Press, pp. 219–39.

Dymski, G.A., and Isenberg, D. (eds) (2001) *Seeking Shelter on the Pacific Rim: Financial Globalization, Social Change, and the Housing Market*. Armonk, NY: M.E. Sharpe.

Fama, E.F. (1980) 'Banking in the Theory of Finance', *Journal of Monetary Economics*, 6(1), pp. 39–57.

Fama, E.F. (1985) 'What's Different About Banks?', *Journal of Monetary Economics* 15, pp. 29–39.

Farmer, J.D., and Geanakoplos, J. (2008) 'The Virtues and Vices of Equilibrium and the Future of Financial Economics'. *Cowles Foundation Discussion Paper No. 1647*, Cowles Foundation for Research in Economics, Yale University, March.

Farmer, R. (1993) *The Macroeconomics of Self-Fulfilling Prophecies*. Cambridge, MA: MIT Press.

Fisher, R.W. (2010) 'Lessons Learned, Convictions Confirmed'. Remarks before the Council on Foreign Relations, New York City, 3 March. Accessed on 31 July 2010 at http://www.dallasfed.org/news/speeches/fisher/2010/fs100303.cfm.

Fleurbaey, M. (2009) 'Beyond GDP: The Quest for a Measure of Social Welfare', *Journal of Economic Literature*, 47(4), pp. 1029–75.

Folbre, N. (1994) *Who Pays for the Kids? Gender and the Structures of Constraint*. London: Routledge.

Fox, J. (2009) *The Myth of the Rational Market: A History of Risk, Reward, and Delusion on Wall Street*. New York: HarperBusiness.

Friedman, M. (1953) 'The Case for Flexible Exchange Rates', in Milton Friedman, *Essays in Positive Economics*. Chicago: University of Chicago Press.

Friedman, M. (1968) 'The Role of Monetary Policy', *American Economic Review*, 58(1), pp. 1–17.

Garnett Jr., R.F. (2006) 'Paradigms and Pluralism in Heterodox Economics', *Review of Political Economy*, 18(4), pp. 521–46.

Geanakoplos, J. (2009) 'The Leverage Cycle', *Cowles Foundation Discussion Paper No. 1715*, Cowles Foundation for Research in Economics, Yale University, July.

Gorton, G., and He, P. (2005) 'Bank Credit Cycles', *NBER Working Paper No. 11363*. Cambridge, MA: National Bureau of Economic Research.

Ingrao, B. and G. Israel (1990) *The Invisible Hand: Economic Equilibrium in the History of Science*. Cambridge, MA: MIT Press.

Johnson, S., and Kwak, J. (2010) 'Too Big for Us to Fail', *The American Prospect*, 26 April.

Kane, E.J. (1989) 'The High Cost of Incompletely Funding the FSLIC Shortage of Explicit Capital', *Journal of Economic Perspectives*, 3(4), pp. 31–48.

Kane, E.J. (2009) 'The Importance of Monitoring and Mitigating the Safety-net Consequences of Regulation-induced Innovation', *Networks Financial Institute, Policy Brief No. 2009-PB-08*, November.

Kane, E.J. (2010) 'Redefining and Containing Systemic Risk', May. Available at SSRN: http://ssrn.com/abstract=1603323.

Kaufman, G.G. (1995) 'The U.S. Banking Debacle of the 1980s: A Lesson in Government Mismanagement', *The Freeman: Ideas on Liberty*, 45(4), April. Published online at http://www.thefreemanonline.org.

Keynes, J.M. (1936) *The General Theory of Employment, Interest, and Prices*. London: Macmillan.

Kiyotaki, N., and Moore, J. (1997) 'Credit Cycles', *Journal of Political Economy*, 105(2), pp. 211–48.

Krugman, P. (2009) 'How Did Economists Get It So Wrong?', *New York Times* (Sunday Magazine), 6 September.

Krugman, P. (2010) 'Financial Reform 101', *New York Times*, 1 April.

Kuhn, T. (1962) *The Structure of Scientific Revolutions*. Chicago: University of Chicago Press.

Kuttner, R. (2010) 'Question for the Tea Party: Why the Free Ride for Republicans Protecting Bankers?', *The Huffington Post*, 11 July 2010, accessed on 1 August 2010 at http://www.huffingtonpost.com/robert-kuttner/question-for-the-tea-part_b_642379.html

Lawson, T. (2006) 'The Nature of Heterodox Economics', *Cambridge Journal of Economics*, 30, pp. 483–505.

Lucas, Jr., R.E. (1986) 'Principles of Fiscal and Monetary Policy', *Journal of Monetary Economics*, 17, pp. 117–34.

Masters, B., and Belton. C. (2010) 'Volcker Seeks Banking Shake-up Alongside New Rules on Capital', *Financial Times*, 14 May.

McCloskey, D.N. (2001) 'The Genealogy of Postmodernism: An Economist's Guide', in S. Cullenberg, J. Amariglio and R. Ruccio (eds), *Postmodernism, Economics, and Knowledge*. London: Routledge: pp. 102–28.

McKenzie, D. (2006) *An Engine, Not a Camera: How Financial Models Shape Markets*. Cambridge, MA: MIT Press.

Minsky, H. (1986) *Stabilizing an Unstable Economy*. New Haven: Yale University Press.

Oldfield, G. (2000) 'Making Markets for Structured Derivatives', *Journal of Financial Economics*, 57, pp. 445–71.

Partnoy, F., and Skeel, Jr., D.A. (2007) 'The Promise and Perils of Credit Derivatives', *University of Cincinnati Law Review*, 75(2), p. 1027.

Rawls, J. (1971) *A Theory of Justice*. Cambridge, MA: Harvard University Press.

Roemer, J.R. (2000) *Equality of Opportunity*. Cambridge, MA: Harvard University Press.

Sen, A. (1999) *Development as Freedom*. Oxford: Oxford University Press.

Shiller, R. (2009) *The Subprime Solution*. Princeton: Princeton University Press.

Shleifer, A. and R.W. Vishny (1997) 'The Limits of Arbitrage', *The Journal of Finance*, 52(1), pp. 35–55.

van Staveren, I. (2011) 'From Gender as Exogenous to Gender as Endogenous in the New Economics', in P. Arestis and M. Sawyer (eds), *New Economics as Mainstream Economics*. Annual IPPE volume. Basingstoke: Palgrave Macmillan.

Wallison, P. (2009) 'The True Origins of This Financial Crisis', *The American Spectator*, February. Accessed online at http://spectator.org/archives/2009/02/06/the-true-origins-of-this-finan/print.

4
From Gender as Exogenous to Gender as Endogenous in the New Economics

Irene van Staveren
International Institute of Social Studies, Erasmus University Rotterdam

Abstract

This paper argues that gender is endogenous to the economic process. It demonstrates a two-way relationship between the economy and gender relations, and emphasises the macro level. It demonstrates that inequality in gender relations can have a negative effect on economic policy and economic outcomes. This integrated understanding of gender in economics, developed in feminist economics, is not possible in neoclassical economics because that treats gender, like any social structure, as exogenous, often as a given constraint on individual choices, or at most as a sex-disaggregated impact variable. Heterodox economics, in particular when applying a contextual view of the economy as embedded in social, cultural and political structures, allows for an endogenous analysis of gender. This chapter shows, with examples from empirical research, how this may be done in a systematic way, by linking feminist economic insights with various key heterodox concepts.

Keywords: Gender, feminist economics, endogenous, inequality, efficiency, trade, institutions.

JEL Classifications: B50, B54, E02, O11

1 Introduction

In neoclassical macroeconomics, gender is often completely absent, either as a variable, or as driving certain institutions, or as underlying the gender division of labour between the paid and unpaid economy. At the same time, the unpaid economy is often ignored completely.

At most, gender is included as exogenous through a sex-disaggregated variable such as male and female labour force participation. For example, in various analyses on EU economic growth in relation to an increasing dependency ratio due to the ageing population, the relatively low female labour force participation rate has been identified as a constraint on economic growth and the financial sustainability of pension systems. Alternatively, some macroeconomic analyses may point at the unequal impacts of macroeconomic phenomena on men and women, for example studies that have shown that cheap labour export strategies of developing countries have generated more employment for women as compared to men, because the kind of industries that have relocated to these countries are typically female-intensive industries (textiles, garments, microelectronics assembly). So, women are recognised as benefiting more than men from the jobs created in export industries. This is simply taken as a differential impact of export growth strategies, as if underlying gender relations – for example, expressed through the gender wage gap – plays no role in bringing about precisely such a female-intensive export strategy. Apart from these examples, in which gender is pictured as an exogenous variable, a constraint, or a social differentiated impact variable of an economic strategy, the far majority of mainstream macroeconomics completely ignores gender.

The reason for the limited attention to the role of gender in economic analysis is that it is not recognised as part and parcel of economic processes and policies. In neoclassical economics, certainly in macroeconomics, agents are assumed to be homogeneous, so that rational economic man (REM) becomes the representative agent in economic analysis. REM, however, is implicitly defined in stereotypically masculine terms (Folbre, 1994). He is competitive, not cooperative; he follows a maximisation algorithm without an eye to social and moral context; he is the default head of household and breadwinner, who performs no unpaid work unless he regards it as leisure. In heterodox economics, gender can be understood as an endogenous variable, shaping and being shaped by economic forces, trends and policies. Gender must be understood as, first, shaping market processes in terms of access to and control over resources, such as education or incomes; second, as shaping people's choices and opportunities and constraints, for example in segmented labour markets with typically feminine and masculine jobs; third, as being inherently part of macroeconomic trends, for example through fluctuations in the female labour force participation rate, and fourth as underlying the household gender division of labour leading to a large female-intensive unpaid economy. Such a more differentiated and layered understanding of the relationship between gender and the economy – as a two-way rather than a one-way relation, as partially positive and partially negative – provides an important social dimension to economic analysis, a form of embedding economic analysis in social behaviour and structures. As a consequence of developing such gender-aware economics, or, to put it more explicitly, feminist economics, simple, straightforward conclusions on the goodness or badness for women and men of certain economic processes or policies can no longer be defended. Economic analysis should no longer reduce important influences on the economic process and from the economic process on social phenomena to exogenous variables. One such important force is gender, which influences the economy and is at the same time influenced by it, in a two-way process.

In this paper, I would like to show that in heterodox economics, particularly feminist economics, but also strands of structuralist economics, social economics and institutional economics, gender has increasingly been recognised as endogenous to the economic process. This implies that not only there are economic impacts that are often different – unequal – for men and women, but also that existing gender relations have an impact on the economy, either positive or negative, and on economic outcomes. Furthermore, these two directions of the relationships between the economy and gender have a mutual influence on each other, directly as well indirectly through feedback effects. In neoclassical economics, gender is at most included as simply sex-disaggregated labour market variables, mostly limited to the labour supply variable. Differences in labour supply and its elasticity are then attributed to exogenous variables such as the availability of childcare or culture. The analysis of gender differences in the labour market, hence, is then reduced to the behavioural question of why women behave differently in the labour market than men, without understanding how gender affects the economic process and is being influenced by dynamic efficiencies, unpaid work, asymmetric institutions, risk strategies of households, path dependence of institutions that generally benefit males over females. At the micro level, there exists already a substantial body of literature on such two-way relationships between the economy and gender, in particular in labour economics and household analysis. At the macro level, however, the literature on this two-way relationship between gender and the economy is still at an early stage of development. But what does emerge from this literature is that for a full understanding of the macro economy, gender can no longer be ignored. In the present paper, I will point out in which ways gender helps to improve macroeconomic analysis, with examples from my own work in development economics.

2 Micro–meso–macro approach, long-run inefficiencies and short-run efficiencies of gender inequality

Elson (1995) has developed the so-called micro–meso–macro approach to studying gender impacts of macroeconomic policies and feedback effects. The approach focuses on the linkages between the micro and macro levels through households, structured labour markets and other structured markets (land, credit), gender asymmetries in institutions (welfare regimes, property rights, childcare arrangements, tax systems), and macroeconomic policies (trade, privatisation, devaluation). At the same time, the micro–meso–macro approach recognizes trends in macroeconomic variables, such as export volumes or GDP growth rates that are partly driven by gender relations (female labour force participation, household-dependent agricultural export supply response, female- or male-intensive employment sectors). So, the micro–meso–macro approach enables a two-way analytical framework for the analysis of gender and the economy, moving back and forth between the micro and macro level of analysis. This framework helps to recognize inefficiencies of gender inequality.

Feminist economists reject the mainstream assumption that economic growth will bring about an automatic reduction in gender inequality. Inglehart and Norris (2003) conclude from their cross-country research that: 'growing affluence does tend to generate the expansion of literacy and schooling, the establishment of a social protection safety net, and the rise of white-collar jobs in the service sector, but this process is not inevitable. Nor does it necessarily automatically benefit women's lives' (5f). At the same time, gender inequality can be bad for growth, because inequality excludes women from production, demotivates efforts for improvement and hence keeps female productivity low, it may cause social conflict chasing away investment, and it allows for male rent-seeking. Hence, there is no straightforward relationship between efficiency and equality in general and gender equality in particular. This insight goes against the standard way of viewing the relationship between efficiency and equity as a trade-off in the welfare theoretical concept of Pareto Optimality.

One of the first economists to propose an alternative efficiency notion that does take equality into account was also the first woman to receive a PhD degree in economics, Margaret Reid. She redefined efficiency in a common-sense way as the minimisation of waste (Reid, 1934, 1943). This basic idea of efficiency as the minimisation of waste had already been recognized by Adam Smith, Karl Marx and Thorstein Veblen. Walsh (2000) reminds us that Smith 'is savage when he sees the surplus being squandered by the profusion of the great' (p. 21) and he also reminds us that Marx's concept of exploitation included the recognition of waste of the surplus on luxury when it is shifted from labour to capital. While the founder of institutional economics, Veblen (1931), has criticised the waste of conspicuous leisure and consumption, arguing that 'the utility of both alike for the purposes of reputability lies in the element of waste that is common to both. In the one case it is a waste of time and effort, in the other it is a waste of goods' (p. 126). Veblen (1931) pointed in particular at the higher-class ideal of the housewife as a luxury and a waste of human resources. His contemporary, Charlotte Perkins Gilman, wrote about women's economic position in a similar way, pointing out that women's household production at an individual basis is inefficient as compared to communal kitchens and other forms of joint production for family consumption (van Staveren, 2003). Hence, the gender norm of the traditional division of labour between a breadwinner and a housewife implies two forms of waste: of female human capital for the labour market and of productivity in ignoring economies of scale in household production.

Reid (1943) referred to her efficiency notion as the minimisation of waste to waste in *consumption* when the rich consume far more than the poor; waste in the *production* of goods that have negative externalities (giving the example of tobacco); waste through inefficient *methods of production* (partially related to economies of scale); and waste through *market equilibria* allowing for the underuse and underinvestment of production factors (leading to suboptimal land-use and unemployment). In her work in agricultural economics, Reid (1943) argued that the partial production for own use among USA family farmers was rational in a dynamic perspective in a context of uncertainty about yields and world market prices, and therefore efficient for the USA food sector. The production for own use protected family farmers from food insecurity and distress sales in bad times and provided a buffer against too high market volatility. Hence, Reid's understanding of efficiency was a pragmatic one, rejecting the welfare-theoretic assumptions of perfect markets, constant returns to scale, and absence of power, while recognising that real-world economies are influenced by uncertainty, power relations and asymmetric institutions. These imperfect conditions of markets require a shift away from efficiency as a static criterion of evaluation – the evaluation of an equilibrium – towards a dynamic criterion, evaluating waste in the economic *process*, rather than in an idealised market *outcome*, as Blaug (2001) has argued. Moreover, it shows that under certain conditions, more equality raises efficiency rather than lowers it, in particular over the long run.

In addition, there is a problem with the libertarian belief that free exchange provides the best incentive structure for efficiency to occur. Because it ignores the real-world situation in which some agents quite often lack the endowments for any beneficial exchange – even in the absence of market imperfections. In other words, libertarianism assumes that exchange is, by definition, voluntary when not forced or constrained from outside. But voluntary exchange may also involve involuntary losses when there is too much imbalance in endowments and opportunities, and, hence, inequality in bargaining power between market parties. That is why genuine voluntary exchange can only exist when there is a feasible non-exchange option (Sen, 1981; Walsh, 2003). Without such a fall-back, exchange of one's last resource or even of non-economic goods such as one's children or bodily integrity, will not be voluntary, but simply the only option available for ensuring short-term survival. This is precisely why we see illegal transactions of women's bodies in the sex trade, as well as involuntary prostitution in many societies where women have limited property rights, where inheritance laws are gender biased, and where investment by parents in their children's human capital is biased against daughters. So, paradoxically, voluntary exchange will only be voluntary with what Sen (1981) has labelled a feasible option for autarky. Distress sales or underinvestment may be regarded by libertarians as voluntary in a static sense, but they undermine an agent's resource base, and, hence, crowd out productive capacity in the long run. This is clearly not voluntarily chosen by agents while it is neither efficient in a dynamic sense, making people dependent on others or the state. Distress sales or underinvestment can only be prevented by trade-independent security, deriving from resources such as savings, wealth, community care, access to commons, public goods or welfare support. Most people who experience a disadvantaged exchange position have very few resources to provide for themselves, except their labour power. And even this may not be in demand, as it may be only potential rather than actual labour power, due to lack of nutrition and health (Dasgupta, 1993), or it may not earn sufficient market value to survive (Kurien, 1996), or a combination of factors including lack of aggregate demand keeping the demand for labour low at any wage rate (Walsh, 1996). Therefore, only an institutional setting of markets that acknowledges equal basic entitlements for men and women alike and other mechanisms that prevent inequality-inducing accumulation will be able to reflect genuine free trade, which may enhance efficiency (van Staveren, 2007c). Below, I will refer to two types of inefficiencies from gender inequality in markets. Through the micro–meso–macro link these inefficiencies tend to have a negative impact on growth, stability, and aggregate productivity because of the sheer size of gender-based inefficiencies.

First, gender inequality is inefficient in the allocation of resources, for example in financial markets. In the experience of the Grameen Bank in Bangladesh, loans to women yield substantially higher household consumption than loans to men. In the case of women, it takes an average of 0.91 dollars lent to generate 1 dollar of household consumption, as compared with 1.48 dollars for men (Morduch 1999: 1593). The Grameen experience shows that lending to women is not less profitable than lending to men – on the contrary, female repayment rates are higher. In 1991, 15.3 per cent of male borrowers from the Grameen Bank missed repayments, compared with only 1.3 per cent of female borrowers (Morduch 1999: 1583). Other research on micro-credit in Bangladesh concludes that loans to women generally yield higher marginal returns than loans to men (Pitt/Khandker 1998). So, discrimination against women in financial markets is not only unfair but also inefficient.

Second, at the aggregate level, gender inequality appears to lead to losses in GDP growth. A regression analysis over the period 1960–92 with GDP growth as the dependent variable and education and employment among the independent variables indicates that Sub-Saharan Africa has suffered considerable growth losses from gender biases in educational investment. If Sub-Saharan Africa had matched East Asia's growth of educational attainment for women, annual per capita GDP growth would have been about 0.5 percentage points higher (World Bank 1999: 15). In addition, if Sub-Saharan Africa had matched East Asia's growth rates in female sector employment, annual per capita GDP growth would have increased by more than 0.3 percentage points (World Bank 1999: 16). So, together, gender biases in investment in education and in employment have reduced annual per capita GDP growth in Sub-Saharan Africa by 0.8 percentage points (World Bank 1999: 17). In a similar study on the economic losses of missing the Millennium Development Goals on gender equality, Klasen and Abu-Ghaida (2004) have calculated that off-track countries are likely to suffer between 0.1 and 0.3 percentage points per capita growth.

The examples point out that discrimination of women is not only unfair but also inefficient. This inefficiency is generated through various mechanisms, in which asymmetric institutions play an important role: institutions that represent power, and protect the interests of the powerful – in this case men and masculine ideals such as being a male breadwinner – over the marginalised – in this case women and the denigration of femininity such as caring roles in the household. Another mechanism is the law of diminishing marginal returns, which is ignored by common gender beliefs held by individual agents as well as by policy makers that male farmers, or male children, are more deserving of scarce investments on their lands or in their human capital than women and girls.

There is, however, also a reverse mechanism which turns gender inequality into a competitive advantage, and, hence, a mechanism for growth. This mechanism occurs when gender inequality reflects exploitation supported by asymmetric institutions of exclusion and discrimination. This is particularly the case for the labour market, in which women's wages tend to be not only lower than men's wages for similar work, but also low relative to women's average productivity. This is generally referred to as the gender wage gap. Seguino (2000a and 2000b) has demonstrated, in two empirical studies on the relationship between growth and the gender wage gap for manufacturing exporting countries in Asia, that growth is positively correlated with the gender wage gap. In other words, her studies have shown that the rapidly growing Asian economies have in effect been able to grow so fast, partially by paying very low wages to women, relative to men: countries with the highest gender wage gap appeared to reap the highest export earnings relative to their GDP, by using low women's wages as a major competitive advantage.

This practice can persist due to imperfections in the labour market, in combination with structural unemployment. On average, for developed and developing countries, women's wages are 75 per cent of men's wages. Some countries do better, with gender wage gaps around 10 per cent (such as Vietnam), whereas other countries have gaps in the range of 30–40 per cent (such as Japan and Korea). Of this gender wage gap, about half cannot be explained by gender differences in human capital or functional characteristics of women's and men's jobs, while the other half is due to gender inequalities in education, and the gender division of labour in the household (expressed in temporary labour market drop-out due to child raising, or part-time or flexible work in order to combine paid work with gender-unequally distributed child care responsibilities).

In the globalised economy, it is hard to undercut this negative mechanism linking gender inequality to growth, when it is used as a competitive advantage. There are, however, two clear policy responses indicated in feminist economic analysis that would help to move away from this short-run growth strategy and help move developing countries to a long-run growth path of increasing value added and increasing levels of productivity in their exports, with a lower gender wage gap. The first policy strategy is a political economy one, recommending a globally agreed minimum labour standards package, such as advocated in the ILO's Decent Work programme (Barrientos, 2007). This package should explicitly include gender equality in wages, the removal of gender-based hiring and firing practices that now keep labour markets gender-segregated, and a revision of education and training systems away from stereotypically feminine and masculine areas of specialisation. The second policy strategy is a macroeconomic one, advocated, among others, by Blecker and Seguino (2002). This policy is geared towards the removal of dynamic inefficiencies arising from wage discrimination. These inefficiencies occur in the long run, and result from reductions in female labour supply and low levels of work motivation which leads to relatively low labour productivity. If the gender wage gap were to be eliminated, female labour productivity would increase, while, through the increase in female labour supply responding to higher wages, the average nominal wage level would not increase proportionally. So, although in the short run women's low wages might be instrumental in keeping production costs competitive, in the long run the disincentives to female labour input are likely to create lock-in effects of cheap female labour, low productivity, low earnings, and, hence, a disadvantaged macroeconomic strategy for a country in the long run, also referred to as 'low road development'. Removing gender inequalities in export sectors would help to prevent such a lock-in into low road development.

3 Gender and trade dynamics

In our book, *The Feminist Economics of Trade*, we have shown how gender inequality can have an impact on trade-related outcomes, such as the terms of trade and the composition of exports and domestic versus export output (van Staveren et al., 2007). Shaianne Osterreich (2007) takes as a starting point the Prebisch–Singer hypothesis that the net barter terms of trade between South and North tend to deteriorate (a hypothesis for which there is ample empirical support). Prebisch and Singer argued that the underlying mechanism for this uneven distribution of gains from trade lies in differences in labour markets in the South and North, with workers in the South having less ability to bargain for rises in productivity to be matched by rises in wages. Osterreich hypothesises that gender inequality is an important aspect of these labour market differences. Using data from a selection of Southern and Northern countries for the period 1975–95, she finds that a decline in the degree of labour market discrimination against women in the South relative to the degree of labour market discrimination against women in the North is associated with an improvement in the net barter terms of trade of Southern countries. So, if governments in the South take action to reduce labour market discrimination against women, this will help to counteract the tendency of their terms of trade to fall, bringing a larger share of the gains from trade to the South.

William Darity (2007) examines the ways in which unequal gender relations in agriculture interact with attempts to stimulate agricultural exports via the devaluation of the currency. He develops a model of gender segregation of labour in smallholder export and subsistence (food) production, based on the empirical literature on Sub-Saharan Africa. Both men and women participate in producing export crops, but only women produce subsistence goods. The model describes three different regimes of gendered power: coercion, in which men exercise power over the time women allocate to export crops, the sales of which are controlled by men; cooperation, in which women (guided by social norms of interfamilial behaviour) willingly agree to allocate unpaid time to export crops; and compensation, in which women will not work on export crops without being compensated by their husbands. Darity models the effect of a currency devaluation, which raises the price that men receive for export crops. Through coercion, co-operation, or compensation, women allocate more time to export crop production. The model illuminates how different regimes of gendered power affect the impact of export expansion. One inference is that if women resist coercion and are unwilling to work without pay, they will not switch into export crop production following devaluation, slowing down export expansion (see also Warner and Campbell 2000), which helps to explain the low supply response to currency devaluations in Africa in the 1980s and 1990s.

Gender segregation in production is also a theme of the model presented by Blecker and Seguino (2002). Their model is based on the stylised facts of semi-industrialised economies, in which women produce a good that is primarily for export, although some is consumed domestically, and men produce a good that is only for the domestic market. Women earn less than men. The model examines the effects on output of an exogenous rise in women's wages, holding male wages and the exchange rate constant. If export markets are price elastic, and workers' consumption of the export good is low, the output of exports is likely to fall, while the effect on the production of domestic goods is ambiguous. On the other hand, if export demand is price-inelastic and the workers' consumption of the export good is high, export production will expand; again, the effect on production of domestic goods is ambiguous. But these conditions are less likely to be met. Given the realistic assumptions of the model, reducing the gender wage gap by raising women's wages is likely to depress exports and may also depress production of domestic goods. If nominal wages of both women and men are flexible, and there is a crawling peg exchange rate, the effects are more complex and an increase in women's wages may be combined with export expansion.

Ozler (2007) uses plant-level data for the period 1986–96 to examine employment by sex and skill level in three types of production: non-tradable, import-competing and export. As expected, net job creation rates were higher in the export sector than the other sectors for all groups of workers. Net job creation rates were higher for females than for males in all sectors, but the biggest gender gap was in the import-competing sector, which had the highest ratio of female to male job creation rates for production workers. Although women benefited from the gender gap in net job creation, women's employment was more volatile than men's, as measured by the female and male gross job reallocation rate (the sum of gross job creation and gross job destruction rates). While the growth of export production increased women's share of the labour force, economy-wide factors contributed to making women's work more precarious than that of men. Hence quantitative gender gaps decreased whereas qualitative gender gaps increased.

Finally, Ebru Kongar (2007) challenges the neoclassical view that increased import competition reduces discrimination against women and the gender wage gap. In a study on the effects of import competition on the gender wage gap in Taiwan and Korea, Berik and van der Meulen (2004) have also challenged the hypothesis that more competition reduces gender discrimination in wages. They found that increased competition was correlated positively with wage discrimination against women, probably due to a reduction in women's bargaining power. Kongar investigates the wage and employment effects (disaggregated by sex and occupation) of increased import competition in the USA in the period 1976–93, distinguishing between concentrated and competitive manufacturing industries. Wages are measured as 'residual wages' net of the impact of the effects of personal characteristics of workers other than sex, such as education, experience, marital status race and location. The study shows that the decline in the residual manufacturing gender wage gap, in a context of declining overall employment, was driven by changes in the composition of the female labour force rather than by a reduction of discrimination against women. In the concentrated industries, female low-wage production workers suffered disproportionately from import-related job losses, raising the average wages of the remaining smaller, more highly skilled, female workforce, and thereby reducing the gender wage gap. By contrast, in the competitive industries, the female share of low-wage production occupations increased and average female wages declined. These differences reflect different firm strategies building on gender-based labour market segmentation in the two sectors, with those in the concentrated sector meeting import competition by adopting more skill-intensive production and those in the competitive sector increasing their use of cheap labour.

The studies on gender and trade show that the gender division of labour in the household, asymmetric gendered institutions affecting the economic behaviour of women and men, and labour market discrimination have significant economic effects. They limit gains from trade, reduce the supply response to exchange rate policy, support an exploitative competitive advantage, generate a trade-off between job gain and job security for women, and allow both competitive and concentrated industry to exploit the gender wage gap and women's weaker labour market position in strategic responses to globalisation. Again, these research results from feminist economics show how varied the two-way relationships between gender and the economy are, and that they often hold each other hostage in a lose–lose situation, with possible short-term gains but long-run allocative and dynamic inefficiencies.

3.1   An example: EU–Mercosur trade agreement

I will illustrate with an example how trade elasticities of gender inequality may be calculated and applied to a particular trade relation in order to detect possible gender–trade relationships (van Staveren, 2007a). I will briefly assess the trade agreement between the European Union and Mercosur, which was initiated in 1995. Trade between the partner regions has increased since 1995, but follows a traditional North–South pattern of specialisation with Mercosur specialising in agricultural exports and EU in manufacturing exports. The data refer to the period 1995–2005.

The denominator can be calculated in three different ways (in which $_i$ refers to a country or a region and $_j$ refers to a bilateral trading partner, or a trading block, or to all trading partners):

- trade volumes as a share of GDP of a country or a region: $[EX_{ij} + IM_{ij}]/GDP_i$
- bilateral or regional trade volumes as a share of total trade of a country or region: $[EX_{ij} + IM_{ij}]/[EX_i + IM_i]$
- openness measured in tariff reductions of x per cent.

In the indicators to be presented in the next section, I will use the first type of trade variable, that is, trade (import and export volumes) as a share of GDP.

For the numerator, there is a potentially wide variety of variables available for measuring gender inequality, but data limitations as well as the limited availability of research on gender effects of trade leaves only a small number of variables to be included in the indicators. These are variables measuring poverty, employment, wages, time use, childcare, and household food security. For many countries these variables are unfortunately only available at the aggregate level, while trade impacts can be expected to differ between sectors of the economy, in particular between export sectors, import-competing sectors and the domestic sector. Nevertheless, they may provide a rough picture of the state of the art of gender inequality among trading partners, and may point out areas for in-depth research at the sector level.

Below follow some examples for numerator variables:

(1)   trade elasticity of the gender gap in earned income

$$d[Y^f/Y]/d[EX_{ij} + IM_{ij}]/GDP_i]$$

(2)   trade elasticity of the gender gap in labour force participation

$$d[L^f/L]/d[EX_{ij} + IM_{ij}]/GDP_i]$$

(3)   trade elasticity of gender inequality in export employment

$$d[L^f_{ex}/L_{ex}]/d[EX_{ij} + IM_{ij}]/GDP_i]$$

(4)   trade elasticity of gender inequality in employment in import competing sectors

$$d[L^f_{imc}/L_{imc}]/d[EX_{ij} + IM_{ij}]/GDP_i]$$

(5)   trade elasticity of the gender gap in unemployment rates

$$d[U^f/U^m]/d[EX_{ij} + IM_{ij}]/GDP_i]$$

(6a)   trade elasticity of gendered job segregation

$$dID/d[EX_{ij} + IM_{ij}]/GDP_i]$$

(6b)   trade elasticity of gendered job segregation in the export sector

$$d[ID_{ex}]/d[EX_{ij} + IM_{ij}]/GDP_i]$$

(6c)   trade elasticity of gendered job segregation in the import-competing sector

$$[ID_{imc}]/d[EX_{ij} + IM_{ij}]/GDP_i]$$

(7)   trade elasticity of relative women's wages in the export sector compared to other sectors

$$d[W^f_{ex}/W^f]/d[EX_{ij} + IM_{ij}]/GDP_i]$$

(8)   trade elasticity of the gender gap in unpaid labour time

$$d[UNPT^f/UNPT^m]/d[EX_{ij} + IM_{ij}]/GDP_i]$$

(9)   trade elasticity of women's purchasing power for food

$$d[[Y^f/\text{female population}]/P_{food}]/ d[EX_{ij} + IM_{ij}]/GDP_i]$$

Filling in data for Mercosur–EU trade and gender inequality in the Mercosur countries, I found that the trade elasticity for food affordability is unity and negative ($-42/41.9 = -1$). Mercosur exports mainly food items – the same that are consumed domestically. This may have led to a crowding out of domestic food supply by foreign demand, following the devaluation of the currency. The indicator suggests that it has become more difficult for women to perform their assigned roles in households as food providers, because women in Mercosur are net food buyers, not growers (more than 80 per cent of the population lives in urban areas). This is even more so the case, because absolute female (and male) income levels have declined over the period.

The indicator for the female employment share in the major export sector, agriculture, is negative and inelastic ($-5.7/77.3 = -0.1$). So, the enormous increase in agricultural exports has not helped to increase the female employment share in this stable and expanding export sector in Mercosur. At the same time, we find that the trade indicator for the male employment share in the major import sector, manufacturing, is negative and elastic ($-28.5/12.6 = -2.3$). Thus there has been an increase in women's share of jobs in the sector that faces import competition. But, whereas in many other developing countries, a move of women from agriculture to manufacturing is generally an improvement of their employment condition since manufacturing is an expanding sector, in Mercosur it implies a shift away from an expanding stable export sector towards a vulnerable import-competing sector.

It is interesting to note that the gender wage gap has worsened for agriculture and improved for manufacturing. This may reflect shifts in relative labour scarcity along gender lines, because, as we have seen, the female employment share in agriculture has declined, while it has increased in the manufacturing sector. Finally, the case study also suggests that there may be impacts from persistent gender inequalities in Mercosur, such as in the labour market, on its trade relationship with the EU. In particular, the data seem to suggest that the 'lock-in' situation of Mercosur in a traditional trade pattern with EU (exports of primary products and imports of manufactures) may actually be reinforced by the gender inequalities in the labour markets of the four countries in South America. Whereas women's average level of education is higher than that of men, they are paid less and find themselves increasingly employed in a sector which is threatened by imported manufactured goods from the EU. This does not seem to be the most efficient allocation of human resources and is not very likely to help Mercosur to move into higher value-added exports, because that would require a better use of human resources, partly through higher returns to female human capital, which in turn would help to stimulate labour productivity. Trade with other external partners, as well as intra-Mercosur trade, appears to be less traditional. Catão and Falcetti (2002), for example, have shown the importance of the Brazilian market for the expansion of Argentinean manufacturing exports, at least during the first seven years of Mercosur (1991–97). A recent Mercosur report shows that, currently, exports to the rest of the world have an increasing share of higher technology (IDB 2004). Hence, it is not unlikely that these other trading partners provide more opportunities for higher value-added exports than the trade relationship with the EU.

In conclusion, the Mercosur–EU trade agreement has not benefited women's economic position whereas the gender division of labour and gender-based labour market segmentation seems to reinforce the traditional trade pattern, in which South America finds itself locked in to a low value-added and low employment-generating trade pattern with the EU. Machismo apparently has a macroeconomic price for the gains from trade – an inefficiency arising from gender inequality.

4   Gendered institutions and access to resources

Recent literature on women's empowerment acknowledges that empowerment involves more than access to resources but also implies agency and an enabling institutional context, which together help women to achieve better well-being outcomes (Kabeer, 2001; Narayan, 2005a; Alsop, Bertelsen, Holland, 2006; Ibrahim and Alkire, 2007). In the light of the recent literature on women's empowerment, I have analysed the role of resources relative to women's agency, captured by gendered institutions that limit this agency (van Staveren, 2007b). One of the definitions of empowerment emerging from the literature has been formulated by Deepa Nayaran (2005b: 5): 'Empowerment is the expansion of assets and capabilities of poor people to participate in, negotiate with, influence, control, and hold accountable institutions that affect their lives.' Although there are some differences, the literature tends to agree that women's empowerment is a process involving *agency* (referred to in the definition above with wordings like 'negotiate', 'influence', and 'control'), access to *resources* (or assets), and *institutions*, which enable women to improve their wellbeing, absolutely, and more importantly, relative to men.

The role of resources for women's empowerment is well understood. For example, access to land (Agarwal, 1994; Doss, 2006; Allendorf, 2007), access to credit (Kabeer, 2001) and access to education (Jejeebhoy, 1995) have all been shown to be important for women's empowerment, and, in turn, for economic development (Klasen, 2002; Lagerlöf, 2003). But next to a lack of access to tangible resources, women also face a variety of intangible constraints to plan their lives, to choose their goals, and to make their own choices, inside and outside households, often more so than men. Such constraints, understood as *gendered institutions* (Goetz, 1997), limit their opportunities in terms of both their access to resources and also their agency (Narayan, 2005b). Institutional economics distinguishes between formal institutions, such as laws and regulations, and informal institutions, which are intangible norms, followed without much questioning (Williamson, 2000; Hodgson, 2006). Both types of institutions reflect power relations since institutions tend to be supported and defended by those who derive advantages from these. For gendered institutions, these power relations are embedded in formal and informal expressions of patriarchy (Folbre, 1994; Goetz, 1997). Formal gendered institutions than can be interpreted as codified gendered social norms such as inheritance laws, property rights, or the fiscal system, with different effects for women and men. On the other hand, informal gendered institutions can be understood as the set of non-codified social norms and cultural practices that impact differently on men and women. Bina Agarwal (1997: 1) has explained how this influence of informal gendered institutions leads to stereotypical masculine and feminine agency by 'ascribing to women and men different abilities, attitudes, desires, personality traits, behaviour patterns, and so on'. This not only results in adaptive preferences (Sen, 1990), which are an internalisation of gender inequalities in one's choices, but experimental research has indicated that gender stereotypes also lead to different self-evaluations, lowering women's self-esteem, motivation and confidence (Biernat et al., 1998; Shih et al., 2006). Hence, women's agency seems negatively affected by gendered rules, laws and rights – formal gendered institutions – on the one hand, and gendered social norms, cultural practices and beliefs – informal gendered institutions – on the other hand.

Given the limitations of working with a cross-country dataset, I employ a simplified model. In this model, variables express gender gaps rather than absolute values. Women's achievements are measured as gender gaps in achievements in health and decision-making power. Resources are defined in terms of women's relative access to education (gender gaps in combined primary and secondary school enrolment rates) and to jobs (female share of the non-agricultural labour force). The two categories of institutions, formal and informal, each consist of three variables, which are taken from the online OECD-GID (Gender, Institutions and Development) database. The two models to be tested reflect the role of gendered institutions in the empowerment literature that gendered institutions not only affect women's and men's access to resources but also impact directly on women's achievements, through affecting their agency, irrespective of their access to resources. This feminist economic analysis of institutions challenges the mainstream view that when women are given access to resources, such as schooling or income, they will automatically achieve similar economic outcomes to men. The macro-level empirical analysis summarised here indicates that such a view of gender as an exogenous variable is too simplistic.

Gender is not only a constraint on women's access to resources, but also affects their economic behaviour – their agency, options, decision-making power and strategies, which in turn perpetuate unequal gender relationships in households, markets and the economy as a whole.

The two resource variables that have been selected are key variables in the women's empowerment literature: access to education and paid employment. They are measured as the gender gap in the combined primary and secondary school enrolment rate (FMedu) and the female share of the non-agricultural labour force (Fnalf). For outcomes, or achievements, the two variables selected are: female/male ratio in life expectancy (FMlife) and female decision-making power (Fdec) in politics and the economy. The variables on gendered institutions lie between zero and one: the more asymmetric the institutions, disadvantaging women, the closer the values are to one. Six variables were chosen from the 13 gendered institutions in the GID database. The variables were grouped into formal and informal institutions, each with three variables. Formal gendered institutions: (1) laws on parental authority (PA), defined as the extent to which parental authority is granted to the mother, both parents equally, or to the father; (2) laws on violence against women (VIO), with laws in three areas: on domestic violence, rape, and sexual harassment; (3) women's land rights (LR), defined as women's access to land ownership. Informal gendered institutions: (1) share of women marrying under 20 years old (EM), defined as the share of girls in the age group of 15–19 years old who are or have been married; (2) prevalence of FGM (FGM): share of women affected by female genital mutilation; (3) missing women (MW), defined as the difference between the number of women that should be alive in a country, with gender equality, and the actual number of women.

The first step in the empirical analysis is the testing of the resource models for education and employment. The two models have independent variables RES_i, with i referring to women's relative access to education (FMedu) and their share in the non-agricultural labour force (Fnalf). The dependent variables are a constant, C, the three formal and three informal gendered institutions, referred to as FGI_j and $IFGI_k$, with ε as the error term:

$$RES_i = C + \beta_1 FGI_j + \beta_2 IFGI_k + \varepsilon \tag{1}$$

The results in Table 4.1 show that both variables have the expected negative sign and are statistically significant. The two resource models have two implications. First, the more asymmetric are the gender norms

Table 4.1   Resource model with aggregate institutions

Independent variables	FMedu	Fnalf
FGI	−0.30***	−0.41***
	(−3.63)	(−5.44)
IFGI	−0.38***	−0.32***
	(−4.50)	(−4.17)
Constant	***	***
	(64.09)	(32.10)
Adjusted R^2	0.36***	0.42***
	(40.88)	(55.04)
N	142	153

Notes: Standardized coefficients (beta) with t-statistics Level of significance for t-statistics for independent variables and for F-statistic for adjusted R^2: * = $p < 0.1$; ** = $p < 0.05$; *** = $p < 0.01$. Sources: GID.
Source: van Staveren, 2007b.

and practices, the less is women's access to resources. This confirms the bivariate results obtained by the initiators of the GID database, Christian Morrisson and Johannes Jütting (2005). Second, the model suggests that informal institutions are a slightly stronger constraint for women's access to education while formal institutions seem to be a little more constraining for women's access to jobs. This, in turn, suggests that both formal and informal gendered institutions are serious constraints for women's economic position, each in their own way for particular resources, which in turn limits a country's economic development through limitations on women's human capital development.

The models for women's achievements can be specified as follows:

$$ACH_l = C + \beta_3 FGI_j + \beta_4 IFGI_k + \beta_5 GDPln + \beta_6 GDPlnSQ + \beta_7 RES_i + \varepsilon \quad (2)$$

Achievements (ACH_l) are measured as the female/male ratio in life expectancy and the average share of women as parliamentarians, administrative persons and managers, and professionals and technicians. GDPln and GDPlnSQ are control variables for level of development, also included as a squared variable in order to account for possible nonlinearity, since the sample includes both developing and developed countries. FMedu and Fnalf are the two resource variables RES_i, as before.

The results for the achievement models as presented in Table 4.2 suggests quite varied relationships for women's empowerment. The achievement model for the gender gap in health, measured as the male/female ratio

Table 4.2 Empowerment model with resources and institutions

Independent variables	FMlife	Fdec
GDPln	3.12**	−0.60
	(2.56)	(−0.53)
GDPlnSQ	−3.02**	0.74
	(−2.50)	(0.66)
FGI	−0.10	−0.31***
	(−0.95)	(−3.09)
IFGI	−0.18*	−0.02)
	(−1.68)	(−0.20)
Fnalf	0.35***	0.26***
	(3.63)	(2.90)
FMedu	−0.16	0.06
	(−1.63)	(0.60)
Constant	***	
	(4.07)	(0.74)
Adjusted R^2	0.30***	0.42***
	(10.05)	(14.75)
N	128	127

Notes: Standardized coefficients (beta) with t-statistics in brackets. Level of significance for t-statistics for independent variables and for F-statistic for adjusted R^2; * = $p < 0.1$; ** = $p < 0.05$; *** = $p < 0.01$.
Sources: GID and World Development Indicators 2006. Empowerment data for the period 2003–05. Irene van Staveren, (2002) 'Global Finance and Gender', in Jan Aart Scholte and Albrecht Schnabel (eds), *Civil Society and Global Finance*. London: Routledge, pp. 228–46.

in life expectancy (FMlife), shows that the level of GDP per capita has the strongest impact. It is a positive impact for most countries (3.12), but negative for rich countries (−3.02), reflecting that men are catching up with women's life expectancy rate when countries get richer, with women adopting less healthy lifestyles, including smoking and obesity, in richer countries (see, for example, on the US: Ezzati et al., 2008). Of the two resource variables, only one is statistically significant, women's access to employment, with a parameter value of 0.35. This suggests that women's own income improves their access to health care. Formal gendered institutions do not but informal institutions do have a small statistically significant negative impact on women's relative health (−0.18). This suggests that gender-biased laws and regulations do not seem to affect women's health outcomes but that informal institutions, namely social norms and cultural practices, do appear to have an impact on health. One possible mechanism through which this may take place may be illustrated with a qualitative study on the effect of social norms on women's use of health care in Burkina Faso (Nikièma, Haddad and Potvin, 2008). The study found that a woman's use of health care does not depend on her having the money to pay for medicine or a hospital visit, but is conditional on the husbands' evaluation of her behaviour, in particular working hard and showing respect to him and his family. The men in the study are also said to suspect their wives feigning illness as an excuse to get out of daily chores – a suspicion which constrained the permission men gave for their wives to seek health care. This is, of course, just an illustration of how the mechanism from informal gendered institutions may affect women's empowerment. In general, however, the model seems to indicate that women's agency to achieve better health in developing countries seems constrained by the lack of an independent income as well as by social norms preventing women to seek health care.

The other achievement model, the model for women's decision-making power, gives a different picture. Here, the level of economic development has no statistically significant impact, nor has women's education relative to men's. Women's relative access to jobs has a moderate positive and statistically significant impact on women's decision-making power (0.26). This may be explained probably not so much by the income effect as by the social participation effect of non-agricultural jobs for women – an effect which is also important for taking up leadership positions in politics, administration, and management. Finally, when looking at the results for gendered institutions, we see that this time the parameter for the informal gendered institutions is small and not statistically significant, whereas the one for formal gendered institutions is negative, relatively large and statistically significant (–0.31). Hence, it is not so much social norms and cultural practices that constrain women's leadership roles but formal constraints to gender equality in politics and the labour market which form hurdles for women to break through the glass ceiling. In many developing countries, positions of power are inextricably connected to wealth and/or families, so that when property rights exclude or marginalise women, they will be disadvantaged when competing for leadership positions. An illustration of this connection is the observation that a relatively large number of female presidents and prime ministers in Asia have achieved their position through their fathers or husbands, despite serious gender biases in these countries' institutions (Thompson and Derichs, 2005).

Three broad conclusions can be drawn from the overall picture that emerges from the two achievement models. First, the level of development has an important impact on women's achievements in health but not on political and economic decision-making power, and the impact of the level of GDP per capita is reversed for developed countries. This suggests that the level of development as such is insufficient to explain women's empowerment, so that development policies should pay attention to the extent to which development implies opportunities for women. This is an indication that gender is more than just an exogenous variable in the development process. Second, depending on the type of achievement, sometimes formal institutions and other times informal institutions appear to be stronger constraints on women's empowerment. Third, the results point out that women's access to resources is important but not sufficient for women's empowerment. Gendered institutions seem to put a serious constraint on women's agency, which prevents them from turning their resources into well-being achievements. As a consequence, women's empowerment requires not only access to resources, but also the dismantling of formal and informal gendered institutions. Such policies would not only help to increase the effectiveness of resources for women's empowerment, but would also have a direct positive effect on women's agency, for example through higher self-esteem or more mobility.

A general implication for policy makers that seems to emerge from the analysis is that shifting the attention from a rather exclusive concern with gender as an exogenous constraint on access to resources towards simultaneously removing gendered institutions as an endogenous influence on women's economic position would make gender policy and economic development more effective.

5   Poverty Reduction Strategy Papers

Poverty Reduction Strategy Papers (PRSPs) are a major macroeconomic policy instrument for developing countries and required by World Bank and IMF as a condition for loans. The macroeconomic framework of PRSPs, however, is not a neutral set of macroeconomic policies but embedded precisely in a wider, neoliberal policy environment supported by the Washington Consensus – referred to as the 'Unholy Trinity' of the IMF, World Bank and WTO, by Peet (2003). It is this PRSP framework of growth, stability, external and internal balance, that constitutes one of the most explicit formulations of this consensus (see also Cammack, 2004), while being complemented by social safety nets as supplementary social policies, as Craig and Porter (2003) have recognised.

> PRSPs, we argue, are best seen as part of a 'Third Way' re-morphing of neoliberal approaches, a new convergence in which governments

and agencies of various stripes in both liberal OECD and developing countries are focusing on optimizing economic, juridical and social governance in order to create ideal conditions for international finance and investment. (Craig and Porter, 2003: 54)

So, while the macroeconomic framework of PRSPs can be regarded as the most concrete manifestation of neoliberal policies, I will argue that the resistance of gender mainstreaming of such policies is part and parcel of this framework, for each of its core elements, leaving gender to the social policies – the equity side – of PRSPs (van Staveren, 2008).

5.1 Domestic price stability and exchange rate policy

A major core element of the PRSP macroeconomic framework is domestic price stability. This is a policy area with inherent contradictions, which clearly have gender dimensions. The stabilisation of the internal price level, aimed at limiting inflation, often makes use of contractionary monetary policy and a high interest rate. However, this will raise problems for holders of debt, and may lead to bankruptcies of, in particular, small and medium-sized enterprises, as happened as a consequence of the high interest rate policies advised by the IMF after the Asian financial crisis (Stiglitz, 2002). In many countries in Africa and Asia, women are the majority of micro and small-scale entrepreneurs, and are therefore very vulnerable to such contractionary monetary policy. Moreover, deflationary policies tend to go hand in hand with increasing female unemployment rates, at higher levels and higher rates of increase than for men, in developing countries as well as in transition economies (UNRISD, 2005). In addition, deflationary policies prevent governments from dealing effectively with recessions due to the high cost of borrowing (Elson and Çağatay, 2000), which induces a substitution effect from paid to unpaid work, largely carried out by women. These gender effects of stabilisation policies reflect the biased emphasis of deflationary policies on security for global investors vis-à-vis workers, small-scale entrepreneurs, and those responsible for meeting household needs.

The macroeconomic framework also often involves exchange rate devaluation. A currency devaluation will benefit export earnings and employment, including women's employment. But, at the same time, imports will become more expensive, so that devaluation can put pressure on basic household expenditures, such as food or agricultural inputs, which, depending on the gender division of labour in households, may hit women harder than men (Warner and Campbell, 2000). In short, whereas exchange rate devaluation may help to expand women's low-wage export employment, but make imports more expensive, the emphasis on internal price stability tends to have negative feedback effects on women's wage employment, survival of small businesses, and support from public services.

5.2   External balance

Another core element is concerned with external balance, often implying the promotion of exports, import tariff reductions, and inviting foreign capital. Export promotion policies tend to increase female employment in labour-intensive manufacturing. While this is a positive effect for women's labour market opportunities, the quality of jobs tends to be low, while labour standards in export production come under the increasing pressure of the unequal bargaining power between globally mobile capital and relatively immobile labour (Palley, 2004). This, in turn, together with the increased competition from imports, leads to an increasing flexibilisation of jobs, particularly for women who work at the lower end of global production systems (Standing, 1999). In agriculture, the incentive is to shift away from food crops to cash crop production. But this shift may not be very effective, precisely as a result of the gender division of labour combined with male control of cash. When women's role as food provider for households is ignored in export promotion policies, the supply response to such policies will be limited and the distribution of benefits within the household will be gender-biased. In conclusion, the external balance policies of PRSPs ignore negative impacts on women through informalisation and flexibilisation on the one hand and increased unpaid workloads on the other hand. Moreover, such policies tend to ignore negative feedback effects for the external position in the long run through lock-in effects in low road development.

5.3   Internal balance

A third core element of the PRSP macroeconomic framework concerns internal balance – the reduction or even elimination of a budget deficit. The contractionary policies that are intended to reduce the budget deficit are likely to hurt those groups in society that are most dependent upon redistributive policies through public expenditures, including women, given their gender role as carers (Elson and Çağatay, 2000). Moreover, women already tend to be disadvantaged by gender biases in public expenditures, as gender audits of government budgets have shown (Norton and Elson, 2002). Hence, budget cuts tend to reinforce the male bias in public expenditures. Indeed, a recent UNRISD (2005) study has shown that fiscal restraint tends to be paralleled by a reduction in social expenditures, which, in turn, tends to shift the responsibility for meeting social needs to women's unpaid workload. Ertürk and Çağatay (1995) have shown in a business cycle model for Turkey how women's unpaid work may indeed substitute for lost household income during downturns in the business cycle, suggesting that anti-cyclical fiscal policy may help to keep social expenditures up and prevent a shift of social services provisioning to women's unpaid work time.

Contrary to an over-concern with internal balance, an increase in social expenditures, including investment in women's health, education, and employment, in order to reduce gender gaps as targeted in the Millennium Development Goals, is likely to crowd-in women's human resources investment, labour force participation, and productivity (Krug and van Staveren, 2002).

The above analysis of how gender is ignored in the macroeconomic framework of PRSPs shows that gender is not regarded as a relevant variable – not as enabling nor as constraining – for the core set of macroeconomic policies. The only place where we do find serious attention to gender in PRSPs is outside the macroeconomic framework, in the social policy sections. The macroeconomic framework ignores that gender equality is often a precondition for poverty reduction: more low-wage jobs increase women's employment but when these are increasingly flexible and informal subcontracting jobs attracted by low female wages, such jobs will hardly contribute to poverty reduction; liberalisation policies may eliminate market distortions, but those distortions that have their roots in discriminatory attitudes on the supply or demand side of markets can only be eliminated by more, not less, state regulation and enforcement; reductions in public expenditures may attract more foreign capital but they conflict with the need to invest in order to meet the Millennium Development Goals by the year 2015, including the elimination of gender gaps as stated in the third MDG goal.

In conclusion, the resistance of the macroeconomic framework to gender mainstreaming is not only constraining the likeliness of reducing women's poverty but also limiting the effectiveness of PRSPs to increase growth and to move a country up the high road of development. In other words, ignoring the endogeneity of gender in the economy negatively affects the effectiveness of PRSPs, so that gender blindness, in fact, becomes an additional reason why 'the macroeconomic frameworks as currently designed do not really support economic growth and poverty reduction in a direct, clear way' (Gottschalk, 2005: 440).

6 Gender inequality and global finance

The gender dimensions in finance occur at all levels: the micro level (including the intra-household level), the meso level (industry, banking, government institutions, taxation), and the macro level, nationally as well as globally (global markets and the role of global-level institutions such as the World Trade Organization (WTO), the World Bank and IMF). This section will discuss three gender biases of global finance (van Staveren, 2002): (1) the underrepresentation of women in financial decision making; (2) increased gender gaps in the economic positions of women and men; (3) gender-based instability of financial markets.

6.1 Undemocratic: underrepresentation of women

Women are hardly represented among the main decision makers in financial markets and institutions, which makes women's issues even more invisible in the decision-making processes on government lending, investment rules, and private sector financial activities. Decisions in relation to World Bank loans and IMF credit are taken by the boards of these institutions, governing bodies that are strongly male dominated (in World Bank less than 10 per cent of Executive Directors and Senior Officers are female). Over the course of the 1990s the G-7 countries have performed the role of the world's lender of last resort, together with World Bank and IMF. G-7 decision making can hardly be regarded as democratic, and certainly not as gender balanced. WTO is almost exclusively a male forum. Decisions on FDI taken in the boardrooms of transnational companies, which are largely, though not exclusively, headed by men. And last but not least, financial traders are largely men – whereas an increasing share of women can be found in financial services in lower-end jobs, the typical financial whizz-kid positions of trading in anonymous financial markets are largely taken up by men. The consequences of these abstract financial decisions are born by women and men as producers, consumers, borrowers, employees, taxpayers, users of public services, and home and community care providers.

A more equal representation of men and women in the boards of international financial institutions national financial institutions, and national and transnational private corporations, would make financial decision making more democratic from a gender perspective. It is likely that a more equal gender balance in decision making on financial governance will represent the experience of both men and women with financial markets and policies and hence prevent the large opportunity costs that women now experience in the realm of global finance. However, consciousness about gender inequalities and interests do not necessarily coincide for elite women and poor women. So, representation of women in boards of financial institutions is a necessary but insufficient condition for gender-aware decision making. Financial decision making should also take poor women's views into account, as stakeholders in the world of finance, for example by consulting women's NGOs. Only then would a more balanced gender distribution in financial decision making – in numbers of men and women as well as in terms of a less dominant masculine management culture – begin to impact positively on the distribution of the positive and negative effects of financial policies over men and women.

6.2   Inequitable: increased gender gaps

Globalisation of finance has had advantages for women: it has increased competition, and hence the supply of credit, to diversified target groups; through this process women have gained more access to credit, although not equally in the formal and informal sectors. Secondly, in some countries it has become easier for women to access foreign exchange markets, for example to receive remittances from partners or relatives abroad, or to send home remittances to family. However, the few studies that have looked into gender effects of finance are not very optimistic about the globalisation gains for women.

Financial markets are clearly not homogeneous markets and in that respect they are no different from goods markets or labour markets. Like other markets, financial markets are characterised by segmentation, involving distortions and transaction costs (Yotopoulos and Floro, 1992). Most texts on distortions in financial markets completely ignore the gender dimension, but there are a few exceptions. In particular, Baden (1996) has distinguished a variety of gender-based distortions in credit markets. These distortions are perceived as transaction costs by the supply side (credit institutions) as well as by the demand side (individual female borrowers as compared with male borrowers), limiting the net gains from financial transactions with women and making financial services for women less accessible and more expensive. The source of the distortions is often not real but irrational, based on a gender ideology that assumes women to be less capable of economic success than men. Just as gender biases in labour markets (masculine and feminine sectors and jobs) and land markets (absent or limited land property rights for women) lead to segmentation to the disadvantage of women, the segmentation of financial markets according to gender creates disadvantages for women. At the same time, segmentation creates inefficiencies in resource allocation – an issue that will be discussed later. From the table it becomes clear how gender biases in society at large (like, for example, the prejudice that 'women are less able to make investments profitable') operate in financial markets and make them gender biased. Apart from transaction costs, some gender distortions lead to costs that are part of the service itself, like administration costs rather than transaction costs that occur outside the exchange. Because of less property and lower earnings of women, and because of their responsibility for household livelihood, women tend to save smaller amounts as well as to save and borrow more regularly compared with men. Women therefore need flexibility in saving and credit. However, credit institutions are not always prepared to provide this flexibility because of the corresponding administration costs.

Moreover, the almost universal norm of the male breadwinner and head of household has benefited men's property rights within households (Blau, Ferber, and Winkler, 1992; Kabeer, 1994; Agarwal, 1994). Women's property rights are often assumed to be included in household rights that are, in turn, often secured in the name of the (male) household head. In some countries, inheritance laws allocate less property to female heirs compared to male heirs, whereas and, similarly, widows are sometimes bereft of all the common property they shared with their husband, by their in-law's family. Women's limited possession of property and their constrained property rights limit their access to financial markets. This may lead to a lack of effective demand for credit by women, and may also discourage the accumulation of savings by women.

Furthermore, there exists gendered segmentation in financial markets. Vertical gender segmentation in financial markets runs along the line of scale: small loans tend to be demanded more often by women, larger loans more by men. Horizontal gender segmentation in financial markets is expressed by the fact that most female lenders lend to women, while most women borrowers borrow from credit institutions that have special programmes for women, or that exclusively target female borrowers, or informally within women's groups. Because of the gendered transaction costs referred to in Table 4.3, credit institutions show adverse selection in their behaviour: they select borrowers on the basis of their gender. This leads to the crowding in of female borrowers into a limited range of credit supply, which drives interest rates up in this sub-credit market. Or, in other words, excess demand for credit

Table 4.3 Gender-based distortions in financial markets

Type of gender-based distortion:	Transaction costs for credit institution:	Transaction costs for female borrowers:
Information constraint	Women are perceived as risky, not creditworthy enough; information gathering might go through an intermediary (husband)	Women have lower literacy rates, and are less mobile, which results in low access to financial market information
Negotiation constraint	Women have less experience in taking formal credit, which requires more time from bank personnel	Women may need husband's permission; have higher opportunity costs to travel to a bank; women may face discriminatory attitude by bank personnel
Monitoring constraint	Women's economic activities may be more difficult to monitor since they are often in different and smaller scale sectors than men's activities that are financed through credit	Women may find it difficult to control their loans in the household when other family members (particularly men) find it in their right to exercise control over this money
Enforcement constraint	Women often lack formal property rights, which makes it difficult for creditors to claim a collateral when a loan is not repaid	Women may be more susceptible to pressure, intimidation, or violence from creditors or their agents; women may lose control over their loans in the household while still being responsible for repayment.

Source: Adapted from Table 1 in S. Baden (1996) 'Gender Issues in Financial Liberalisation and Financial Sector Reform'. Paper prepared for EU (DG VIII) and OECD DAC/WID. Sussex: BRIDGE. See also van Staveren (2002).

leads credit institutions to use quantity rather than price rationing to allocate funds (Yotopoulos and Sagrario Floro, 1992: 304), which in a context of gender segmentation of credit markets, leads them to exclude women and women's activities (like home-base production) from their portfolios (Baden, 1996). Gender segmentation in the division of labour thus reinforces gender segmentation in financial markets, indicating the relatedness of gendered institutions throughout the economy, with various feedback effects.

Discriminatory views held by credit institutions' personnel that women would be risky borrowers, that they would be less skilled entrepreneurs than men, and hence, less profitable, or that they would spend borrowed money on consumption without being able to repay, is a significant constraint on women's interactions in financial markets. The reality is different, however. First, women tend to have high repayment rates, which defeats the prejudice against female borrowers: the repayment rates of credit programmes that exclusively or in majority lend to women are around 97 per cent (Women's World Banking at http://www.swwb.org/, see footnote 12). Second, when women borrow for consumption purposes it is often to overcome short-term liquidity problems that they can solve by long-run cash flows, not endangering repayment (Baden, 1996).

At the macro level, gendered institutions impact on financial markets as a whole: through the savings rate, interest rate, and investments. As Baden (1996) concludes from the literature that she reviewed, the globalisation of financial markets through liberalisation has not succeeded in substantially raising savings rates. Investments have increased in some developing countries, depending on the inflow of FDI and World Bank loans and IMF credits, albeit insufficiently. Liberalised interest rates have moved in the direction of international market rates, but nevertheless they have been unable to generate effective and efficient financial markets in many developing countries. Aghion, Caroli, and Garcia-Penalosa (1999, p. 1621) conclude from a review of inequality and global markets that: '(a) inequality reduces investment opportunities (b) inequality worsens borrower's incentives (...)'. As an elaboration of this argument, the point can be made that gender inequality in financial markets reduces investment opportunities even further since it constrains women's ability to invest and it worsens borrowers' incentives since it discriminates against female borrowers. So gender inequality is likely to contribute to aggregate low savings rates, low investment rates, and distorted interest rates. Hence, also at the macro level, gender appears to be an endogenous variable. affecting monetary variables.

6.3   Unstable: gender-based instability in financial markets

The lack of democracy in financial governance and the inequities that financial markets create are not only problematic in themselves, but also have an impact on the stability of financial markets (Aghion, Caroli, and Garcia-Penalosa, 1999, p. 1628). The annual volume of foreign exchange transactions is about fifty times the volume of international trade in goods and services. The Asian financial crisis created reductions in the monetised real economy of more than 10 per cent cf GDP, whereas the 2008 financial crisis led to lower, but still significant reductions in GDP in the developed world. The instability that occurs along with these changes is increasingly perceived by some economists as having endogenous roots, rather than as occurring from outside shocks as is commonly supposed under mainstream economics. Endogenous causes of market instability are inherent in the structure of financial markets and financial institutions.

The burden of excessive financial risk is, however, not only shifted to taxpayers and the public sector, but also to another part of the economy that is invisibly and silently called in at a crisis to balance the losses of financial markets: the care economy. Here, there is a need to include a gender perspective in the analysis. The shift of the burden of excessive risk by financial market actors incurring debts to finance increasingly risky investments and speculative transactions is almost exclusively a male strategy. As I have argued above, the decision-making positions in the world of finance are held by men, transactions with larger amounts of money are carried out mainly by men, and speculation is principally a male activity. This is important to note because the burden of risk is predominantly shifted to females, and, hence, the mechanism underlying the extent and impact of recent financial crises is highly gender biased. The burden of excessive risk that is shifted to the state concerns not only taxpayers but, more importantly the burden is shifted to the users of public services, since, in most developing countries, government budget deficits are approached through budget cuts rather than through (politically often infeasible) increases in tax revenue. Because of a gender division of labour in most economies in North and South, women are made responsible for household food security, family health care and securing household supplies such as energy for cooking and safe drinking water. Cuts in the health budget, or in budgets concerning the provision of clean drinking water in poor urban districts and far away villages, and the abolition of food subsidy to the urban poor or of input subsidies to food farmers (who in Sub-Saharan Africa are in the majority female), affect women more than men; in addition, cuts in educational budgets do not help to reduce the school enrolment gap between boys and girls, as studies on the effects of Structural Adjustment Programmes in Africa, Latin-America and Asia have shown (see, for example, Elson, 1998).

Yet this is not the main gender bias of the shift of the burden of excessive risk in global finance. Apart from a shift of the burden to states, there is a parallel shift of the burden of excessive risk to the non-monetised sector of the economy, or the care economy, which functions principally on the basis of female unpaid labour. States, in both the North and the South, and through states the taxpayer and receiver of public services is one sector of the economy to which excessive risk burdens are shifted, burdens that have been quantified above as lying between 4 and 9 per cent of GDP. The care economy is another sector that incurs the costs of balancing financial instability, although in non-monetised terms. UNDP (1995) has quantified the market value of labour in the care economy at around 50 per cent of GDP, the majority of which is female labour. Lack of research on the relations between the monetised (real and financial) and non-monetised economy makes it impossible to make a reasonable estimation of the costs from financial market cycles shifted to female unpaid labour. An increasing number of case studies, however, point out that increases in women's unpaid labour time are significant in periods of crisis in the developing world (Moser, 1989; Bakker, 1994; Sparr, 1994; Elson, 1995; UNDP. 1995). In fact, the burden of shifting excessive risks from financial markets to the care economy might be captured in two ways.

First, production in the care economy can act as a substitute for production of public services that have been either cut back or made too expensive by governments seeking ways to reduce their budget deficit through cost recovery measures (Elson, 1998). This substitution effect prevents that the effect of a financial crisis on the real economy leads to an unacceptable fall in well-being at the household level. The types of public services that are substituted by female unpaid labour in times of crisis are health care (home care of the sick rather than hospitalisation); home-made medicine rather than market-bought medicine; a reduction in doctor visits), education (children are used for household labour rather than send to school), and public utilities (electricity is substituted for firewood, kerosene, or cow dung, whereas clean drinking water is substituted for unhygienic sources of water). This substitution of public services for services in the care economy helps the government to reduce its fiscal deficit and enables households to continue consumption, although at lower-quality levels, without increasing monetary expenditure.

Second, production in the care economy can act as a substitute for production for the market. This can be analysed as savings but can also be regarded as production, albeit non-monetised. The motivation is then not to save on household expenditures, but to reduce risks attached to production for the global market. In particular in developing countries, exports are vulnerable to instability in world market prices, since most developing countries have a relatively homogenous export package. Moreover, in the agricultural sector, export crop varieties tend to be more vulnerable to climatic circumstances and crop diseases than indigenous crops. Hence, in a situation of economic crisis, and given the risk averseness of the poor who have no social security ensured by the state, it is rational for female producers to shift part of market production back to subsistence production, or at least to production for local markets rather than for the high-risk world market. Moreover, even when women, such as female farmers in Sub-Saharan Africa, are prepared to take the risk on world market production, they are unlikely to do so because of gender distortions. This is because women face another risk that prevents them from benefiting from production for the global market, which is a lack of control over the receipts of such production in the household (World Bank 1999).

7   Summary and conclusions

The emphasis of this paper has been on demonstrating, with results from empirical research in feminist macroeconomics, that gender is endogenous to the economic process, and that inequality in gender relations often has a negative effect on economic (and economic policy) outcomes. What is important to emphasise here is that gender is not only a micro-level variable, but also an important macro-level variable and perspective. Just as, for example, inequality as measured by the Gini coefficient is a macro variable featuring in some growth equations, the gender wage gap is a macro variable explaining growth differences between labour-intensive export economies on the one hand, and capital intensive or less export oriented economies on the other hand.

As a recapitulation, let me briefly sketch the main theoretical paths through which these gendered economic processes occur. A first mechanism is through a gendered response to uncertainty. Whereas a liquidity preference is generally seen as the major household response to uncertainty, such as unemployment, a substitution of market demand for consumer goods by self-production through unpaid work is often overlooked as another response. When this response is combined with the additional worker effect, often through additional hours of female labour supplied, these responses may actually aggravate a crisis, by reducing aggregate demand and increasing unemployment. A second mechanism is through the interconnectedness of aggregate supply and demand in the household, through the multiple roles that household members play, differentiated through the gender division of labour: consumer, paid worker, unpaid worker, entrepreneur, saver, investor, taxpayer, and receiver of public services. This may result, for example, in different propensities to consume and save for men and women, even at the same level of income. In turn, such gendered economic roles in the household may also lead to gendered patterns of expectations, which may result in different levels of risk-taking by men and women, and possibly the shifting of risks from males to females in the shape of additional paid and unpaid female labour time during downturns. A third mechanism is through asymmetric institutions, which work out differently for men and women, or even benefit one group to the disadvantage of the other group. This mechanism runs largely parallel to that of class, with the important addition that gendered institutions differentiate not only between households but also within households. If for wage-earners, the propensity to consume is higher than for capital earners (and the proportion of imported goods lower), a well-known implication may be that economic stimulus packages would prove more effective by stimulating wage income rather than capital income. In analogy, aggregate demand may be stimulated more effectively by expanding employment for women and/or increasing women's wages relative to men's wages.

In conclusion, gender has clear economic dimensions, affecting economic variables, decisions, constraints, opportunities, and outcomes. Therefore, treating gender as only an impact variable relevant from a social perspective – are women affected differently, and perhaps more negatively, than men by a particular economic policy? – is an important question but a far too limited way to treat gender in economics. Good economic analysis also includes questions on how social inequalities, such as gender, impact upon micro- and macro-economic behaviour, variables, relationships and policy effectiveness. New economic thinking can only emerge when it builds on inclusive economic thinking, which implies a far deeper understanding of how gender affects economic processes. This requires a move well beyond neoclassical economics into pluralist and contextualised economic analysis. This chapter has argued that such analysis is possible not only at the micro level but even at the macro level, so that positive and negative relationships between gender inequalities on the one hand and inefficiency on the other hand are taken into account in the study of trade, fiscal and monetary policy, financial crises, and growth strategies.

References

Aghion, P., Caroli, E. and Garcia-Penalosa, C. (1999) 'Inequality and Economic Growth: The Perspective of the New Growth Theories', *Journal of Economic Literature*, 37(4), pp. 1615–60
Agarwal, B. (1994) *A Field of One's Own: Gender and Land Rights in South Asia.* Cambridge: Cambridge University Press.
Agarwal, B. (1997) '"Bargaining" and Gender Relations: Within and Beyond the Household', *Feminist Economics*, 3(1), pp. 1–51.
Allendorf, K. (2007) 'Do Womens Land Rights Promote Empowerment and Child Health in Nepal?', *World Development*, 35(11), pp. 1975–88.

Alsop, R, M.F. Bertelsen, and J. Holland (2006) *Empowerment in Practice: From Analysis to Implementation*. Washington, DC: World Bank.

Baden, S. (1996) 'Gender Issues in Financial Liberalisation and Financial Sector Reform'. Paper prepared for EU (DG VIII) and OECD DAC/WID. Sussex: BRIDGE.

Bakker, I. (ed.) (1994) *The Strategic Silence: Gender and Economic Policy*. London: Zed Books.

Barrientos, S. (2007) 'Gender, Codes of Conduct and Labour Standards in Global Production Systems', in I. van Staveren et al. (eds), *The Feminist Economics of Trade*. London: Routledge, pp. 239–56.

Berik, G. and van der Meulen Rodgers, Y. (2004) 'International Trade and Gender Wage Discrimination: Evidence from East Asia', *Review of Development Economics*, 8, 237–54.

Biernat, M., Ch. Crandall, S. Halpin, D. Kobrynowicz, and L. Young (1998) 'All That You Can Be: Stereotyping of Self and Others in a Military Context', *Journal of Personality and Social Psychology*, 75(2), pp. 301–17.

Blau, F., M. Ferber, and A. Winkler (1992) *The Economics of Women, Men and Work*, 3rd edition. Upper Saddle River, NJ: Prentice Hall.

Blaug, M., (2001) 'Is Competition Such a Good Thing? Static Efficiency versus Dynamic Efficiency', *Review of Industrial Organization*, 19, pp. 37–48.

Blecker, R., and S. Seguino (2002) 'Macroeconomic Effects of Reducing Gender Wage Inequality in an Export-Oriented, Semi-Industrialized Economy', *Review of Development Economics*, 6(1), pp. 103–19.

Cammack, P. (2004) 'What the World Bank Means by Poverty Reduction, and Why it Matters', *New Political Economy*, 9(2), pp. 189–211.

Catão, L. and Falcetti, E. (2002) 'Determinants of Argentina's External Trade', *Journal of Applied Economics*, 5(1), 19–57.

Craig, D., and Porter, D. (2003) 'Poverty Reduction Strategy Papers: a New Convergence', *World Development*, 31(1), pp. 53–69.

Darity, W. (2007) 'The Formal Structure of a Gender-Segregated Low-Income Economy', in I. van Staveren et al. (eds), *The Feminist Economics of Trade*. London: Routledge, pp. 78–90.

Dasgupta, P. (1993) *An Inquiry into Well-Being and Destitution*. Oxford: Clarendon Press.

Doss, Cheryl (2006) 'The Effects of Household Property Ownership on Expenditure Patterns in Ghana', *Journal of African Economies*, 15(1), pp. 149–80.

Elson, D. (1995) *Male Bias in Economic Development*. Manchester: University of Manchester Press.

Elson, D. (1998) 'Sector Programme Support'. A collection of papers published by the Graduate School of Social Sciences, Genecon Unit. Manchester: University of Manchester. For OECD/DAC – WID.

Elson, D. and N. Çağatay (2000) 'The Social Content of Macroeconomic Policies', *World Development*, 28(7), pp. 1347–64.

Ertürk, K. and Çağatay, N. (1995) 'Macroeconomic Consequences of Cyclical and Secular Changes in Feminization: an Experiment at Gendered Macromodeling', *World Development*, 23(11), pp. 1969–77.

Ezzati, M., A. Friedman, S. Kulkarni, and Ch. Murray (2008) 'The Reversal of Fortunes: Trends in County Mortality and Cross-County Mortality Disparities in the United States', *PLOS Medicine*, 5(4), pp. 557–68.

Folbre, N. (1994) *Who Pays for the Kids? Gender and the Structures of Constraint*. London: Routledge.

George, D. (2001) *Preference Pollution: How Markets Create the Desires we Dislike*. Ann Arbor, MI: University of Michigan Press.

Goetz, A.M. (1997) *Getting Institutions Right for Women in Development*. London: Zed Books.

Gottschalk, R. (2005) 'The Macro Content of PRSPs: Assessing the Need for a More Flexible Macroeconomic Policy Framework', *Development Policy Review*, 23(4), pp. 419–42.

Hodgson, G. (2006) 'What are Institutions?', *Journal of Economic Issues*, 60(1), pp. 1–25.

Ibrahim, S., and S. Alkire (2007) *Agency and Empowerment: A Proposal for Internationally Comparable Indicators*. Oxford: OPHI Working Paper Series. Oxford Poverty and Human Development Institute.

IDB (2004) *Mercosur Report 2003–2004*. Euenos Aires: IDB-INTAL.

Inglehart, R., and P. Norris (eds) (2003) *Rising Tide: Gender Equality and Cultural Change Around the World*. Cambridge: Cambridge University Press.

Jejeebhoy, S. (1995) *Women's Education, Autonomy, and Reproductive Behavior Experience from Developing Countries*. New York: Oxford University Press.

Kabeer, N., (2001) 'Conflicts over Credit: Re-Evaluating the Empowerment Potential of Loans to Women in Rural Bangladesh', *World Development*, 29(1), pp. 63–84.

Kabeer, N. (1994) *Reversed Realities: Gender Hierarchies in Development Thought*. London: Verso.

Khwaja, A.I. (2005) 'Measuring Empowerment at the Community Level: An Economist's Perspective', in D. Narayan (ed.), *Measuring Empowerment. Cross-Disciplinary Perspectives*. Washington, DC: World Bank, pp. 267–84.

Klasen, S. (2002) 'Low Schooling for Girls, Slower Growth for All? Cross-Country Evidence on the Effect of Gender Inequality in Education on Economic Development', *World Bank Economic Review*, 16(3), pp. 345–73.

Klasen, S., and D. Abu-Ghaida (2004) 'The Costs of Missing the Millennium Development Goal on Gender Equity', *World Development*, 32(7), pp. 1075–107.

Kongar, E. (2007) 'Importing Equality or Exporting Jobs? Competition and Gender Wage and Employment Differentials in US Manufacturing', in I. van Staveren et al. (eds), *The Feminist Economics of Trade*. London: Routledge, pp. 215–36.

Krug, B., and I. van Staveren (2002) 'Gender Audit: Whim or Voice?', *Public Finance and Management*, 2(2), pp. 190–217.

Kurien, C.T. (1996) *Rethinking Economics. Reflections Based on a Study of the Indian Economy*. New Delhi: Sage.

Lagerlöf, N. (2003) 'Gender Equality and Long-Run Growth', *Journal of Economic Growth*, 8(4), pp. 403–26.

Morduch, J. (1999) 'The Microfinance Promise', *Journal of Economic Literature*, 37(4), pp. 1569–614.

Morrisson, Ch. and J. Jütting (2005) 'Women's Discrimination in Developing Countries: A New Data Set for Better Policies', *World Development*, 33(7), pp. 1065–81.

Moser, C. (1989) 'The Impact of Recession and Adjustment Policies at the Micro Level: Low Income Women and Their Households in Guayaquil, Ecuador', in

UNICEF, *The Invisible Adjustment: Poor Women and the Economic Crisis.* Second Revised Edition. Santiago: UNICEF, pp. 137–66.

Narayan, D. (2005a) *Measuring Empowerment: Cross-Disciplinary Perspectives.* Washington, DC: World Bank.

Narayan, D. (2005b) 'Conceptual Framework and Methodological Challenges', in *Measuring Empowerment: Cross-Disciplinary Perspectives.* Washington, DC: World Bank, pp. 3–38.

Nikièma, B., S. Haddad and L. Potvin (2008) 'Women Bargaining to Seek Healthcare: Norms, Domestic Practices, and Implications in Rural Burkina Faso', *World Development*, 36(4), pp. 608–24.

Norton, A. and D. Elson (2002) *What's Behind the Budget? Politics, Rights and Accountability in the Budget Process.* London: ODI.

OECD (2006) Gender Institutions Database. URL: http://stats.oecd.org/WBOS/default.aspx?DatasetCode=GID&lang=en.

Osterreich, S. (2007) 'Gender, Trade and Development: Labor Market Discrimination and North–South Terms of Trade', in I. van Staveren et al. (eds), *The Feminist Economics of Trade.* London: Routledge, pp. 55–77.

Ozler, S. (2007) 'Export-led Industrialization and Gender Differences in Job Creation and Destruction: Micro Evidence from the Turkish Manufacturing Sector', in I. van Staveren et al. (eds), *The Feminist Economics of Trade.* London: Routledge.

Palley, T. (2004) 'The Economic Case for International Labour Standards', *Cambridge Journal of Economics*, 28, pp. 21–36.

Peet, R. (2003) *Unholy Trinity: The IMF, World Bank and WTO.* London: Zed Books.

Pitt, M. and S. Khandker (1998) 'The Impact of Group-Based Credit Programs on Poor Households in Bangladesh: Does the Gender of Participants Matter?', *Journal of Political Economy*, 106(5), pp. 958–96.

Reid, M. (1934) *Economics of Household Production.* New York/London: Wiley/Chapman & Hall.

Reid, M. (1943) *Food for People.* New York/London: Wiley/Chapman & Hall.

Seguino, S. (2000a) 'Accounting for Gender in Asian Economic Growth', *Feminist Economics*, 6(3), pp. 27–58.

Seguino, S. (2000b) 'Gender Inequality and Economic Growth: A Cross-Country Analysis', *World Development*, 28(7), pp. 1211–30.

Sen, A. (1981) *Poverty and Famines: An Essay on Entitlement and Deprivation.* Oxford: Clarendon Press.

Sen, A. (1990) 'Gender and Cooperative Conflicts', in Irene Tinker (ed.), *Persistent Inequalities.* Oxford: Oxford University Press, pp. 123–49.

Shih, M., T. Pittinsky, and A. Trahan (2006) 'Domain-Specific Effects of Stereotypes on Performance', *Self and Identity*, 5(1), pp. 1–14.

Sparr, P. (ed.) (1994) *Mortgaging Women's Lives: Feminist Critiques of Structural Adjustment.* London: Zed Books.

Standing, G. (1999) 'Global Feminisation Through Flexible Labor: a Theme Revisited', *World Development*, 27, pp. 583–602.

Stiglitz, J. (2002) *Globalization and its Discontents.* New York: Norton.

Thompson, M., and C. Derichs (2005) Frauen an der Macht. Dynastien und Politischen Führerinnen in Asien. University of Passau. Available online at http://www.phil.uni-passau.de/die-fakultaet/lehrstuehle-professuren/suedostasien/suedostasien/publikationen/frauen-an-der-macht.html.

Truong, T. (1999) 'The Underbelly of the Tiger: Gender and the Demystification of the Asian Miracle', *Review of International Political Economy*, 6(2), pp. 133–65.

UNDP (1995) *Human Development Report 1995*. Oxford: Oxford University Press.

UNRISD (2005) *Gender Equality: Striving for Justice in an Unequal World*. Geneva: UNRISD.

van Staveren, I. (2002) 'Global Finance and Gender', in Jan-Aart Scholte and Albrecht Schnabel (eds), *Civil Society and Global Finance*. London: Routledge, pp. 228–46.

van Staveren, I. (2003) 'Feminist Fiction and Feminist Economics – Charlotte Perkins Gilman on Efficiency', in D. Barker and E. Kuiper (eds), *Toward a Feminist Philosophy of Economics*. London: Routledge, pp. 56–69.

van Staveren, I. (2007a) 'Monitoring Gender Impacts of Trade', in I. van Staveren, D. Elson, N. Cagatay and C. Crown (eds), *The Feminist Economics of Trade*. London: Routledge, pp. 257–76.

van Staveren, I. (2007b) 'Gender Inequality and Policies: Why More Labour Force Participation, Education, and Credit Do Not Always Help'. Paper presented at the EAEPE conference held in Porto, 1–2 November.

van Staveren, I. (2007c) 'The Ethics of Efficiency'. SCEME working paper no. 18, 2007. Stirling: Stirling Centre for Economic Methodology, University of Stirling.

van Staveren, I. (2008) 'The Gender Bias of the Poverty Reduction Strategy Framework', *Review of International Political Economy*, 15(2), pp. 289–313.

van Staveren, I., D. Elson, N. Cagatay, and C. Grown (eds) (2007) *The Feminist Economics of Trade*. London: Routledge.

Veblen, T. (1931) [1899] *The Theory of the Leisure Class*. New York: Dover Publications.

Walsh, V. (1996) *Rationality, Allocation, and Reproduction*. Oxford: Clarendon Press.

Walsh, V. (2000) 'Smith after Sen', *Review of Political Economy*, 12(1), pp. 5–25.

Walsh, V. (2003) 'Sen after Putnam', *Review of Political Economy*, 15(3), pp. 315–94.

Warner, J. and Campbell, D. (2000) 'Supply Response in an Agrarian Economy with Non-Symmetric Gender Relations', *World Development*, 28(7), 1327–40.

Williamson, O. (2000) 'The New Institutional Economics: Taking Stock, Looking Ahead', *Journal of Economic Literature*, 38(3), pp. 595–613.

World Bank (1999) *Gender, Growth, and Poverty Reduction: Special Program of Assistance for Africa*, 1998 Status Report on Poverty in Sub-Saharan Africa. Technical Paper no. 428. Washington, DC: World Bank.

Yotopoulos, P. and Sagrario Floro, M. (1992) 'Income Distribution, Transaction Costs and Market Fragmentation in Informal Credit Markets', *Cambridge Journal of Economics*, 16, pp. 303–26.

5
Long-Term Uncertainty and Social Security Systems

Jesús Ferreiro and Felipe Serrano
Department of Applied Economics V, University of the Basque Country

Abstract

The existence of ageing processes in the developed economies has led mainstream economics to defend a radical reform of pensions – from the current pay-as-you-go (PAYGO) systems to funded pension systems. The argument is that the latter, in addition to being sheltered from the ageing problem, generate better macroeconomic performance. In our opinion, this view is completely flawed, because it is based on a set of assumptions that are not reflected in the real world. Moreover, it is also based on the consideration that the main objective of a pension system is to generate a market-clearing equilibrium outcome. On the contrary, we argue that this should not be the objective of a pension system; rather, it should be focused on providing individuals with sufficient income to maintain a socially acceptable level of consumption. Starting from this objective, and accepting the existence of uncertainty problems, we argue that current PAYGO pension systems are more efficient than unfunded systems. Moreover, by reducing uncertainty about the future, the PAYGO systems help to stabilise the working of the economy. Therefore, in our opinion, any reform of the current PAYGO pension systems intended to face the challenges of ageing must necessarily maintain the essential nature of these systems.

Keywords: Social security, pensions, uncertainty, information problems, ageing

JEL Classifications: B59, D81, H55

1 Introduction[1]

The phenomenon of population ageing we are witnessing in most developed countries, and, particularly, in the countries of the European Union, is the subject of special attention, promoted both by economic research and by sociology and political science. The terms of this debate, on the other hand, are not free from tensions and contradictions. Times of change are always times of conflict, since they are confronting different reforming options fostered by contradictory interests (not only economic). It is hardly surprising, for example, that political science has a particular interest in studying how population ageing is contributing to the development of different political behaviour (between population groups of different ages) in such aspects as the composition of public expenditure or fiscal pressure. But the reforming agenda that we are dealing with is not being designed solely by these different political behaviours. The reform proposed by the economists who use the analytical tools of the neoclassical theory are biasing the debate on the reforms demanded by an ageing population. Their proposals for 'more market and less state', which are disguised by the appearance of economic efficiency, are helping to create a favourable opinion towards some specific reforming measures (for example, fiscal incentives for individual saving or co-payment of certain social items as health) which would be the only possible measures liable to be implemented if we want to prevent population ageing from giving rise to unsustainable public finances or from using up the growth potential of the economy.[2]

The present financial crisis and, in particular, the processes of fiscal consolidation which have begun to be implemented in most European countries are contributing to a reinforcement of the reforming line. The restraint first and the subsequent reduction of the public debt imposed by financial markets are accelerating reforms of the social protection systems in general and of the pension systems in particular, with the aim of moderating the future growth of public spending. In respect of pension systems, in some European countries (Spain, Germany, Portugal, France, Italy or Sweden), these reforms are being carried out, at the moment, with the aim of making the current pay-as-you-go (PAYGO) systems feasible in the future. But the reforming rhetoric, which demands greater importance for individual saving plans, that is to say, a greater presence of defined contribution systems, has not failed as a consequence of the devastating effects the present financial crisis has had upon pension plans. The problem, it is argued, is not in the methods of saving but in the problems of financial regulation, which have emerged during this crisis. Once these problems have been resolved, individual saving methods will recover their primacy over the PAYGO systems as the most adequate method to make provisions for old age.

For developed countries, an ageing population is an unprecedented phenomenon. Consequently, the study of its economic effects is subject to large elements of uncertainty. On the other hand, the analysis of these effects is always the result of the theoretical framework in which they are considered. Neoclassical theory has added the basic analytical assumptions which characterise it (instrumental rationality, perfect information, rational expectations, market efficiency and economic equilibrium) to the analyses of population ageing effects, and, above all, to the analysis of pension systems and their relationship to ageing. The commitment to these assumptions has made this paradigm develop an analytical framework, which excludes some of the most relevant aspects that must guide any reflection of pension systems. Among them, the most important ones for this paper are those related to the problems of information we have to face. In the world in which we live, knowledge about the future is always uncertain. The decisions we make are affected not only by information asymmetry but also, and especially in relation to the topic with which we are concerned, by an uncertain knowledge of future events, which affect our present decisions.

The neoclassical paradigm cannot give an answer to the multiple questions that arise from the consideration of the problems of information. How can we estimate the optimum level of saving we need during our working life if we have no certainty about the age at which we will die, the future evolution of prices or the profitability we can get from our savings? Do individuals have the rationality taken for granted by the neoclassical models in order to modify their savings in the face of unexpected life events? Does not the permanent adaptation to these changes have macroeconomic consequences?

The questions the neoclassical theory cannot answer in the microeconomic field are not the only analytical gaps which characterise the neoclassical paradigm in terms of the issue with which we are concerned. Their belief that saving is always equal to investment and, therefore, the increase of saving fostered by individual plans to make provisions for old age are a guarantee of future economic growth, is far from obvious. But even if we accept this were true, the aspect that neoclassical theory cannot explain is that this connection must necessarily happen in the country that increases its level of saving. The ageing problem affects private saving plans. The only way to escape this problem would be by transferring savings to other countries so that the geographical area where saving is promoted is not the same as the geographical area where investment and economic growth will take place.

The capital export just mentioned places the problem of national and international markets performance, and, in particular, the effect that investment strategies followed by pension plans have had upon the performance of such markets, at the centre of the reflection on how to choose the best option to make provisions for old age. Given the aim of our work, we will not focus our attention either on this point or on another problem also related to the role of these funds in the financial system: the effects that bank disintermediation may have had upon the monetary policy. A process of financialisation, which has been driven by the growth and development of such funds over the past two decades.

Our work has two main objectives. On the one hand, we want to show that the present theoretical arguments used by the neoclassical paradigm to oppose the current PAYGO systems do not justify a radical change in the model of old age benefits provision. Secondly, we want to present some ideas that, from our point of view, help to shape a framework of theoretical reflection (a framework alternative to the one offered by the prevailing paradigm) in order to understand up to which extent institutions need social security.

2   The microeconomic dimension of pension systems

There has always been a conflict between neoclassical economic theory and pension systems based on the PAYGO method. At first, criticism of such pension systems focused on how to demonstrate the negative effects such systems had on the aggregate saving of the economy and, by extension, on economic growth, as well as on labour supply. The theory of the life cycle provided the theoretical framework which allowed an end to be put to the depressive effect of these systems upon individual saving and, by extension, though beyond reasoning, upon the aggregate saving of the economy (Ando and Modigliani, 1963; Feldstein, 1974 and 1976). Population ageing, as well as the difficulties of empirically testing the conclusions reached by the theory, relegated this criticism to second place, although the main idea about the increase of aggregate saving caused by individual saving plans has been preserved. However, now it is presented as a possibility rather than as an irrefutable conclusion of the analysis.

It could be said that the present criticism of pension systems based on the PAYGO approach has adopted a more pragmatic form, although it is still openly critical of the effects of the nature of those systems. On the one hand, it is suggested that population ageing generates a problem of financial sustainability in the long run, which demands a change in the model of provision. On the other, it is pointed out that, even if we accept that such a problem did not exist, the change would also be necessary since, as Feldstein (1997) said

> the real reason for shifting from a PAYGO system to a prefunded program is that doing so would raise the economic welfare of population. The key to this is the fact that the rate of return in a funded system is much higher than the implicit rate of return that is produced by a PAYGO system. That, in turn, implies that the funded system can provide any given level of benefits at a much lower cost to working-age people than a PAYGO system can. (p. 3)

Firstly, we will focus on showing that population ageing is not a solid argument to justify the transition from one system to another. In saying this, we are not trying to argue that the problem does not exist, nor that it has the desired effects upon the pension systems based on the PAYGO system. The only thing we are trying to point out is that the ageing problem does not justify the shift from a system based on the PAYGO to another based on the capitalisation of individual saving. Secondly, we will try to show that Feldstein's (1997) reasoning, in a world characterised by uncertainty, is also weak in justifying such change.

Before advancing our arguments, we want to make it very clear, although this may appear quite obvious, that the aim of any pension system is to provide an income that allows retired citizens to have a socially acceptable level of consumption. It is important to keep this idea in mind because, when mention is made of the future risks that will be faced by the present public pension systems, this is not the idea being dealt with. Such risks are associated with a problem of financial sustainability – that is, with an imbalance between income and expected expenses. Systems based on capitalisation and particularly defined contribution systems do not face this problem, because of their very nature. This is a problem of financial sustainability as it happens with the PAYG systems. This problem only arises when there is a legal obligation to guarantee some pension funding streams for which there are insufficient resources. Nevertheless, individuals whose pensions depend on the savings accumulated during their working life, may find themselves at their retirement age with an insufficient income to guarantee the desired level of consumption if, for example, there is a financial crisis which causes the disappearance of a substantial proportion of their savings. Therefore, the only way to develop a comparative analysis of the advantages of different systems that make provisions for old age is to take as a reference the guarantees offered by each of them about the future availability of the income which permits access to the same level of consumption.

Bearing this idea in mind, we will start by pointing out how population ageing affects this future income in a PAYGO system.

3   Population ageing and pension plans

Population ageing affects pension systems based on the PAYGO system on both the expenditures and the revenues sides. On the one hand, ageing means that a larger number of people (during a larger average number of years) will be the beneficiaries of a pension, which implies an increase in the total pension expenditure. Ageing also implies (ceteris paribus) a lower number of contributors and, consequently, of revenues as a result of the deceleration of the future labour supply caused by lower birth rates. The financial disequilibrium that this different behaviour of expenditures and revenues brings about obliges the system to tackle reforms, whether they affect expenditures or revenues or both at the same time.

The connection between population ageing and the appearance of problems of financial sustainability in the PAYGO systems is based on some assumptions, which should be noted. These assumptions, under the hypothesis of a closed economy – that is to say, one not open to migration flows – affect future economic growth rates as well as a subset of legal conditions, which influence the future expenditure and income flows of the system. More precisely, for such a connection to take place, it is necessary to assume that economic growth rates will decelerate in the future as a consequence of the process of population ageing itself, in such a way that the expected revenues (linked to economic growth) will be lower than the expected growth rate of expenditures on pensions. This assumption implies, on the one hand, accepting that it is impossible to increase the current activity rates above the present values or that, even if we accepted this were possible, the revenues obtained from that rise would not be enough to compensate the expected increase in pension expenditure. On the other hand, it means accepting that the greater pension expenditure cannot be compensated by the revenues obtained (for a given active population) from an increase in the productivity rates as a consequence of the technical change.

Moreover, financial sustainability appears in the assumed presence of certain legal constants. Above all, it is necessary to assume, on the one hand, that there are no changes in the legal age from which people have access to their retirement pensions; and, on the other, that the increase of the expected expense cannot be financed by an increase in social contributions, since this rise, supposedly, would have a negative effect on the labour supply and, therefore, the potential growth of the economy.

Most of the models that have dealt with the prediction of future financial problems in pension systems are founded on these assumptions. Evidently, there is room for disagreement on the results they reach, but we do not consider the selected method as incorrect.[3] Our disagreement with the prevailing paradigm does not lie here, but in the assumption that systems based on capitalisation are the solution to financial problems caused by the PAYGO systems for population ageing. This consideration conceals the fact that such systems are also affected by demographic changes and, consequently, are subject to the same strains as PAYGO systems.

Actually, systems based on capitalisation, and, in particular, defined contribution systems, as we have already pointed out, do not face a problem of financial sustainability. Nevertheless, if we approach the problem from the point of view of the welfare of the retired population (measured exclusively in terms of the incomes pensioners receive from the pension system) it is not difficult to notice what we are trying to explain. Pension systems, whether PAYGO or funded systems, are a mechanism to transfer income from the working population to the non-working population. In a PAYGO system, this transfer is explicit and visible, since it is made by means of the payment of compulsory social contributions. In a funded system, however, this transfer is more opaque since it is made indirectly. The non-working population has accumulated rights to financial and/or real assets, which allow getting a part, proportional to the volume of the income of the period generated by the working population either in the form of interests or by the sale of accumulated assets. Therefore, pensions in either system depend on income or, in other words, on the rate of economic growth (Barr, 2000). If there is a weakening of economic growth, the amount of income to be distributed will also decrease and the pensions received through either method will also be affected. If not, there will not be any reason for concern.

In order to explain more clearly what we are trying to demonstrate, we can imagine a world consisting of pension systems based on capitalisation and we can also imagine that we are facing a problem of population ageing. If we keep the same assumptions used to project the future financial disequilibrium of the present PAYGO systems, it is not difficult to understand how future pensioners' income will become affected. In a system of funded individual accounts, and under the assumption of a closed economy – that is, one that is not open to capital outflows – the effects of population ageing would be seen as a growth rate of the financial or real asset supply (retired population sells their assets to consume) higher than the growth rate of the demand (the one which working population makes to place their savings). This situation would lead to a slump in the value of the asset and with it the income of retired population (Brooks, 2002; Takáts, 2010). Only a rise in the saving rate of working population[4] could guarantee the maintenance of the value of the assets accumulated by retired population.[5] This increase in the saving rate would be equivalent to an increase in the flow of incomes of the present PAYGO systems caused by an increase in activity rates or productivity resulting from a technical change or a rise in social contributions.

On the other hand, both systems can 'avoid' the ageing problem by opening themselves to capital outflows, that is to say, looking for income beyond borders. In the PAYGO system, immigration, would allow increasing the labour supply and eliminating the scarcity of taxable wage income. In the case of capitalisation, the solution would lie in placing saving overseas. However, this solution is neither definite nor exempt from problems.

Immigration has a two-way effect on pension systems. At first, immigrants provide new income for the system, but once they retire they start receiving a pension. The net effect, from a theoretical perspective, is considered positive under certain assumptions (Sinn, 1997; Razin and Sadka, 1999). However, few empirical investigations have dealt with the study of the likely net impact which immigration may have on the different national social security systems. In a recent paper, Serrano, Eguía and Ferreiro (2011) have tried to simulate this impact for the case of the Spanish Social Security system and the results we have obtained leave no room for optimism. Immigration flows permit, at best, delaying the emergence of problems, but they are not the solution to the income deficit the system will bear as a consequence of population ageing.

In the case of funded systems, the solution to the demographic constraint depends necessarily on capital exports to economies with potential growth rates and with population pyramids different from the ageing populations of developed countries. The problems associated with this solution, following the behaviour of the international financial system in the past decade, which has led to an unprecedented financial crisis, do not require detailed comments.

Therefore, population ageing, bearing in mind the hypotheses made to simulate its impact on pension systems, makes developed countries confront the need to tackle reforms, since external transfers are not the solution to demographic pressures. Present PAYGO systems show obvious advantages in relation to the capitalisation of individual savings. In the PAYGO systems the necessary adjustments to restore financial balance are not determined by the market, but by political decisions which may regulate the solidarity that a society is willing to have towards their elderly population. In a system of individual accounts, the retired population, who witness how their income decreases as the value of their saving decreases due to the excess of assets supply is the only group negatively affected by the ageing process. In a PAYGO system, this loss can be distributed among the whole society through different channels. For example, the financial equilibrium can be restored by means of different combinations of reductions in the amounts of the benefits, an increase in the level of social contributions or an increase in the transfers from the general tax system to social security systems. In both systems a rise in the retirement age (that is, an extension of the working life) would have similar effects. Nevertheless, whereas in the PAYGO systems this measure could be one more part of the solidarity effort of society, in the individual account systems it would be the most acceptable option to avoid welfare losses.

4 Problems of information and pension systems

4.1 On return differentials

We have given above, quoting Feldstein (1997), what can be considered the traditional argument to defend the supremacy of capitalised accounts over PAYGO systems: namely, the different returns provided by each of the systems for the same target pension. We will see if this argument justifies a radical reform of the present public systems.

Returns (to an individual) on a PAYGO system, as pointed out by Samuelson (1958), are equal to the addition of the labour growth rate and the growth rate of productivity – that is, the growth rate of the base social security contributions from which the latter are extracted. This return is proxied through the growth rate of the GDP in the long run. In a system based on capitalisation, such return could be identified with the interest rate or with any index reflecting the evolution of profits generated by an asset portfolio which may be understood as representative of the kind of investment towards which saving from retirement should be channelled. Aaron's (1966) paradox argues that the selected system should be the one that yields highest returns. If the rate of interest, in the long run, were above the economic growth rate, then the funded method would be better than the PAYGO system. If not, that is, if the expected economic growth rate in the long run were higher than the expected financial rate of return, the pay-as-you-go system is the one which would offer a greater welfare level to retired population.[6]

The use of expected rates of return as a selection process is not, however, a good discriminatory practice. Aaron's (1966) paradox, in fact, poses a false theoretical problem. This problem originates in the impossibility of making an accurate estimate of the future value of the real or financial returns due to uncertainty. This uncertainty rises from the non-stationary and evolutionary character of the economic process, and we must distinguish it from the concept of risk. Risk reflects a situation where the distribution of probabilities of the potential results produced by some events can be known in the present moment. However, the relaxation of the stationary hypothesis prevents the use of past relative frequencies to estimate the future distribution of probabilities, consequently making it impossible to reason in terms of risk and compelling the inclusion of the concept of uncertainty.

The risk/return relationship, characteristic of investment decisions, is blurred, however. The present financial crisis, as well as its gestation, provides a good example of what we are trying to highlight. During the years of the financial boom, the supporters of individual saving accounts used to get expected rates of return (adjusted by risk) that were substantially higher than the expected economic growth rates (Blake, 2000; McMorrow and Roeger, 2002). These rates of return were obtained by projecting into the future the returns obtained during the previous years from an average portfolio including assets with different risks. This differential was presented as the main argument for justifying the abandonment of the present pension system. Today, it can be seen that those rates of return were the result of a financial bubble which, on bursting, reduced the value of capital accumulated by savers. We also know the adjustments of estimated rates of return for risk were wrong. Actually, the mistake does not occur necessarily because actuaries are unable to handle the theory of probability but because the economic process is supposed not to be evolving and, therefore, this theory is used to estimate the risk/return relationship in the long run.

The use of return differentials to discriminate systems of provisions has other weaknesses, which, though they have lower theoretical intensity than the one mentioned, also contribute to an erosion of its usefulness in the justification of the change of the system. When a financial rate of return higher than the GDP rate of growth is calculated, there is a tendency to ignore, at least, two costs whose consideration can result in the reduction of the return differential. This results in the disappearance of the hypothetical advantages of one system over another, in respect of the rates of return provided by each of them. The costs to which we are referring are as follows.

Firstly, transition costs: the costs to be incurred by the generation supporting the reforms for the payment of accrued pensions in the moment of change to the new system based on funded individual accounts. These costs will have different intensity depending on the depth of the reform, but they will be unavoidable. The transition generation would bear those costs in the form of an *overfunding* of their future pensions, since their individual saving for retirement should be added to the corresponding amount of taxes or precise contributions to pay the existing pensions. Extending such costs in the time by means of debt issuance cannot solve the problem. In this case, the burden would be distributed among more generations, which would, consequently, affect the real return obtained by other generations besides the one that begins the transition.

Secondly, management costs: the simple comparison of rates of return implicitly assumes administrative costs are identical in both systems. Although it is not easy to have clear and accurate information about the management cost applied by pension funds, the evidence we have suggests they are substantially higher that those of the present public systems (Shiller, 2005).

4.2   Adjustment costs due to information problems

The main objective of any pension system is to provide a pension high enough for the retired population to keep a socially acceptable standard of living. In a world characterised by uncertainty, to reach this goal implies, first of all, the need to anticipate in the present the future value of the variables that are relevant; and, secondly, the need to correct the estimation mistakes which may occur, which causes cost rise. *It is precisely the capacity to minimise such costs that makes one pension system better than another.* In order to demonstrate what we want to argue, and taking for granted that both systems have the same difficulties in predicting the future (which is not totally correct given their different informative necessities), we will focus our attention exclusively on the correcting mechanisms, whose main characteristic is to face information mistakes.[7] Posing the problem as a question, the aim is to give a satisfactory answer to the following: do mechanisms by means of which each of the systems is adjusted to deviations happening between estimated and necessary values to preserve the target pension have the same efficiency to reach the desired objective?

We can give a first answer beginning with the traditional way we use to cover ourselves against risk: insurance. The essence of insurance is in the transfer, distribution and grouping of risk. Individuals who protect themselves transfer their individual risk to the whole group of members insured, sharing among all of them the objective risk they aim to cover. Insurance exists, from a technical point of view, because individuals have different individual probabilities of incurring the risk covered by insurance. If this were not the case, that is to say, when there is interdependence of probabilities, resorting to insurance is impossible, since all individuals would be affected by the same problem at the same time and, consequently, there would be no chance to transfer risks among different insured agents. A second technical restriction on the existence of a potential insurance market relates to the capacity of estimating probabilities. In the presence of uncertainty, obviously, it does not make any sense to speak about a figure like this.

Individuals can group together to share their risks either voluntarily or by legal imperatives. In this last case we would find ourselves in the presence of a measure directed to deal with a typical problem of adverse selection. Individuals of low objective risk, as they are obliged to get and buy insurance, subsidise the insurance of high-risk individuals in such a way that the balance obtained by grouping is actually stable; this is so since there is no possibility that individuals will give up the insurance. The fact that it is compulsory means that there is an imposition to transfer income among individuals with different risk probabilities.

Retirement benefits cannot be treated strictly as an insurance, for, among other reasons, the probability for the insured event to happen is equal to the unit for all the potential insured. However, and this is the most relevant aspect, individuals face the future risks that can affect their pensions in the same way as any other risk susceptible of being insured through the market. The effects that a fall in the financial return of saving, for example, may have upon the future welfare of a pensioner are similar to the effects of the loss of income due to an industrial accident. In both cases individuals have to cope with a decrease in their consumption against which they logically wish to protect themselves.

If grouping is the optimum mechanism available to minimise costs caused by future events which affect us, then the PAYGO system has unquestionable advantages over capitalised individual accounts. It preserves the essence of the classical figure of the insurance: grouping and, in this case, intergenerational risk transfer. It could be said active workers cover the different 'risks' of retired population of that time. Nevertheless, it could be argued that this generic advantage attributed to the PAYGO system is the result of the fact that affiliation is compulsory rather than of a specific peculiarity of the method. In other words, could the same results be obtained in a world with individual accounts if the state legislated the obligatory nature of the insurance? For some risks that have to be faced by the retired population, the answer could be affirmative but the costs would be higher than in the present system. Longevity can be a valid example of what we are trying to show.

4.2.1 Longevity risk

The classical mechanism of planning savings for retirement, for a target pension previously fixed, consists of estimating the necessary contributions which, for a high given rate of return and a determined life expectancy (keeping constant the rest of variables), allow us to have access to the desired level of consumption during our retirement years. Any deviation arising as a result of the effective life being longer than the estimated life, automatically implies unplanned losses of welfare. This deviation can be the result of a simple estimation error (for instance, exact death dates can never be reckoned) or of a simple alteration in average life expectancy of the whole retired population caused, for example, by health improvements.

Insurance companies can manage this kind of risk by offering life annuities and, as a result, avoiding welfare losses mentioned above. Individuals turn their accumulated savings into a monthly income for the remainder of their lives. Consequently, they are transferring their risks to the insurance company. For its part, the insurance company can manage that individual risk as long as it has groups big enough to compensate the different individual probabilities of death. It is at this point that a typical problem of adverse selection appears. This means that the insurance cost rise substantially, as we can see at present. The high price of this coverage lies in the scarce offer of this kind of insurance that can be observed in those countries where pension funds have a wider implementation.

The obligatory nature of insurance does not necessarily have to help eliminate the problem of adverse selection mentioned above.

Nevertheless, it seems logical to think that, in a world where private saving methods for retirement predominate, private companies should offer coverage against longevity risk at a lower price than they are actually doing, since the group of people potentially affected would increase considerably. However, the cost would still be higher than that of the current PAYGO systems. The grouping provided by these systems allows the distribution of risks and compensation for the differences existing in individual probabilities of death, without significantly affecting the cost of offering this coverage. Marginal cost is practically zero due to the returns to scale generated from handling large groups of population.

On the other hand, an estimated alteration in the average life expectancy of retired people cannot be managed by resorting to classical insurance forms because of the problem of interdependence of probability that arises. When there is a general increase in life expectancy, it is impossible to face the new situation. The present PAYGO systems, however, can actually manage this form of longevity risk, since they deal with the problem mentioned by connecting generations which, though can be affected by the same variation in life expectancy, are not affected at the same time.

The risk of outliving individual savings permits some comparative reflection between systems, since there is a theoretical possibility of anticipating life expectancies for population groups by means of the theory of probability. Nevertheless, this reflection disappears when we face risks, which cannot be anticipated and, therefore, the costs they may cause cannot be managed through the market. We will focus on two risks: unanticipated inflation and, above all, alterations in returns and salaries.

4.2.2 Unanticipated inflation risk

The purchasing power of any kind of income is measured in real terms, that is to say, in terms of the amount of goods which can be purchased with such income. Pensions are no exception to this rule. The concern of pensioners is not the possibility of getting a certain amount of money every month, but rather the possibility to purchase the goods they wish to consume. The influence of price fluctuations has a particular importance in the welfare of the retired population. This kind of risk is similar to longevity risk, which we mentioned in the previous paragraph: in the absence of mechanisms to correct it, inflation may end up exhausting the purchasing power of pension income.

The long-run estimation of the evolution of prices is a task as impossible as the estimation of the individual probability of death of any person. Nobody can guarantee an individual who contracts a pension fund the exact trend of prices during retirement years. In addition, in this case private insurance faces an interdependence of probabilities. Inflation, when it occurs, has a simultaneous effect on all of the members of a pension system. Uncertainty and interdependence of probabilities make it impossible for the market to offer not just an insurance against the 'risk' of old age, but an insurance against any kind of risk. If probabilities cannot be estimated, there is no way to calculate the premium, and if, in addition, risk cannot be managed through grouping because there are no individuals with different probabilities, there cannot be any efficient form of private insurance in this contingency.

However, the obligatory nature of insurance in current PAYGO systems does allow, in the same way as occurred with the problem of longevity, a transfer of individual risk towards the group of insured people, in this particular case towards the group of the currently working population. The reason lies in the fact that, even if all individuals are affected by price fluctuations, some groups have certain advantages over others to cover themselves against such variations. Provided wage incomes are updated in line with price changes, we can have the necessary group to transfer the income we need. Apart from that, the process is almost automatic. The revenues the social security system receives from employed population by means of contributions are indexed as a result of the collective bargaining. We could say that the system collects capacity of real purchase that it distributes among retired population.[8]

Obviously, this automatic change to which we refer is not strictly technical, since updating pensions to price fluctuations conceals a political decision. As long as there is a political decision, the present system can guarantee the objective without any difficulty. However, if there is no such decision, if it is not desirable to maintain the purchasing power of pensions, the system would adjust the collection to the amount necessary to face an expenditure which, while the rest remains constant, would decrease gradually in real terms over the years – that is to say, the expenditure on pensions would decrease as a percentage of GDP. In other words, the participation of retired population in income distribution would be lowered gradually. Maintaining the purchasing power of pensions is, among others, one of the strongest expressions of solidarity of PAYGO systems.

4.2.3   *Bounded rationality and adjustments to deviations*

One of the most acute problems faced by individuals when planning their retirement income through individual saving (but at the same time, one of the least considered aspects in the discussion on pension reform) is their myopia about the future.

The term myopia refers to the incapacity of individuals to consider their whole life horizon when planning their present decisions on consumption and saving. They are encouraged to give up present systems and replace them with private pension funds because it is assumed that, as a result of their myopia, there would be a risk that they did not get insured. Compulsory insurance tends to be presented as the mechanism that permits correcting costs generated by individuals' lack of planning.

However, by making it compulsory the only costs that can be avoided, at best, would be those that are generated from the absence of income once the retirement age has been reached; that is to say, it would even prevent pension incomes from falling below poverty thresholds at the time they stop their working life. These limited effects of the obligatory nature of insurance are due to the fact that such measures only help correct one of the multiple forms in which bounded rationality of agents is expressed.

Bounded rationality includes the entire range of decisions taken by individuals, since the impossibility of processing all of the information required (even if this exists) in each moment to obtain optimum results is at the root of this process. With regard to the subject we are dealing with here, one of the most dramatic effects of this myopia emerges when individuals feel the need to adjust their contributions at a time when there are either deviations between the estimated and the obtained income or changes in wages. In both cases, individuals must adjust their decisions on saving in order to keep the path which will allow them to reach the target pension.

Any deviation between the estimated and the obtained rate of return demands modifications in the contributions to avoid undesirable situations. If the return obtained is below the rate necessary to guarantee the target pension, individuals will have to increase their contributions, otherwise they would end up paying for their lack of provision with a lower quantity of goods than the initially desired for retirement age. Another possible option would be to keep the planned provision of goods and extend the years of working life. If the relation is the opposite, that is to say, if the return obtained is higher than planned, individuals should decrease their contributions in the following period. If they did not take this direction, they would be incurring excess savings over the ones initially planned or, in other words, they would be slowing down their present consumption below their optimum level.

The rule that expresses the desired income for the retirement years in terms of the income obtained during the years of active life requires the inclusion of the wage variable in the calculation of contributions. Therefore, contributions, for a given expected rate of return on saving, can be expressed as a proportion of wage. Any wage variation will generate automatically the corresponding variation in the contributions. If wage increases, so will contributions and vice versa. Obviously, if these adjustments are not carried out, individuals will end up paying for it, as in the previous case, in the form of a smaller amount of goods or a working life extension.

In a system based on individual saving accounts, there is no guarantee that individuals will adjust their decisions in the most adequate manner, since, contrary to what is proposed by the neoclassical theory, individuals are not characterised by having instrumental rationality. The only way to correct the lack of provision would be by some form of public intervention, which, for example, could fix the intervals of compulsory contributions annually depending upon the changes which may have occurred, at least, in financial returns which may be regarded as representative. This kind of intervention is practically equivalent to fixing by law the compulsory family saving rate of each period, which is more interventionist, and, undoubtedly, more complicated than annually fixing the amount of social contributions required to finance the expenditure on pensions.

The remarks we have just made are based on an implicit hypothesis: there is the possibility to adjust contributions because individuals have enough time to react to unforeseen events. However, if there is not sufficient time, individuals will pay for any sharp downward alteration between the necessary return to reach the desired consumption and the return obtained with lower levels of welfare once retirement age is reached or with a working life that extends beyond the planned date. The cost of adjustment always, and exclusively, falls on the insured. In a hypothetical world ruled by capitalised individual accounts, the most critical years are those closest to the retirement age, since there is less time to make adjustments to pensions arrangements. If deviations were not intense, the problem would not be particularly serious. However, any financial crisis could have the effect of ruining the efforts made throughout the whole of a working life. The present crisis provides a clear example of what we are trying to show.[9]

4.3   Political risk

Public pension systems are also under risks that cannot be ignored, although they have a different nature from the ones we mentioned in the previous subsection. This whole group of risks is are under the general heading of 'political risks'. Conventional doctrine understands political risk as the risk that benefits, promised by the pension system, may become altered (downwards) through the political process. This alteration can adopt multiple forms: an increase in the number of years considered to fix the amount of the pension, a modification of the indexes of reference used to maintain the purchasing power of the pension, changes in the legal retirement age, and so on. It is usually argued that this kind of risk is exclusive of present public pension systems, since, as has been mentioned before, benefits provided by PAYGO systems are determined by a political process.

The reflection on this kind of risk is not usually as clear as would be convenient, since quite frequently this reflection mixes performances that tend to rationalise the system with clearly arbitrary measures that imply an obvious risk for the solvency of the system itself. This disturbance has its origin in the very concept of political risk. This is identified exclusively with alterations in the promised benefits, no matter where the alterations stem from: and fundamentally what information affected people have about their effects, or their level of participation in the legal changes that give rise to them.

Nobody argues that in the crisis of the social security systems in Latin America, for example, unjustified privileges of some groups of workers, or the 'political' use made of the benefits provided by pension systems from the different countries, were a permanent source of instability and disturbances in their performance, which ended up failing. The inefficiency of the different social security administrations also helped to plunge them in an irreversible crisis (Jimenez, 1998). It is actually relevant to speak about political risk in these cases, since the outcomes of the political process were not leading towards the maintenance and reinforcement of public provision systems.

However, it is more problematic to use the idea of political risk with the aim of speaking about potential cutbacks in future benefits as a consequence of population ageing, as stated, for instance, by McHale (1999). For this author, the trend observed in most developed countries to reduce the expenditure on pensions through the hardening of access conditions to retirement benefits, is a clear example of cutback in expected benefits which fully fits the generic heading of 'political risk'. However, can we really identify parametric reforms with political risk?

In these pages we have already had the opportunity to make reference to the possibilities that present pension systems have to adapt to the demographic change we are living through. One adjustment option would be not to modify access conditions to pensions and to transfer the main part of the increase in spending towards higher social security contributions.[10] A second option would be just the opposite; that is, to adjust expenditure exclusively while keeping contributions constant. A third option would be some combination of the two previous ones. It is the case that the predominant option in most developed countries is the second. Measures already implemented – as well as those which are being discussed at the moment – are clearly oriented to curb the pace of expenditure expansion by acting on the amount of benefit. This does not mean, however, that in future these reforming measures cannot be combined with increases in social contributions in case future growth rates are not high enough to cope with the expected rise in pensions expenditure. Are these reforms actually a risk? Should they not be interpreted as the guarantee that public pension systems will still cover the need for income of retired population in the future?

In any case, political risk would exist if the information we have today was ignored and reforms were prevented under the assumption that future economic growth will provide a solution to everything. It is also a political risk to direct the reform towards uncontrollable situations, radicalising the scope of the reform by promising results that are uncertain of being obtained. Political risk, then, should be identified not so much with a cutback on benefits but with the responsibility on the part of the administration and political powers to guarantee the future of pensions. The guarantee of democratic control, however, is not enough if the social security administration is opaque and inefficient or if political decisions are based on cronyism and immediate political returns. The aim is to neutralise both lines of disturbance. The demand for wide social and political agreements to tackle reforms in pensions can be a good antidote against a political power controlled by short-run (economic, political or electoral) considerations.

The best possible regulations cannot prevent a potential future scenario with pessimistic profiles. The economic growth rate, as we mentioned before, is the strategic variable for both insurance methods. Consequently, if the future economic growth rate were insufficient, possibilities to minimise the adjustment costs that such a situation would demand are higher in the PAYGO system than in the capitalisation method. Whereas in the latter the whole adjustment cost would be borne by individuals, the present system would allow a redistribution of costs with increased solidarity, which brings about more positive macroeconomic effects than those that can be expected from a system based on individual saving.

5   The Macroeconomic dimension of social security systems

5.1   Uncertainty, institutions and equilibrium

Economic history has shown the evolutionary nature of market economies. Economic expansion cycles are followed by periods of crisis. It is during these episodes that we witness in a clearer way, on the one hand, the 'destruction' of 'old things', that is to say, of the structural features that characterised the expansion stage, and, on the other, the construction of something new on which a new growth stage can be settled. Post Keynesian economics uses the concepts of historical time and logical time to refer to this dynamic process of change (Davidson, 1991, 2002, 2007; Robinson, 1962). With the concept of historical time, it tries to explain the evolutionary nature of such economies – that is, the succession of different economic stages with different characteristics. The concept of uncertainty we referred to in previous pages stems precisely from this point: from the analytical necessity to consider the effects upon economies of structural changes gradually taking place.

The concept of logical time tries to capture the idea of stability without having to identify it with the concept of neoclassical economic equilibrium. We understand stability as a situation where relationships among economic variables are susceptible to being predicted without falling into serious estimation errors. Logical time is a time when tensions caused by historical time have been temporarily neutralised. The concept of risk based on probabilistic calculus, which we also mentioned in the previous section, has a direct relationship with this concept of logical time.

In the economic world described by neoclassical theory only logical time is considered. In addition, stability among variables is identified with situations of economic equilibrium, which are reached through decisions made by rational agents who try to optimise their decisions. The hypothesis of 'rational expectations' is used to close the model when the time variable is included, that is, when information about the future has to be included in the decisions made in the present time. Intertemporal optimisation of decisions made by rational agents generate stability situations in the present time (and, therefore, they produce economic equilibrium, more accurately, a succession of equilibrium results) because, as pointed out by Muth (1961), subjective distribution of probabilities, which agents make, is the same as the objective distribution of such probabilities. Disequilibrium situations are always the result of a mistake in the expectations of agents caused by an eternal agent (usually the state and public policy) but which are only temporary, since agents are supposed to have the capacity to learn how to come back to equilibrium once they modify their expectations by including the new information.

In the Post Keynesian paradigm, stability of relations among economic variables is a result of the interaction between non-rational agents (in the neoclassical sense), who have different and contradictory information. The information these agents are provided with is not perfect, however. They encounter a variety of information failures. Certainly, agents face a problem of the asymmetric distribution of information. But they also face problems of uncertainty, which arise both from the evolutionary nature of the economic process and from their bounded rationality – that is, their incapacity to process all the information they are provided with correctly. In a world with these characteristics, the neoclassical concept of equilibrium does not fit at all, which does not mean we should abandon the idea of equilibrium.

The concept of equilibrium in the economic theory is a normative concept. Interaction among agents always brings about results. Goods, as well as productive factors, are permanently being exchanged in the market, producing results in terms of employment and unemployment rates, price level or quantities of saving and investment. The normative dimension of the concept of equilibrium appears when some assessment criteria are imposed on these results, that is, when we discriminate among results considering that some are preferable than others. Since the publication of Keynes' General Theory (1936), the criterion of full employment has become the main criterion to discriminate – that is, to identify relations among variables which may be regarded as the cause of equilibrium situations (and consequently desirable) and non-desirable situations.[11] Furthermore, in the General Theory, Keynes (1936) showed that there could be situations characterised by the stability of relations between variables but they had to be considered non-desirable, since they contributed to the generation of a situation of full employment (Kregel, 1976). Stability and equilibrium, then, are not necessarily synonyms, as it happens in the neoclassical paradigm.

The economic analysis of institutions has revealed institutions are not an exogenous variable for the economic analysis. Relations between agents happen within some fixed rules of the game, which establish the limits of what can and cannot be done. They inform about how to establish the relations or about what can or cannot be exchanged in the market. Institutions do not come up necessarily as a derived product; they are not determined by the demands of economic relations defined regardless of institutions. The conflicting process of generation of institutions can be partly influenced by certain economic behaviours but it is also a process fed by speeches about how we want or how we understand the development of economic relations. So that they bring about the desired results, that is to say, an equilibrium situation generating full employment.

The analysis of institutions is one of the compulsory steps that has to be taken when we intend to base macroeconomic relations on microeconomics (Ferreiro and Serrano, 2009). This is especially true when the hypothesis of instrumental rationality and perfect information get relaxed. Limited rationality, as well as information problems, causes a priori, (and from a theoretical perspective) unexpected individual behaviour. Stability in causal relationships between variables is not a true result, as it is not, either, the fact that if there is actually stability, this is a synonym of equilibrium. Institutions are, fundamentally, a source of information for individuals. By means of institutions, we partly correct problems connected with information asymmetry and, at the same time, they help to shape behaviour patterns, which allow us to solve problems arising from our bounded rationality. Institutions do not eliminate uncertainty problems, but they may help to ease their effects – at least, temporarily. When setting the rules of the game, they make agents' behaviours predictable, and consequently the results of such behaviours. In short, through institutions the effects of historical time are neutralised (at least, temporarily) helping, thereby, the stabilisation of relationships between economic variables and making possible the use of logical time as a working tool. If economic results are foreseeable, it is because it has been possible to stabilise the relationships between variables. In other words, stability is always a result, not the natural state of economy, as it happens in neoclassical theory (Ferreiro and Serrano, 2007, 2008).

Nevertheless, in the same way stability situations are different from situations of economic equilibrium. We must consider the possibility of good and bad institutions to achieve situations of full employment. Bad institutions bring about stability situations but not equilibrium situations whereas good institutions generate situations of equilibrium with stability.

5.2   Public pension systems and macroeconomic effects

A public pension system can be considered an institution that helps to stabilise economic relations. On providing us with information on the availability of future income, it influences our present decisions on consumption and saving. If we assume the premises of the neoclassical theory, we could say that the present system is a bad institution, since it raises present behaviour that generates worse results than those which would be obtained with a system based on individual saving. In fact, for the neoclassical theory the only good institutions are those that guarantee a market-clearing equilibrium outcome or, at least, the closest possible to it, that is, a second-best outcome.[12] The results they refer to are a lower level of savings and, consequently, of investment, employment and economic growth. Therefore, strictly speaking, the economy has been living in a situation of economic disequilibrium since these systems appeared.

This conclusion, which nobody has been able to demonstrate empirically, however, does not rise necessarily as a logical corollary of the neoclassical model. In a virtual reality as the one described by the neoclassical theory there may be a place for a different hypothesis, provided rational and optimising behaviour of the agents and the commitment with equilibrium is respected. In order to base the depressive effect of these systems upon saving, and, consequently, upon investment and economic growth, it is necessary to presume that their existence depresses the saving rate in relation to the levels that would be reached in a world where there were no public pension systems at all. If, on the contrary, we assume that in their decisions individuals make on saving, the income they will receive in the future from the social security system is being correctly considered, then their contributions to the system could be identified with the dissaving that retired population would make in a world without public pensions, in such a way that the saving rate that would be generated in each moment would be the best. In other words, the macroeconomic dimension of these systems in the neoclassical paradigm depends on the hypothesis made about their effects, since the latter are not a decisive element of the model, but an exogenous variable which will be later included once the necessary restrictions to reach the equilibrium are already fixed.

The neoclassical relationship between economic growth and pension systems can be presented in a wider perspective, that is, showing either the positive effects that the funded individual accounts could produce on the economic activity or the negative effects arisen from the current PAYGO public systems. In the latter, in addition to the consequences on the savings and the labour force, special attention is paid on the positive impact that a private insurance system based on individual savings has on capital markets. A narrow perspective of that relationship, the dominant one in the literature, focuses only on the two first variables mentioned.

From a theoretical point of view, the argument is the following: public pension systems have depressed the rate of national savings and, subsequently, the investment and the rate of economic growth. The ultimate effect of these systems has been a lower welfare than the one that could have been reached with private systems based on individual saving accounts. The change to funded capital accounts would, therefore, lead to the opposite effects.

That latter system is open to a number of criticisms. The first one is: how can we calculate the optimal saving rate to be used as a benchmark? The way to calculate the optimal rate of saving that an economy without social security would reach is by aggregating the behaviour of a representative individual. This individual is assumed to have rational behaviour: that is, there are no limits on her ability to process the information and she also maximises her utility throughout her life cycle. By definition, the information available is perfect. In sum, the model is constructed under the assumption of rational expectations. With the latter and other assumptions, the critics of the PAYGO system build a model of equilibrium where saving rates are optimal. Finally, this virtual world is compared to the real world to detect the differences. If the observed saving rate is lower than that estimated in the model, the conclusion is that public systems are squeezing the savings.

The empirical results are key to reaching any conclusion. The empirical research has been very extensive and the only clear conclusion is that a clear conclusion has not been reached because of the opposite results of those researches (Danzinger et al., 1981; Kessler et al., 1987; Graham, 1987; Kotlikoff, 1979). The reason is that this kind of research poses a false theoretical problem. The estimation of the optimal rate of saving is a pure speculative exercise that it is impossible to test empirically. The information that it is assumed to be managed by individuals when they maximise their intertemporal utility is not the available statistical information existing in the real world. In theoretical models, individuals work with perfect information, but the world we are living in provides only imperfect information. Thus, the optimal rate of saving is arbitrarily calculated, using, for instance, the average income of a certain number of years as a proxy of the permanent-life income. Obviously, the outcomes reached will be different depending on the kind of proxies used.

Moreover, in the economic models on which criticisms to public pension systems are based, the aggregated supply is the dominant economic variable. The investment is constrained by the availability of saving, that is, any increase of saving is automatically transformed in an equivalent increase of investment. In these models, market economies do not face any long-run constraint coming from the demand side. The aggregate demand is automatically adjusted to the changes in the aggregate supply. The adjustment can be more or less slow, depending on the rigidities in the goods or inputs markets, but in the long run, economies will always be in equilibrium. The trend to the equilibrium is the outcome of the interactions among individuals that behave in a rational manner.

In this framework, the change from the current PAYGO system to a system based on individual accounts will automatically increase the savings and the rates of economic growth. From a theoretical point of view, there is no clear answer. It could be argued that the outcome would be a decomposition of the different motives of saving, keeping constant the aggregated rate of savings. This rate could also fall as a consequence of the myopia of individuals. But even assuming an increase in the rate of saving, this increase would be transitory, lasting until the new system matures. In that moment, the dissaving of the retired population would equal the savings of the working population, changing the initial outcomes (Toporowski, 2000; Sawyer, 2003).

An increase of the savings rate will not automatically lead to an increase in investment, because the latter depends basically on the profit expectations and not on the current supply of loanable funds. Furthermore, a simple national income accounting shows us that:

$$(S - I) + (T - G) = (X - M),$$

and, further,

$$S = I + (G - T) + (X - M)$$

Therefore, an increase in savings will lead to a similar increase in investments if and only if $(G - T) + (X - M) = 0$. If the increase in savings does not come with an equivalent increase in investment, the higher rate of savings will necessarily come with a higher public deficit and/or with a surplus in the current account and with a deficit in the capital account (Sawyer, 2003). In the first case, the higher public deficit involves a fall in public savings in the short run. The fall in public savings will (partially) offset the higher private savings, thus reducing the impact of the increase of private savings on total national savings, the relevant variable. Furthermore, in the long run, the higher public deficit, and the consequent higher debt burden, can lead to raise taxes, thus affecting private savings (Cessarato, 2002, 2006; Sawyer, 2003).

If higher savings do not come with higher investment and/or a higher public deficit, it must come with a higher current account surplus and, therefore, with a higher deficit in the capital account. The economy will become a net capital flow exporter, and in this case economies with lower savings, those where their savings are below investments, will be those who will benefit from the higher capital supply.

6   Reforms of the public pension systems: implications on the stability of the expectations and the macroeconomic stability

Public pension systems are the result of a complex historic process whose need began to be felt once the nuclear family failed and could not fulfil the function of assistance of elderly people. At their inception, these systems were only intended to replace the nuclear family by supplying people with survival incomes. Their macroeconomic dimension begins to gain relevance as systems evolve and individual benefits increase as a result of the social demands to improve the life of older population. Evidence shows that these pension systems have been the ones that have helped to decrease poverty rates among the older population (Engelhardt and Gruber, 2004; Sainsbury and Morissens, 2002).

How should we understand this macroeconomic dimension? As we pointed out at the beginning of this paper, the analysis of this institution is based on the economic paradigm chosen for each study. Neoclassical connection of this institution with economic growth, through its influence on individuals' saving, is coherent with an equilibrium model where it is assumed that every supply creates its own demand. However, in a world where there may actually be problems of demand caused by lower investment expectations in relation to the generated savings, which bring about unemployment situations, the macroeconomic dimension of this institution has different profiles to the ones supported by the neoclassical theory.

Savings exists because the future is uncertain and thrifty people wish to protect themselves against unexpected future situations of lack of income or necessity following consumption. Every decision to save a part of the income generated in the present means the inability to purchase goods in the present time. Situations characterised by uncertainty, as can be seen in the present financial crisis, increase savings, slow down investment and reinforce situations of depression. Savings does not imply, automatically, an increase in investment as it happens in the neoclassical paradigm, but a contraction of the supply so that it can adjust itself to the existing demand. On the contrary, with lower uncertainty, consumption, investment and employment increase. If public pension systems have been part of our economic model for so many years, it has not only been for the unquestionable social benefits they have produced but because they have also clearly contributed to the economic growth. These systems have generated in the population, stable (and positive) expectations that they would be provided at their retirement age with the sufficient income to meet their spending needs during those years, regardless of the length of the retirement period. This stability has strengthened the connection between income and consumption, as it eliminates one of the biggest sources of uncertainty individuals have to face when planning their decisions on savings.

Public pension systems, on reinforcing the relation between income and consumption, can also be seen as a powerful fiscal tool, although with their own specific characteristics. Fiscal policy stems from the need to move the existing savings when the expectations of benefit do not generate enough investment to absorb such savings. When we eliminate one of the main sources of uncertainty that affect individuals' decisions on savings, these systems complement the traditional fiscal policy. Without them, fiscal policy would have had to be developed more intensely, because it would have been necessary to absorb a larger quantity of savings and, probably, with a more erratic behaviour, since it is influenced by the general state of expectations during each period.

Implementing and developing public pension systems was not a macroeconomic objective. The usefulness of institutions, and this is no exception despite the economic dimension it has reached, is not necessarily determined by the demands imposed by the rules of the game which in each historical moment ruled the performance of economic relations. Instead, these rules of the game begin to take shape as a result of the interactions that take place both on the political and on the economic ground. What we are trying to show is that the strong social anchoring this institution has is due, without doubt, to its contribution to eliminate an important source of uncertainty for individuals. This may be the only support for the institution. Nevertheless, when through Keynes (1936), we have come to understand the economic importance of this informative problem, it is then that we have also been able to understand that this institution links unquestionable social benefits to economic benefits (Ferreiro and Serrano, 2008). The reform of these pension systems, and, exceptionally, their replacement by a system based on individual savings, cannot ignore what we have just mentioned. In addition, the present crisis can contribute to strengthen some of the effects that a change of model can presumably produce. The risks we face are clear: an increase of individual uncertainty, with direct negative effects on the economic aggregates and on the international financial system, will inevitably deepen the current crisis.

In previous sections we made reference to the probable effects a change of system could have on the savings of individuals, without considering the present level of expectations. During the period before population ageing starts to be felt, there would be an increase in the saving rates of economies above the average levels observed in the past. After that, as ageing begins to have its effects, savings rates would start decreasing, for an identical given state of future expectations.

In a situation like the present one, with a high level of uncertainty, the reform would only contribute to an increase in that uncertainty, raising the already too high savings rates for the economic situation we are going through. This increase is most likely to be absorbed by a considerable increase in public debt, which would be caused, in part, by the need to abandon the existing pensions and, in part, because of the incapacity of the financial system to recycle the savings that would be generated if developed economies undertook this kind of reform. The present financial crisis has shown the difficulties the financial system has to face in order to provide non-speculative solutions to the increase of liquidity observed during the past few years. These difficulties were actually already well known before the outbreak of the crisis. Even some of the international institutions which had most clearly declared themselves in favour of a change of the pension system, openly admitted that such change could not take place if it were not followed by a reinforcement of the international financial system (Bank for International Settlements Group of Ten, 1998).

The financial crisis has contributed to alter some aspects of the debate on the reform of pension systems, as it crudely shows the effects that financial risk may have upon the incomes of the pensioners (Impavido and Tower, 2009). Now it is not possible to appeal to the good aspects of individual saving as an alternative to present pension systems, arguing that the efficiency of markets of capitals in the resource allocation provides rates of return (with low risk) higher than the rates of economic growth. Has the present crisis put an end to the debate on the change of the potentially ideal model of the pension system? The answer is likely to be negative, although we will have to wait until the crisis has been overcome to know whether this hypothesis is true or not. At the moment, the crisis has not substantially modified the influence of the prevailing paradigm.[13] The origins of the financial crisis are still related to regulation deficits, in such a way that once these deficits have been solved, there are no objective reasons for supporters of the change to take up their traditional view again. Even pressure could increase unless the model of economic globalisation we know is changed.

Financial globalisation has been the typical feature of capitalist economies for the past two decades. The enormous increase of financial relations that have taken place during these years has strengthened the position of power of international financial agents (banks and pension funds, mainly) (Arestis, Baltar and Cavalcante, 2009; Esteban, Ferreiro and Serrano, 2010; Freeman, 2010; Lapavitsas, 2009; Palley 2009). The savings that emerging economies and economies exporting raw materials channelled towards financial markets of developed countries, as well as the savings generated in these countries (caused by population ageing), have been the main sources of worldwide liquidity around which their businesses revolved. An acceptable solution, though partial, to the international financial crisis depends on the correction of the disequilibria in the balance of payments by developing growth models in emerging economies focused on the development of their respective domestic demands (Altuzarra, Ferreiro and Serrano, 2010; Yueh, 2010). This option would eliminate one of the two sources of international financial business in recent years. Therefore, it is not a risk to think that in the next years, if the neoclassical paradigm still prevails, we will witness an increase in pressures, coming mainly from certain sectors of the financial system, to privatise present pension systems. Privatisation would be a new source of world liquidity that would enliven financial business and, probably, a new speculative bubble similar to the one which has led us to the present situation. Privatisation, otherwise, does not have to be total; that is, it does not have to imply replacing one system with another. Present systems need to be reformed to face the problem of population ageing. Depending on how this reform is carried out, cutbacks in incomes may be more or less intense and, consequently, the need for resorting to private forms of saving can be more urgent. On the other hand, fiscal benefits enjoyed by these forms of saving act as a powerful booster for their development.

The combination of a model of financial globalisation as the one we know with a partial privatisation of pension systems (which would substantially modify behaviour patterns of individuals and, as a corollary, the connection between income, savings and consumption boosted by present pension systems) would open new sources of economic instability. The most evident change that would take place in the present situation would be the leading role of the financial income to make decisions on consumption and savings (Serrano and Ferreiro, 2007). As we pointed out in previous pages, deviations between the estimated return and the one obtained would make it necessary to readjust the decisions on savings and consumption in order to continue in the path of savings compatible with the consumption wished to be reached at retirement age. This is valid for individuals who are able to see the changes and, then, readjust their decisions. Those who are not may react either raising their savings rate considerably due to the increase of uncertainty (as it happened in China after the reforms of the social protection system), or ignoring the future and paying for this ignorance in terms of a low future consumption which, socially, would be seen as an increase in poverty rates among elderly population.

The increased influence that financial income would exercise would be an added source of economic instability. The weight of financial income in the decisions on consumption, at least in Europe, does not have a great influence at the moment, due partly to the present pension systems. Its partial privatisation, however, would modify this situation, closely connecting consumption to the evolution of such return, because of the influence of financial return on decisions on saving for reasons of retirement. The influence of financial markets upon the general economic evolution, then, would increase above the present situation. The instability that characterises these markets would become the core of the economic activity, which determines the volume of jobs.

The need for a change in the economic paradigm is urgent. This change will be the result of multiple actions, in relation to both the theory and practice of economic policy. In the problem with which we are dealing here, a reasonable way to advance towards change is admitting that the problem of ageing has effects on public pension systems and that, therefore, reforms are necessary. The focus on the problematic nature of the present paradigm must be centred in the nature of reforms, not so much in the need for them.

7   Summary and conclusions

Neoclassical economics argues that the preferential solution to the problems that ageing processes generate in relation to public pension systems based on a PAYGO system is their (partial or total) replacement by accumulation systems based on individual accounts. From this perspective, this radical reform of pension systems would eliminate financial unsustainable problems of present systems at the same time as having a stimulating effect upon economic activity.

The truth is that neoclassical economics deals inadequately with this problem, and, in general, with the effects of pension systems. On the one hand, it evades the fact that both accumulation systems and PAYGO systems are equally affected by ageing processes. However, its analytical framework depends on some assumptions, which keep neoclassical economics detached from the real world. The problems of asymmetric information, limited rationality and fundamental uncertainty mean that the micro- and macroeconomic effects of pension systems are far from the effects proposed by orthodox economics.

Consequently, in our opinion the validity and efficiency of any pension system must be judged not by its capacity to reach an equilibrium result of market clearing but by its capacity to provide their beneficiaries with an income flow. This should allow them to have a consumption level socially acceptable during their retirement and by its capacity to give individuals some certainty about the economic future.

All pension systems, both funded and unfunded, are negatively affected by the ageing process. The neoclassical argument that funded pension systems are sheltered from ageing is simply false. Moreover, the presumed positive effects on economic activity from a radical reform of pension systems depend dramatically on a set of assumptions – such as the existence of perfect information or the perfect working of financial markets – which do not happen in the true world.

We can, thereby, argue that radical reforms of pension systems would not only fail to produce the results their supporters claim for them. They would also have a negative impact upon both economic activity and economic stability (real and financial); and the capacity to implement the necessary macroeconomic policies to act on economic cycles on top of it all.

Public pension systems based on a PAYGO scheme have proven their capacity not only to provide beneficiaries with the certainty of future income during the retirement period. It has also helped individuals to reduce their uncertainty about the future and, therefore, has helped them to make more efficient decisions. As a result of this, they have also contributed to a stabilisation of the working of the aggregate economy and to implement a macroeconomic policy that smooths the short-run economic fluctuations. This does not mean that this system does not face problems, given the evolutionary nature of economic activity. Public pension systems need to be reformed when structural changes occur that endanger the fulfilment of the main objective of the system: providing individuals with a socially acceptable income. In this situation, parametric reforms must be necessary, but always under the constraint of keeping the nature of the system.

Notes

1. Comments from participants of the conference on 'The New Economics as "Mainstream" Economics', Cambridge, 28–9 January, and the 7th international conference on 'Developments in Economic Theory and Policy', Bilbao, 1–2 July, and the editors are welcome. This work has been supported by the Basque Government (Consolidated Research Group GIC10/153).
2. A good example in the context of the text is the 2009 Ageing Report of the European Union (European Commission, Directorate-General for Economic and Financial Affairs, 2009).
3. The need to make estimations and/or simulations on the future evolution of expected expenses and incomes in pension systems rises from the very nature of the correcting measures that a social security system demands. Such measures cannot be implemented when events have already taken place, among other reasons because it could be too late to correct the non-desired effects or because the cost of such correction could be too high in terms of the welfare of the retired population. The anticipation of results allows implementing reforms and, thus, having enough time to measure the intensity and the most suitable direction of the measures to be implemented. Anticipation also permits managing the time to provide affected people the necessary information on the scope and the moments they will start to notice the changes intended. However, carrying out long-run projections of future expenses and incomes of the social security is not an easy task. The non-stationary character of the economic process generates information problems, which must be solved by resorting to assumptions and scenarios whose choice is discretionary and, most of the time, reflects the subjective opinion of those who make them. Therefore, it is not surprising that there are strong discrepancies about the moment and intensity with which systems may encounter financial problems.
4. Which means a deterioration of their current consumption and consequently, of their welfare level.
5. It would be important to highlight that the effects on the prices of the assets of population ageing would only take place once the system were generalised and the process of assets de-accumulation started to occur. During the transition process from a system to another, what we would witness is the opposite effect, that is, a rise of the asset prices due to the increase in demand. However, the transition period is not the relevant time to understand the effects of population ageing upon the system, in the same way as the present time is not the relevant moment to understand the effect of demographic tensions upon present PAYGO systems. The analytically relevant period is the time when population ageing starts to be felt in the form of an increase in the asset offer (an increase in expenditure on pensions if we speak about

PAYGO systems) and a slowing down in savings rates (a deceleration in the growth rates of social contributions in PAYGO systems).

6. In the recent past there have been attempts to overcome Aaron's (1966) paradox by assuming that a dynamically efficient economy always has to provide higher financial rates of return than real rates of return. The evident corollary to this assumption, for the subject here under discussion, is that pension funds, which invest savings of individuals in financial assets will always have better results than PAYGO systems.

7. In order to clarify some of the arguments we will develop, it is convenient to keep in mind that private pension funds are individual mechanisms of provision for old age. Decisions, beyond the advice that may be given through the market, exclusively correspond to the insured themselves. The insured are the ones who determine the level of consumption they are going to maintain during their lives, the ones who establish the part of the income they wish to save and to consume, who decide to adjust their contributions or their future spending in the face of the non-estimated changes which may occur. On the contrary, in present public systems based on the PAYGO system, all decisions affecting pensions are made through a political process. By means of this process, it is decided on the total amount of income which will be transferred from working population to retired population as well as the distribution of such income among different individuals of different generations and, of course, the level of solidarity the society wants to have with their retired population.

8. Social contributions actually tax a total wage bill, which may have changed due both to price fluctuations and/or productivity. Therefore, the system could generate an automatic update of pensions not only in relation to prices but also in relation to changes in productivity.

9. Impavido and Tower (2009) provide data about the losses produced by pension funds as a result of the crisis. The effects these losses have had on welfare of retired population, as well as on decisions made on extending working life in those countries where individual saving plays a more important role, are still to be assessed.

10. A related option would be to transfer revenues from the general tax system to the social security.

11. The concept of Keynesian full employment is also conceptually different from the neoclassical concept of full employment. Thus, for neoclassical economics full employment is identified with that situation where the job market is cleared, a result obtained when for a real salary (of equilibrium), supplied and demanded job quantities are equivalent. This equality means that marginal productivity of work and marginal relationship of substitution between work and leisure are the same as equilibrium real wage, so unemployment would have a voluntary nature. In this scenario, the level of full employment can be any figure of employment. On the contrary, from a Keynesian perspective, full employment is identified with that situation where, for the prevailing market wage, all those workers who are willing to work do have a job. This implies that unemployment has now an involuntary nature and the level of employment can be measured as a particular figure (usually a percentage of the job supply deducting that part of unemployment which has a frictional nature).

12. In fact, the only institution necessary and sufficient to guarantee an equilibrium result is the market, always under that assumption that it works under the principles of perfect competition.
13. Blanchard and Cottarelli (2010), Blanchard, Dell'Ariccia and Mauro (2010) or Poole (2010), among others, are a good example of these approaches.

References

Aaron, H.J. (1966) 'The Social Insurance Paradox', *Canadian Journal of Economics and Political Science*, 32, pp. 371–4.

Altuzarra, A., Ferreiro, J. and Serrano, F. (2010) 'The Role of Global Imbalances as a Cause of the Current Crisis', *Journal of Innovation Economics*, 6, pp. 25–48.

Ando, A. and Modigliani, F. (1963) 'The "Life Cycle" Hypothesis of Saving: Aggregate Implications and Tests', *American Economic Review*, 53(1), part 1, pp. 55–84.

Arestis, P., Baltar, C.T. and Cavalcante, A. (2009) 'Current Financial Crisis: The End of Financial Liberalisation?', *Ekonomiaz*, 72, pp. 12–31

Barr, N. (2000) 'Reforming Pensions: Myths, Truths and Policy Choices', *IMF Working Paper*, No. 00/139.

Bank for International Settlements Group of Ten (1998) *The Macroeconomic and Financial Implications of Ageing Populations*. Basel: Bank for International Settlements.

Blake, D. (2000) 'Does It Matter What Type of Pension Scheme You Have?', *The Economic Journal*, 110, pp. 46–81.

Blanchard, O. and Cottarelli, C. (2010) 'Ten Commandments for Fiscal Adjustment in Advanced Economies', *VoxEU.org*, 28 June.

Blanchard, O., Dell'Ariccia, G. and Mauro, P. (2010) 'Rethinking Macroeconomic Policy', *IMF Staff Position Note*, SPN/10/03.

Brooks, R.J. (2002) 'Asset-market Effects of the Baby Boom and Social Security Reform', *American Economic Review*, 92(2), pp. 402–6.

Cessarato, S. (2002) 'The Economics of Pensions: A Non-conventional Approach', *Review of Political Economy*, 14(2), pp. 149–77.

Cessarato, S. (2006) 'Transition to Fully Funded Pension Schemes: A Non-orthodox Criticism', *Cambridge Journal of Economics*, 30(1), pp. 33–48.

Danzinger, S., Haveman, R.H. and Plotnick, R. (1981) 'How Income Transfer Programs Affect Work, Savings, and the Income Distribution: A Critical Review', *Journal of Economic Literature*, 19, pp. 975–1028.

Davidson, P. (1991) 'Is Probability Theory Relevant for Uncertainty? A Post Keynesian Perspective', *Journal of Economics Perspectives*, 1, pp. 129–43.

Davidson, P. (2002) *Financial Markets, Money and the Real World*. Cheltenham: Edward Elgar.

Davidson, P. (2007) 'Strong Uncertainty and How to Cope With It to Improve Action and Capacity', in J. McCombie and C. Rodriguez Gonzalez (eds), *Issues in Finance and Monetary Policy*. Basingstoke: Palgrave Macmillan, pp. 8–27.

Engelhardt, G.V. and Gruber, J. (2004) 'Social Security and the Evolution of Elderly Poverty', *NBER Working Paper*, No. 10466.

Esteban, M., Ferreiro, J. and Serrano, F (2010) 'Financial Liberalization, Growth and Financial Crisis', in G. Fontana, J. McCombie and M. Sawyer (eds), *Macroeconomics, Finance and Money: Essays in Honour of Philip Arestis.* Basingstoke: Palgrave Macmillan, pp. 282–94.

European Commission, Directorate-General for Economic and Financial Affairs (2009) 'The 2009 Ageing Report: Economic and Budgetary Projections for the EU-27 Member States (2008–2060). Joint Report Prepared by the European Commission (DG ECFIN) and the Economic Policy Committee (AWG)', *European Economy*, 2/2009, Luxembourg: European Communities.

Feldstein, M. (1974) 'Social Security, Induced Retirement and Aggregate Capital Accumulation', *Journal of Political Economy*, 82(5), pp. 902–26.

Feldstein, M. (1976) 'Social Security and Saving: The Extended Life Cycle Theory', *American Economic Review*, 66(2), pp. 77–86.

Feldstein, M. (1997) 'Transition to a Fully Funded Pension System: Five Economic Issues', *NBER Working Paper Series*, No. 6149.

Ferreiro, J. and Serrano, F. (2007) 'New Institutions for a New Economic Policy', in E. Hein and A. Truger (eds), *Money, Distribution and Economic Policy. Alternatives to Orthodoxy.* Cheltenham: Edward Elgar, pp. 141–57.

Ferreiro, J. and Serrano, F. (2008) 'Institutions, Welfare State and Full Employment', in P. Arestis and J. McCombie (eds), *Missing Links in the Unemployment Relationship.* Basingstoke: Palgrave Macmillan, pp. 182–99.

Ferreiro, J. and Serrano, F. (2009) 'Institutions, Expectations and Aggregate Demand', in G. Fontana and M. Setterfield (eds), *Macroeconomic Theory and Macroeconomic Pedagogy.* Basingstoke: Palgrave Macmillan, Hampshire, pp. 309–22.

Freeman, R.B. (2010) 'It's Financialization!', *International Labour Review*, 149(2), pp. 163–83.

Graham, J.W. (1987) 'International Differences in Saving Rates and the Life Cycle Hypothesis', *European Economic Review*, 31, pp. 1509–29.

Impavido, G. and Tower, I. (2009) 'How the Financial Crisis Affects Pensions and Insurance and Why the Impacts Matter', *IMF Working Paper*, WP/09/151.

Jimenez, A. (1998) 'La reforma de los sistemas públicos de pensiones en América Latina', *Ekonomiaz*, 42, pp. 132–45.

Kessler, D., Masson, A. and Strauss-Kahn, D. (1981) 'Social Security and Saving: A Tentative Survey', *The Geneva Risk and Insurance Review*, 18, pp. 3–50.

Keynes, J.M. (1936) *The General Theory on Employment, Interest and Money.* Cambridge: Macmillan Cambridge University Press, for Royal Economic Society.

Kotlikoff, L.J. (1979) 'Testing the Theory of Social Security and Life Cycle Accumulation', *American Economic Review*, 69, pp. 233–53.

Kregel, J. (1976) 'Economic Methodology in the Face of Uncertainty: The Modelling Methods of Keynes and the Post-Keynesians', *The Economic Journal*, 86p. 209–25.

Lapavitsas, C. (2009) 'Financialisation, or the Search for Profits in the Sphere of Circulation', *Ekonomiaz*, 72, pp. 98–117.

McHale, J. (1999) 'The Risk of Social Security Benefit Rule Changes: Some International Evidence', *NBER Working Paper Series*, No. 7031.

McMorrow, K. and Roeger, W. (2002) 'EU Pension Reform. An Overview of the Debate and an Empirical Assessment of the Main Policy Reform Options', *Economic Papers*, 162. Brussels: Directorate General for Economic and Financial Affairs, European Commission.

Muth, J.F. (1961) 'Rational Expectations and the Theory of Price Movements', *Econometrica*, 29, pp. 315–35.

Palley, T.I. (2009) 'The Macroeconomics of Financialization: A Stages of Development Approach', *Ekonomiaz*, 72, pp. 34–51.

Poole, W. (2010) 'Principles for Reform', *Finance and Development*, 47(2), pp. 28–9.

Razin, A. and Sadka, E. (1999) 'Migration and Pension with International Capital Mobility', *Journal of Public Economics*, 74, pp. 141–50.

Robinson, J. (1962) *Essays in the Theory of Economic Growth*. London: St Martin's Press.

Sainsbury, D. and Morissens, A. (2002) 'Poverty in Europe in the Mid-1990s: The Effectiveness of Means-tested Benefits', *Journal of European Social Policy*, 12(4), pp. 307–27.

Samuelson, P.A. (1958) 'An Exact Consumption-loan Model of Interest with or without the Social Contrivance of Money', *Journal of Political Economy*, 56, pp. 476–82.

Sawyer, M. (2003) 'An Economic Evaluation of Alternative Arrangements for Retirement Pensions', mimeo. Available at http://www.epoc.uni-bremen.de/pdf/Vienna_Sawyer_2003.PDF.

Serrano, F., Eguía, B. and Ferreiro, J. (2011) 'Can Immigration Solve the Future Financial Problems from Ageing in Public Pension Systems?', *International Labour Review*, forthcoming.

Serrano, F. and Ferreiro, F. (2007) 'Does an Ageing Population Justify a Radical Reform of Public Pension Systems in the European Union', in J. McCombie, and C. Rodriguez (eds), *The European Union. Current Problems and Prospects*. Basingstoke: Palgrave Macmillan, pp. 111–34.

Shiller, R.J. (2005) 'The Life-cycle Personal Accounts Proposal for Social Security: An Evaluation', *NBER Working Paper Series*, 11300.

Sinn, H.W. (1997) 'The Value of Children and Immigrants in a Pay-as-you-go Pension System: A Proposal for a Partial Transition to a Funded System', *NBER Working Paper Series*, No. 6229.

Tákats, E. (2010) 'Ageing and Asset Prices', *BIS Working Papers*, No. 318.

Toporowski, J. (2000) *The End of Finance: Capital Market Inflation, Financial Derivatives and Pensions Fund Capitalism*. London: Routledge.

Yueh, L. (2010) 'A Stronger China', *Finance and Development*, 47(2), pp. 8–11.

6
Finance-dominated Capitalism in Crisis – The Case for a Keynesian New Deal at the European and the Global Level*

Eckhard Hein
Berlin School of Economics and Law and Institute for International Political Economy (IPE) Berlin, Germany

Achim Truger
Macroeconomic Policy Institute (IMK) at Hans Boeckler Foundation, Duesseldorf, Germany

Abstract

We analyse the long-run imbalances of finance-dominated capitalism underlying the present crisis, which began in 2007, with a focus on developments in the USA, on the one hand, and in Germany and the Euro area, on the other hand. We argue that beyond inefficient regulation of the financial sector, the severity of the present crisis has been caused principally by increasing inequalities of income distribution and rising imbalances in the world economy as well as in the European economy associated with finance-dominated capitalism. From this it follows that in the near and not so near future, the USA will no longer be able to act as the driving force for world demand. In order to avoid a period of deflationary stagnation in major parts of the world economy and a disintegration of the Euro area, we finally propose the policy package of a Keynesian

*Paper presented at the 7th International Conference 'Developments in Economic Theory and Policy', Bilbao, Spain, 1–2 July 2010. This paper extends our earlier analysis (Hein, Truger 2010a), which was presented at the conference 'The New Economics as "Mainstream" Economics', Murray Edwards College, Cambridge, UK, 28–29 January 2010, by including the intra-European imbalances which are at the roots of the 2010 euro crisis. We would like to thank the participants in both conferences for helpful comments and Petra Dünhaupt and Matthias Mundt for the assistance in collecting data and preparing some of the figures.

New Deal at the global and at the European level which should consist of: (i) the re-regulation of the financial sector; (ii) the re-orientation of macroeconomic policies along (Post-)Keynesian lines; and (iii) the re-construction of international macroeconomic policy coordination, in particular in the Euro area, and a new world financial order.

Keywords: Finance-dominated capitalism, financial crisis, macroeconomic policies, Keynesian New Deal

JEL code: E32, E44, E61, E63, E65

1   Introduction

The world economy is still struggling with its most severe crisis since the Great Depression of the late 1920/early 1930s. On the one hand, the present crisis is a financial crisis which started with the collapse of the subprime mortgage market in the USA in summer 2007, which then gained momentum with the breakdown of Lehman Brothers in September 2008 and which reached another climax with the euro crisis in early/mid-2010. Under the conditions of deregulated and liberalised international financial markets the financial crisis has spread rapidly across the world. On the other hand, the present crisis is a real crisis, which started well before the financial crisis with an economic downswing in the USA. The financial crisis and the real crisis have reinforced each other, and the world economy has been hit by a decline in real GDP in 2009 – something not seen for generations. Major regions in the world are only slowly recovering from this decline, in particular the Euro area, the UK and Japan.[1]

A complete breakdown of the world economy could be halted by monetary policy interventions providing liquidity on a massive scale to the money market, thus preventing a meltdown of the financial sector, and, in particular, by massive fiscal expenditure programmes. We will argue, however, that the present global crisis, with serious future deflationary risks, marks a structural break in the long-run development since the early 1980s. This development has been dominated by the neoliberal model of deregulated labour markets, reduction of government intervention and social policies, redistribution of income from (lower) wages to profits and high management salaries, and deregulated international financial markets. In the USA and the UK this model, in combination with expansive monetary and partly fiscal policies, has been able to generate sustained periods of high growth rates and low unemployment, and these economies performed far better than the Euro area and, in particular, Germany as the largest Euro area economy.[2] The neoliberal model has also been consistent with a long period of sustained growth of the world economy, with the USA as the demand locomotive until recently. However, as the crisis has made clear, this model has been built on considerable imbalances, at national, European and global levels.

In Section 2 of this paper we will analyse the long-run imbalances associated with the neoliberal model of finance-dominated capitalism underlying the present crisis. We will focus on developments in the USA, Germany and the Euro area. As a result of this analysis we argue that, in both the short and the long run, the USA will no longer be able to act as the driver of world demand and that the present policy model pursued in the Euro area will not allow Europe to replace the USA. On the contrary, the Euro area itself will be threatened by serious risks of stagnation and deflation. This has major implications for economic policies far beyond immediate responses to the crisis, in particular for those countries which have benefitted from soaring USA demand in the past – that is, the countries with huge current account surpluses, in particular China, Japan and Germany. Against this background, Section 3 will provide a brief review of the short-run economic policy reactions towards the crisis, and will outline some perspectives for future development. In Section 4 the long-run requirements for economic policies preventing sustained deflationary depression in major parts of the world, in particular in the Euro area, will be described, and the components of a Keynesian New Deal for Europe and the world will be outlined. We will argue that such a Keynesian New Deal will have to tackle the three main sources of the present crisis: inefficient regulation of financial markets, increasing inequalities in income distribution, and imbalances in the current accounts at the European and the global scale. Section 5 will summarise and conclude.

2   Long-run inequalities and imbalances of finance-dominated capitalism and the present crisis

The present crisis is often seen as a consequence of liberalised financial markets, wrong incentives, personal greed, fraud, naïve beliefs, and herding behaviour by economic actors, which have given rise to housing price bubbles, and their subsequent bursting.[3] It is certainly true that, on the one hand, inefficient regulation of financial markets is an important source of the present crisis. But on the other hand, there are at least two further sources which explain the severity of the present crisis: increasing inequalities in income distribution and imbalances in the current accounts, both associated with finance-dominated capitalism.[4]

We will focus on these causes, which have started to develop in the USA, where increasing financial market orientation began in the early 1980s, and which have fed worldwide imbalances since then.[5] Although the term 'financialisation' – often used in this context – has many facets,[6] from a macroeconomic perspective we prefer to see financial market orientation and 'financialisation' through the lenses of the effects on income distribution, consumption and investment and thus on aggregated demand, capital accumulation and growth (Hein 2010a, 2010b; Hein and van Treeck 2010). From this perspective, we will briefly sketch the long-run development up to the present crisis in the USA, on the one hand, and in Germany and the Euro area, on the other.[7] The USA and Germany can be seen as two main representatives of the global current account imbalances, the USA being the primary deficit country and Germany – together with China, Japan and the oil-producing countries – being one of the main surplus countries.[8] The particular role of Germany is also a major cause for the imbalances in the Euro area, the present euro crisis and the threat of deflationary stagnation in Europe and disintegration of the Euro area, as will be shown below. As can be seen in Figure 6.1, the current account imbalances at the global level have exploded, in particular, since the early 2000s when the recovery from the New Economy crisis began.

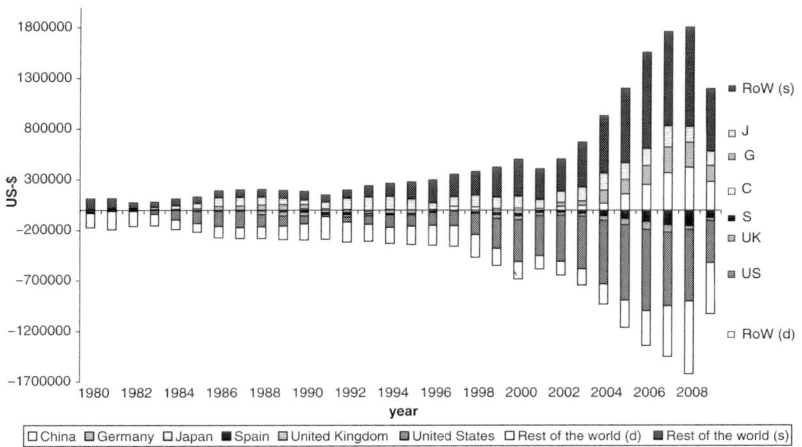

Figure 6.1   Current account balances, 1980–2009 (in millions US$)
Source: IMF World Economic Outlook Database, authors' calculations.

2.1 'Financialisation' and the unstable debt-led consumption boom in the USA

Increasing financial market orientation in the USA since the early 1980s has been associated with considerable redistribution. On the one hand, high unemployment, anti-labour policies, increasing shareholder value orientation of management, induced by stock-market-oriented remuneration schemes and a market for corporate control – favouring management strategies of 'downsize and distribute' in order to keep stock prices high instead of Fordist/Golden Age type 'retain and invest' strategies (Lazonick and O'Sullivan 2000) – have increased pressure on workers' and trade unions' wage demands and have contributed to the tendency of the wage share to fall, which had already started in the early 1970s (Figure 6.2).[9] On the other hand, inequality in personal income distribution has increased remarkably to a level not seen since the 1920s, mainly due to increases in top-management salaries (Piketty and Saez 2003, 2006) (Figure 6.3).

Against the background of these trends in redistribution, real investment in the business sector remained weak, with the exception of the

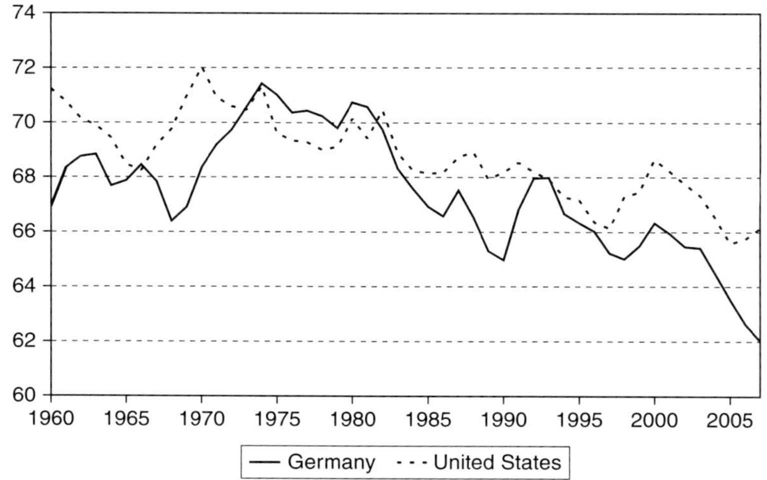

Figure 6.2 Labour income share in per cent of GDP at factor costs in the USA and Germany, 1960–2007
Source: AMECO Database of European Commission.

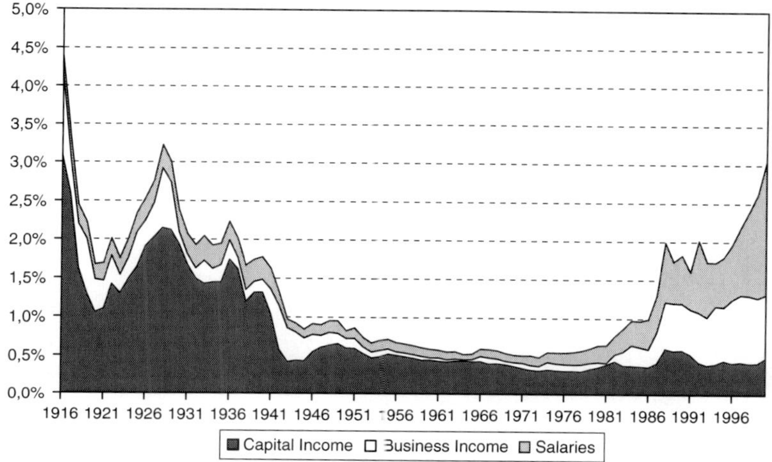

Figure 6.3   The top 0.01 per cent income share and composition in the USA, 1916–2000
Source: Data from Piketty and Saez (2006), provided on Emmanuel Saez's website (http://elsa.berkeley.edu/~saez/).

New Economy boom in the second half of the 1990s. Since the early 1980s, a decoupling of the development of investment and profits can be observed, accompanied by a dynamic increase in share prices until the New Economy bubble burst in 2000 (Figure 6.4). Two features of 'financialisation' have contributed to the weak tendency of real investment: First, the rising dominance of shareholders vis-à-vis management changed the preferences of the corporation as a whole: short-term maximisation of shareholder value via the distribution of profits and share buybacks was favoured, compared to real investment projects which promised only long-term gains ('preference channel'). Second, increasing dividend payouts and share buybacks in order to keep share prices high – and to prevent hostile takeovers – reduced internal means of finance for real investment projects ('internal means of finance channel').[10]

A macroeconomic constellation of 'profits without investment' (Cordonnier 2006), as in the USA since the early 1980s, however, can only arise if weak investment is compensated for by high consumption out of profits or wages, by a high public budget deficit, or by a high current account surplus (Kalecki 1954: 45–52). In the USA, rising profits in the face of weak investment were generated by soaring private consumption. Since the early 1980s relatively high GDP growth, by international standards, was driven mainly by private consumption expenditure.

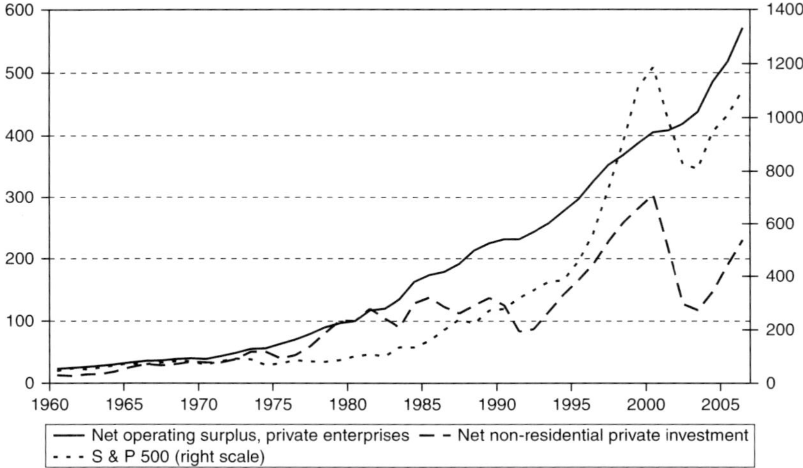

Figure 6.4   Investment, profits and share prices, USA, 1960–2006 (1980 = 100)
Source: Data from van Treeck (2009a), provided by the author.

The growth contribution of private investment diminished – with the exception of the New Economy boom – and the growth contribution of net exports has been negative since the mid-1990s (van Treeck 2009a). In recessions, government deficits up to 6 per cent of GDP stabilised GDP growth and hence profits (Hein and Truger 2007a).

In the face of weak real wage growth, dynamic consumption demand meant a decreasing propensity to save out of current income, and increasing indebtedness of major parts of the private household sector (Figure 6.5).[11] The stock market boom in the second half of the 1990s, followed by the house price boom until the recent crisis, (seemingly) generated collateral against which households could borrow.[12] Liberalised credit standards and the trend towards securitisation ('originate and distribute') decreased creditworthiness standards and allowed for increasing household debt. The boom of property-based and credit-financed consumption was driven by rich households first, but then low-income households followed this pattern, too (Joint Center for Housing Studies 2006). When housing prices stopped rising in the face of increasing interest rates, the subprime mortgage market – covering mortgages to low income households – triggered the present crisis.

Taken together, below the surface of a seemingly robust and dynamic development in the USA since the early 1980s, major imbalances have been generated, which are responsible for the severity of the present

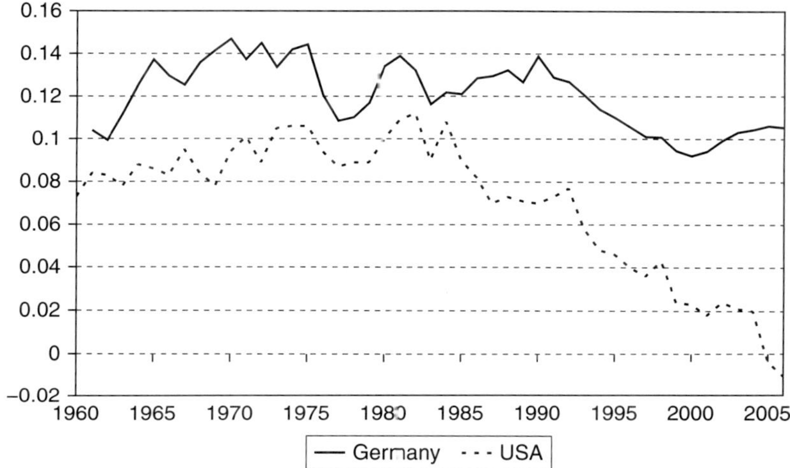

Figure 6.5 Savings rate of private households in Germany and the USA, 1960–2006
Source: OECD Economic Outlook Database; NIPA; authors' calculations.

crisis spreading across the world. Figure 6.6 shows these USA imbalances using sectoral financial balances as a share of nominal GDP, which, by definition, have to sum up to zero. In particular, with weak private investment after the collapse of the New Economy boom, the private sector balance nonetheless turned negative due to the debt-financed consumption boom. The financial balance of the public sector also became negative because of countercyclical fiscal policies. Consequently, the balance of the rest of the world had to be positive: High and rising current account deficits meant increasing capital imports financing the USA-consumption boom and government deficits.

Such a constellation is highly fragile, because domestically it has to rely on rising property prices in order to allow for rising indebtedness fuelling steady increases in consumption demand under the conditions of a falling labour income share and rising inequality in household incomes. Regarding the relationship with the rest of the world, a sharp depreciation of the US dollar, which would have been required in order to improve the international price competitiveness of USA producers and thus the current account, had to be prevented in order to guarantee steady capital imports without necessitate the raising of domestic interest rates, which would in turn have increased the possibility of a collapse of the domestic demand boom. When such a constellation erodes – as in the aftermath of the subprime mortgage crisis and the following downswing – this affects not only the USA, but also the rest of the world. In particular, the current

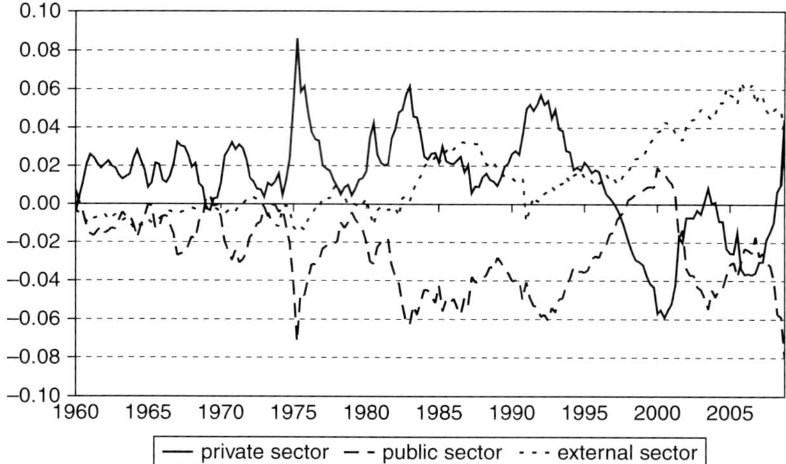

Figure 6.6   Financial balances as a share of nominal GDP, USA, 1960–2008
Source: NIPA, tables 5.1, 1.1.5; authors' calculations.

account surplus countries have to suffer twofold. On the one hand, capital exports into highly speculative USA markets associated with the current account surpluses of some countries are devalued by the financial crisis, and therefore the financial crisis quickly infects these surplus countries. On the other hand, the markets for exports collapse and current account surplus countries are thus infected by the real crisis, too.[13]

2.2   Dysfunctional mercantilism in Germany – a counterpart to the USA development and a main contribution to the euro crisis

2.2.1   *Dysfunctional mercantilism as a counterpart to the USA development*

Against the background of a falling labour income share since the early 1980s (Figure 6.2) and increasing inequality in household income distribution during the 1990s (Bach, Corneo and Steiner 2009; OECD 2008), economic development in Germany has also been dominated by a decoupling of profits and private investment in capital stock since the early 1980s, which was only interrupted by the unification boom in the first half of the 1990s (Figure 6.7). For the development since the mid-1990s this can also be attributed to increasing financial market orientation. Major steps towards the liberalisation and deregulation of financial markets took effect in this period: in 1991 the abolition of the stock exchange tax, in 1998 the legalisation of share buybacks, in 2002 the abolition of capital gains taxes for corporations, and in 2004 the legalisation of hedge funds.

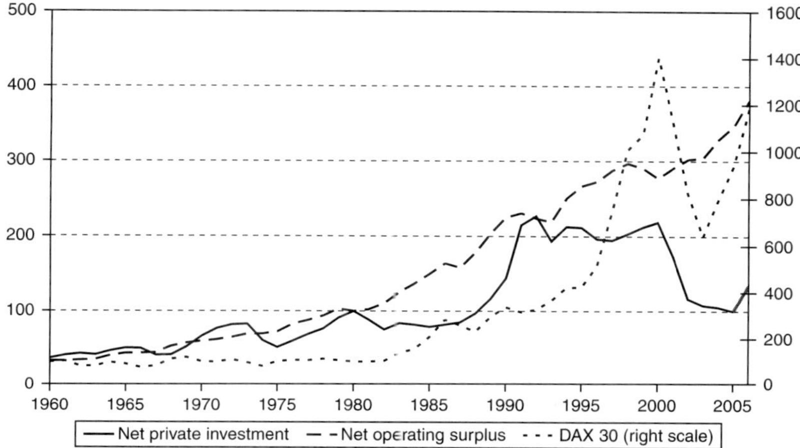

Figure 6.7   Investment, profits and share prices, Germany, 1960–2006 (1980 = 100)
Source: Data from van Treeck (2009a), provided by the author.

Furthermore, as we have analysed elsewhere in more detail, restrictive macroeconomic policies and weak domestic demand have contributed significantly to weak investment, and hence to the weak growth and employment performance in Germany since the middle of the 1990s, and in particular after the 2000/01 recession (Hein and Truger 2005a, 2007a, 2009). Increasing uncertainty, caused by policies of 'structural reforms' and deregulation in the labour market (Agenda 2010 and Hartz-laws), subsidies for capital-based private pension schemes ('Riester'- and 'Rürup'-pensions), and redistribution at the expense of (low) labour income and in favour of profits and high-income receivers associated with nominal wage moderation, have led to an increase in the propensity to save of private households since 2001, contributing to weak consumption demand (Figure 6.5). Pressures on trade unions caused moderate wage increases and contributed to inflation rates below the Euro area average, leading to above-average real interest rates. This made Germany particularly vulnerable to restrictive monetary policies by the European Central Bank (ECB). And the attempts of fiscal policies to balance the budget, by means of expenditure cuts in periods of weak private demand, have reinforced weak domestic demand without reaching the consolidation target.

As the only driving force of mediocre growth there remained high and increasing export surpluses. The degree of openness of the German economy increased significantly: In 1995 the ratio of nominal exports to nominal GDP was 24 per cent, but it increased to 47 per cent in 2008 (European Commission 2010). Current account surpluses quickly reached more than 4 per cent in the years after the recession of 2000/01, peaking at 7.9 per cent of GDP in 2007. The reasons for rising net exports were extreme wage moderation, on the one hand, which increased the price competitiveness of German producers in international markets, and low domestic demand making imports fall short of rising exports, on the other hand.

As can be seen from the sectoral financial balances – each in relation to nominal GDP – in Figure 6.8, Germany has been a counterpart to the USA development, in particular since the 2000/01 recession. Weak investment was not compensated by strong private consumption, and the private financial balance was thus strongly positive. High and rising German current account surpluses, and hence a negative financial balance of the rest of the world, acted as a stabiliser for weak domestic economic activity and profits. The government's financial balance has remained negative since the early 1990s. One major difference from the USA, however, was that government deficits were not the result of active and expansive fiscal policies, but the macroeconomic result of restrictive fiscal policies in a period of slow growth (Hein and Truger 2009).

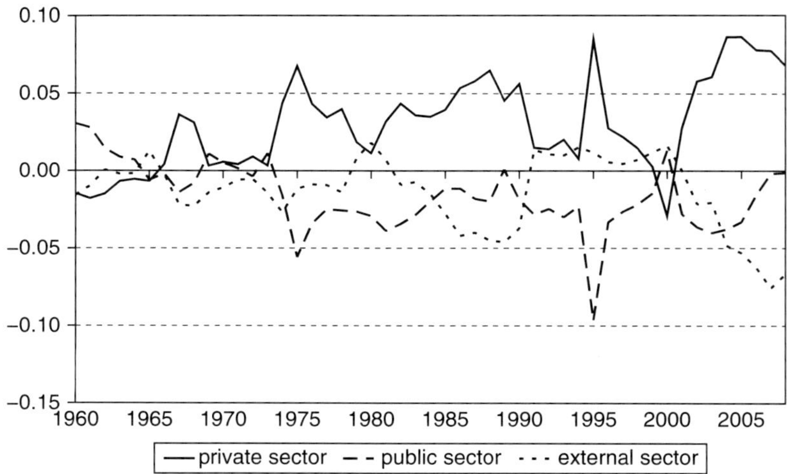

Figure 6.8　Financial balances as a share of nominal GDP, Germany, 1960–2008
Source: National Accounts of the German Statistical Office; authors' calculations.

Whereas the dynamic consumption-driven model of the USA had to rely on the willingness and the ability of private households to go into debt (and of the rest of the world to supply credit), the stagnating German neo-mercantilist model had to rely on the willingness and the ability of the rest of the world to go into debt. Contrary to public opinion before the crisis, this German model has been as fragile as the USA model. On the one hand, the moderate growth rates were dependent on the dynamic growth of export markets, and hence on the expansion of the world economy. On the other hand, increasing capital exports to the more dynamic economies carried the risk of contagion in the case of a financial crisis in these markets. And both channels became effective during the present crisis.

2.2.2 Dysfunctional mercantilism in Germany as a main contribution to the euro crisis

Not only does the German neo-mercantilist low-growth regime explain part of the global imbalances. It is also, to a large extent, responsible for the perhaps even more serious economic imbalances within the Euro area that have recently become apparent in the euro crisis. This crisis began with the public debt problems in Greece in early 2010 and the dramatic emergency measures taken in order to prevent a Greek government default – and possibly defaults of other governments (Portugal, Spain, Ireland and Italy?) as well, and therefore an end to the euro as a currency.

Mainstream economics and economic policy debates see the high and rising government debts, and the failure of the Stability and Growth Pact (SGP) to contain government deficits and debt, as the main reasons for the crisis and therefore the most important problems to be tackled in the Euro area. From that point of view the main threat for the euro is caused by governments which have run irresponsibly high deficits leading public finances to the brink of default. However, even a casual look at the data raises many doubts about this point of view: For example, both Ireland and Spain looked perfectly well before the crisis as they seemed to follow the SGP in an almost ideal manner. Ireland ran a budget surplus of 3 per cent of GDP in 2006 and Spain had a surplus of 1.9 per cent in 2007. In 2007 gross government debt in relation to GDP was only 25 per cent in Ireland and 36 per cent in Spain. Therefore, from the perspective of the SGP nobody would have suspected any risk of government default in these countries. The fact that nevertheless they came into trouble is thus due to other imbalances: Very similar to the USA, in both Spain and Ireland, it was the private sector which

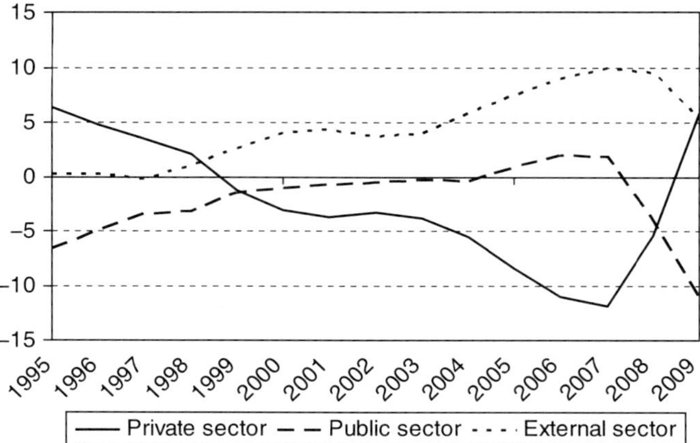

Figure 6.9   Financial balances as a share of nominal GDP, Spain, 1995–2009
Source: AMECO Database of European Commission, authors' calculations.

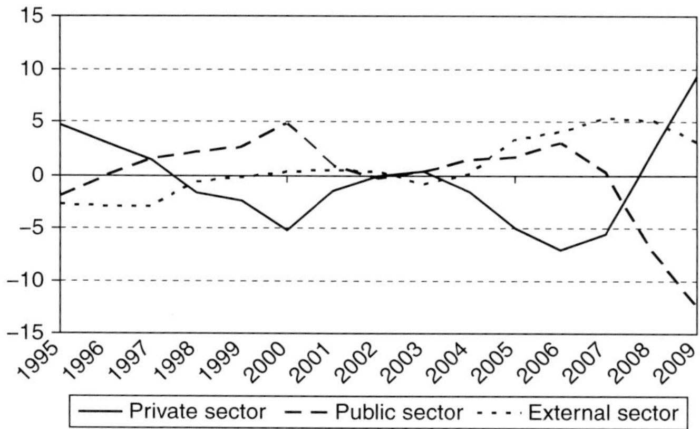

Figure 6.10   Financial balances as a share of nominal GDP, Ireland, 1995–2009
Source: AMECO Database of European Commission, authors' calculations.

had gone deeply into debt before the crisis unfolded, partly as a consequence of a house price bubble.

Figures 6.9 and 6.10 show the financial balances of the private sector, the public sector and the external sector for Spain and Ireland respectively. Although the figures are more striking for Spain, in both countries huge private sector deficits (more than 5 per cent of GDP in Ireland for some years and more than 10 per cent of GDP in Spain) were associated with surpluses in the government balance and – to a much larger extent – with current account deficits against the rest of the world. When the bubble growth came to a sudden end as the result of the crisis, the private sector balance quickly turned into surpluses and governments stabilising the economy had to accept a dramatic rise in government deficits. Therefore, the 'unsustainable' government deficit turns out to be a consequence of unsustainable private and external sector balances in the first place.

In fact, if one takes a look at two other, of the – disrespectfully – so-called 'PIIGS countries', it turns out that the picture is very similar for them. In Portugal and Greece (Figures 6.11 and 6.12), both the private sector and the government sector had run continuous deficits since the start of the euro. Those deficits had to be financed by capital inflows and hence current account deficits of about 10 per cent of GDP in the case of Portugal and even about 12 per cent of GDP in the case of Greece before the crisis. After the crisis, in both countries the government stepped in to prevent the economy from collapsing when the private sector reduced deficits or turned into surplus again, leading to rising public deficits and the 'problems of government debt' currently in the focus of public attention.[14]

Therefore, it seems that the current euro crisis can better be interpreted as the consequence of preceding private debt and current account imbalances and not as a result of excessive public deficits. In the four countries outlined above, the private sectors tended to spend beyond their means. This was associated with government surpluses (Ireland,

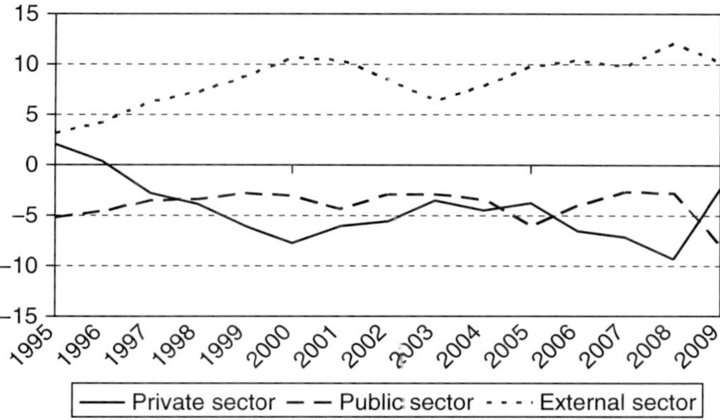

Figure 6.11   Financial balances as a share of nominal GDP, Portugal, 1995–2009
Source: AMECO Database of European Commission, authors' calculations.

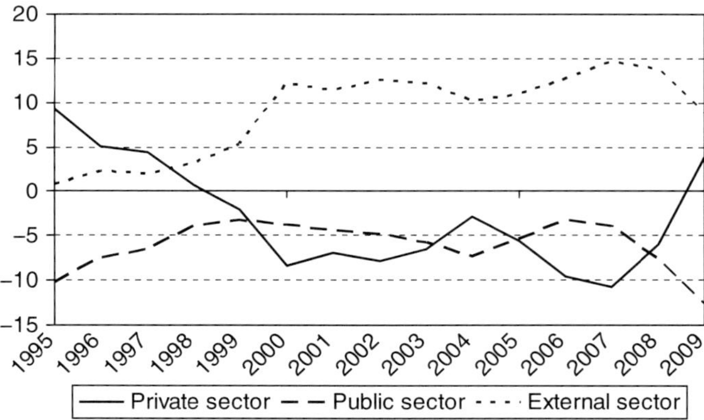

Figure 6.12   Financial balances as a share of nominal GDP, Greece, 1995–2009
Source: AMECO Database of European Commission, authors' calculations.

Spain) or amplified by government deficits (Portugal, Greece), which led to very high and unsustainable current account deficits in the four countries. Obviously, there must be a counterpart for these developments. And in fact, since the current account of the Euro area as a whole has been roughly balanced, these counterparts are to be found in the Euro area: There are other countries in which the private sector tends to spend much less than it earns. If in such cases the government is not willing to run a correspondingly high deficit (or is prevented from doing so by the SGP), then this will correspond with a deficit of the foreign sector, that is, a current account surplus – taking GDP as given. Within the Euro area there are at least four countries for which such characteristics hold: Germany, the Netherlands, Austria, and Belgium, with Germany as the largest Euro area country being the most important one.

The economic imbalances in the Euro area as expressed by the current account developments can be summarised with the help of Figure 6.13. As can be seen, the imbalances have increased almost continuously since the start of the euro in 1999, peaking in 2007 – just before the crisis. For most of the countries (with the notable exception of Ireland) the current account is dominated by the balance of goods and services, that is, the net exports of goods and services. As can be seen from Table 6.1, with the exception of Ireland, the current account deficit countries in trouble have had negative growth contributions of their net exports, whereas the surplus countries on average from 1999 to 2007 had positive growth contributions of net exports. Since the development of the balance of goods and services (in real terms) depends mainly on two factors – the growth

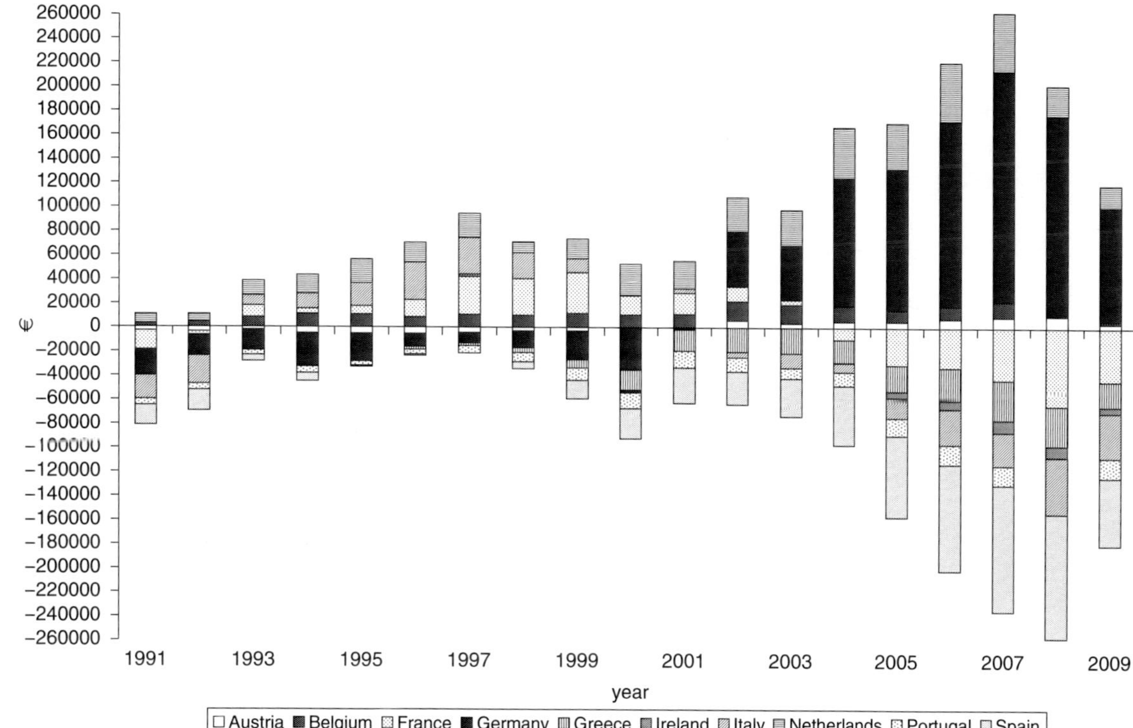

Figure 6.13 Current account in millions ECU/euro, selected Euro area countries, 1991–2009
Source: AMECO Database of European Commission, authors' calculations.

of domestic demand (relative to foreign demand) and on international price competitiveness (relative to trading partners) – we next take a look at indicators of these factors.

As a proxy for the first factor we look at the growth contributions of real domestic demand on average over the period from 1999 to 2007 and compare it to the average for the old Euro area (EU-12) (Table 6.1). Concerning the current account surplus countries, in Germany the GDP growth contribution of domestic demand was considerably below the average of the EU-12. In addition, Austria had a well below EU-12 average growth contribution to domestic demand, and in Belgium and the Netherlands it was also slightly below the EU-12 average. In relation to the second group, the troubled deficit countries, the case is very clear for Ireland, Spain and Greece, where the growth contribution of domestic demand greatly exceeded the EU-12 average. Portugal and Italy, however, were slightly below EU-12 average and over the whole period even a little bit below Belgium and the Netherlands.

In respect of the second indicator, international competitiveness, we use the development of nominal unit labour costs since the start of the Euro area in 1999 until 2007 (Table 6.1). Obviously, from the surplus countries Germany is the country with the slowest unit labour cost growth; between 1999 and 2007 unit labour costs almost stagnated. Austria used to follow the German example until 2004, since then its unit labour cost growth has accelerated a little, but it is still well below the Euro area average. Belgian unit labour costs grew almost perfectly in line with the EU-12 average, whereas in the Netherlands it was faster, although this is almost entirely due to a rather steep increase in the first years of the euro; since 2003 there has been a remarkable deceleration. Taking a look at the current account deficit countries, the picture is very clear for all of them: Their unit labour cost growth is much faster than that of the EU-12 average. The relative inflation rates mostly reflect the differences in unit labour cost growth: the current account surplus countries mostly have inflation rates below EU-12 average, whereas in the current account deficit countries inflation exceeds EU-12 average.[15]

On the basis of our analysis so far, we can draw the following conclusions: The neo-mercantilist macroeconomic policy regime followed by the largest Euro area country, Germany, can be identified as a major reason for the currently observed (current account) imbalances within the Euro area underlying the euro crisis. Germany's consistently slow domestic growth as well as its ever rising international competitiveness, due to extremely moderate wage developments, have both been a drag for many other Euro area economies, driving their balance of goods and services, and ultimately

Table 6.1 Key macroeconomic indicators for imbalances, selected Euro area countries, average values, 1999–2007

	Austria	Belgium	Germany	Netherlands	EU-12	Greece	Ireland	Italy	Portugal	Spain
GDP, average annual growth, in per cent	2.4	2.3	1.5	2.5	2.2	4.1	6.6	1.5	1.7	3.7
Domestic demand, average annual contribution to GDP growth, in percentage points	1.5	1.9	0.6	1.9	2.1	4.6	5.2	1.6	1.8	4.8
Balance of goods and services, average annual contribution to GDP growth, in percentage points	0.8	0.4	0.9	0.6	0.1	−0.5	1.5	−0.2	−0.1	−1.0
Nominal unit labour costs, average annual growth, in per cent	0.6	1.6	0.2	2.2	1.6	2.8	3.1	2.4	2.8	3.0
HICP, average annual growth, in per cent.	1.7	2.0	1.6	2.4	2.1	3.1	3.4	2.3	2.9	4.2
Current account balance, average, in per cent of GDP	1.4	4.4	2.9	6.8	0.4	−11.4	−1.5	−0.6	−9.2	−5.7
Balance of goods and services, average, in per cent of GDP	3.6	4.3	3.9	6.7	1.6	−11.2	13.7	0.6	−8.7	−3.8

Source: AMECO Database of European Commission, authors' calculations.

also their current accounts, into deficit. The situation has been worsened by the fact that Germany had some followers within the EU-12, certainly Austria and, to a lesser extent, the Netherlands and Belgium. This is not to say, of course, that the macroeconomic policy regime of Germany and its followers is the only cause of the dramatic imbalances within the Euro area. Certainly, the bubbles, particularly in Ireland and Spain, as well as inadequate fiscal policies and wage developments in the deficit countries have also contributed to those imbalances. However, the German neo-mercantilist policy regime has been a major underlying and still active force which will make it very hard to overcome the imbalances in the future.

3   Economic policy reactions in the crisis and perspectives for development[16]

The global financial and real economic crisis has led to remarkably fast and strong economic policy reactions in many countries (OECD 2009). As an immediate measure central banks have provided massive liquidity to money markets, thereby meeting their lender of last resort function. In many cases the financial sector had to be bailed out in order to prevent a breakdown of the whole financial system. And to differing extents in different economies monetary policy and fiscal policy switched to expansion in order to tackle the crisis of the real economy. Although many details of the measures chosen may be open to criticism, it cannot be doubted that the general direction of most of the measures was appropriate.

From the point of view of the current paper, however, the crucial question is whether the macroeconomic policy measures taken also address the long-run inequalities and imbalances of finance-dominated capitalism. If they do not, the major causes of the current crisis will still be in place after the crisis, which in turn will mean that the future prospects for sustainable and prosperous development of the world economy will be doubtful. As the following short remarks reveal, at least for the two important economies in the focus of the current paper, the USA and Germany – and with it the Euro area – no significant change in the general economic policy patterns is discernible yet.

The recession in Germany was considerably stronger than in the USA, where the crisis originated. In 2009 annual real GDP fell by 5 per cent in Germany, but only by 2.4 per cent in the USA (IMF 2010). The major reason for this was that Germany, as a neo-mercantilist economy mainly driven by export demand, was affected particularly severely by the global slowdown and the dramatical fall in export demand.

Regarding the macroeconomic policy response, the ECB in its role as a lender of last resort acted in a very fast and internationally coordinated manner, thereby saving the financial system from collapse. However, ECB interest rate policies have been less favourable and have shown a similar pattern as in the recession 2000/01 when compared to the US Federal Reserve (Hein and Truger 2007c). Whereas the Federal Reserve started to lower interest rates quickly and drastically from 5.25 per cent in the second half of 2007 to 0.25 per cent in early 2009, the ECB followed the 'wait and see' stance it had already adopted in the previous recession. In July 2008, when the dramatic economic slowdown could no longer be ignored, the ECB even increased the key interest rate by 25 basis points to 4.25 per cent with recourse to inflationary dangers. However, it was clear that the strong increase of the HICP since autumn 2007 had been almost entirely the result of the rise of oil prices. There were no clear signs of second-round effects, because nominal unit labour cost growth remained moderate. The ECB then only started to lower interest rates in late 2008 when the recession took effect, and oil prices – and consequently HICP growth – had started to fall. In 2009 the main refinancing rate finally came down to 1 per cent where it has remained since then.

Regarding fiscal policies, we have seen a quick and massive discretionary reaction in the USA with an expansionary package of close to 6 per cent of GDP for the period 2008–10, according to the estimates of the OECD (2009). Unlike in previous recessions (Hein and Truger 2007a) fiscal policy in Germany has also reacted in a remarkably countercyclical way. After some hesitation and some merely 'cosmetic' measures in the first months of 2009 a substantial stimulus package was enacted. Overall, the expansive discretionary fiscal policy stance amounts to 1.5 per cent of GDP in 2009 and 1.0 per cent in 2010 (OECD 2009). Compared to the usual German fiscal policy reaction which used to be pro-cyclically restrictive in times of crises, this is certainly remarkable progress. However, there are two drawbacks: First of all, both the discretionary reaction and the overall impact of the USA fiscal policies have again been stronger. Additionally, fiscal policy in the USA was not only more expansive with respect to the discretionary stimulus packages, but also on an overall basis, taking into account the working of automatic stabilisers. Second, as a political precondition to the German stimulus package, a so-called 'debt brake' was introduced into the constitution. This will limit the room of manoeuvre for German fiscal policy in the future and will set it on a restrictive consolidation path irrespective of the economic situation from 2011 onwards. And from 2016 onwards the federal budget will only be allowed to run a cyclically adjusted deficit of 0.35 per cent of GDP.

The federal states' (Länder) budgets will have to be structurally balanced from 2020 onwards. As the cyclically adjusted or 'structural' deficit will be determined by a variation of the European Commission's method of calculating structural deficits, they will exhibit the same strong sensitivity to short-term revisions of GDP forecasts and will therefore prevent the full working of automatic stabilisers.[17] Discretionary fiscal policy will only be allowed under very restrictive conditions.

Regarding wage policies and unit labour cost development, as a major determinant of prices and inflation, there is a serious threat of deflation, for the USA, Germany and the Euro area. Weak labour unions and the increasing (threat of) unemployment have imposed downward pressure on the growth of compensation of employees in the USA, and with acceleration of productivity growth in the course of recovery this will generate negative nominal unit labour cost growth and hence deflationary pressure (European Commission 2010). Although unemployment has been remarkably stable in Germany since the beginning of the crisis, in particular the developments in German wage trends remain a major source of concern. Since the end of the 1990s this has been very weak, it showed little recovery even in the last upswing in 2006 and 2007, and it is expected to become weaker again over the next years (European Commission 2010). Therefore, taking the expected negative fiscal policy stance, there is a high risk of deflation in Germany where the unit labour cost growth rate for 2010 is already expected to be negative.

The prospective development in Germany means that the imbalances within the Euro area are very unlikely to be moderated over the next years. Of course, it cannot be doubted that the fiscal policy reaction to the crisis was substantially stronger in Germany than for the Euro area average (OECD 2009). Additionally, as a consequence of the successful stabilisation of employment during the crisis, labour productivity fell sharply in 2009, leading to a steep increase in unit labour costs in international comparison in that year. However, the trend since the end of the 1990s of German wage growth continuously undercutting average Euro area wage growth (Hein, Schulten and Truger 2006) will continue (European Commission 2010). What is worse, with the exception of Ireland, none of the countries with current account problems is expected to be gaining international competitiveness in relation to Germany.

Therefore, German wage moderation will continue to exert a substantial downward pressure on wages in the other Euro area countries which causes a risk of deflation not only for Germany but for the Euro area as a whole. The unit labour cost growth rate in 2010 for the Euro area is already expected to be negative and stagnation is expected in 2011

(European Commission 2010). If fiscal and monetary policy stimuli are withdrawn too early, the Euro area as a whole will also face the risk of becoming trapped in deflationary stagnation. Unfortunately, there are clear signs that the fiscal policy stimuli will, indeed, be withdrawn too early: Euro area member countries' governments have announced ambitious consolidation plans in their stability programmes which would amount to a negative fiscal stance of about 1 per cent of GDP in the Euro area (Brecht et al. 2010). It is very telling in this context that the European Commission's (2010) spring forecast sees a rather slow recovery of the Euro area economy, with GDP growth rising from 1.2 per cent in 2010 to 1.6 per cent in 2011. However, in this forecast, the assumed negative fiscal policy stance is only 0.3 per cent of GDP as the Commission did not include measures that have not definitely passed legislation in the respective countries. Therefore, if countries meet their structural consolidation targets, a substantially weaker growth for 2011 and even a relapse into stagnation or worse may occur.

Summing up this brief survey of short-run macroeconomic policy reactions towards the crisis we have to acknowledge that, although the macroeconomic anti-crisis policies have again been very expansionary in the USA, there is still a serious risk of future deflation for the USA economy. And it remains an open question when the expansionary fiscal policy stance will have to be terminated for political reasons and therefore aggregate demand will be dampened again. Whereas ECB interest rate policies have again failed to contribute to stabilising the economy, fiscal policies in Germany and the Euro area have been more expansionary than in past recessions, but will most probably become restrictive again. Together with the pressure on wages this might cause a deflationary stagnation. If this occurs, Germany and the Euro area will certainly not contribute to replacing the USA as a world engine of demand and growth in the future. And if the current macro-economic regime is not replaced by a more functional alternative, the serious problem of current account imbalances within the Euro area is also unlikely to be solved – and the threat of a disintegration of the currency area will persist.

4   Requirements for a Keynesian New Deal at the global and the European level

Given our analysis so far, even if the present anti-crisis policies are effective in stabilising the economy in the short run, we cannot expect the world economy to return to the dynamic pre-crisis growth path driven by debt-financed consumption in the USA. Private sector financial balances in the USA have already switched quickly from a substantial deficit of almost 4 per cent of GDP in 2006 to a surplus of 4 per cent of GDP in 2008 (Figure 6.6). And while the USA government may run fiscal deficits of around 10 per cent of GDP for a few years, thereby compensating for the fall in private consumption spending, it will not be able to do so for a longer period of time. Therefore, the USA will not be able to continue as the engine for world demand and it will have to be relieved by other countries, in particular the current account surplus countries.[18] Our analysis of the problems and the economic policy reactions in the Euro area, however, have revealed that Europe is currently far from replacing the USA as a world demand engine and rather suffers from internal contradictions caused mainly by the German strategy of pursuing a neo-mercantilist economic policy.[19] What is required is therefore a Keynesian New Deal at the global level which addresses the three main causes of the present malaise, that is, the inefficient regulation of financial markets, the inequalities in income distribution, and the imbalances in the current accounts at the global scale.[20] This global Keynesian New Deal has to be supplemented by a New Deal at the European level tackling the imbalances which have piled up over the first decade of the euro and overcoming the restrictive macroeconomic policy regime imposed by the Maastricht Treaty, the SGP and the monetary policy strategy of the ECB. The Keynesian New Deal should be considered as policy package[21] containing first, the re-regulation of the financial sector in order to prevent future financial excesses and financial crises; second, the re-orientation of macroeconomic policies, in particular in the current account surplus countries; and third, the re-construction of international macroeconomic policy coordination – in particular, on the European level – and a new world financial order. In what follows we will sketch the main building blocks of such a Keynesian New Deal for the global and the European level.

4.1   Re-regulation of the financial (and the real) sector

Re-regulation of the financial system requires a host of measures which should aim at orienting the financial sector towards financing real economic activity, namely real investment and real GDP growth.[22] It has at least three dimensions:

First, it should include measures which increase transparency in financial markets in order to reduce the problems of asymmetric information, asymmetric expectations and hence fundamental uncertainty, moral hazard, and fraud, which are inherent to this sector in particular and which have contributed to the present crisis. These measures include the standardisation and supervision of all financial products in order to increase transparency in the market. Off-balance sheet operations should be abolished and national and international regulation and supervision of all financial intermediaries (banks, insurances, hedge funds, private equity funds, and so on) should be introduced. Since rating can be considered a public good, independent public rating agencies will have to be introduced replacing the private ones. Diversity in the banking sector should be increased in order to increase resilience. Therefore public and cooperative banks supplying credit to households and small firms and thus competing with private banks should be strengthened. Financial institutions with systemic relevance should be in public ownership, because stability of these institutions can be considered to be a public good, too.

Second, re-regulation should generate incentives for economic agents in the financial and non-financial sectors encouraging them to focus on long-run growth rather than short-run profits. This has again several dimensions. First of all, securitisation should be reduced in order to prevent 'originate and distribute' strategies which were at the root of the US subprime mortgage crisis. Banks should be induced to do what banks are supposed to do, i.e. evaluate potential creditors and their investment projects, grant credit and supervise the fulfilment of payment commitments by the debtor. For the financial and non-financial corporate sector, share buybacks in order to drive share prices up should be reduced or even abolished. The short-termism of managers in the corporate sector should be minimised by means of reducing stock option programmes and by extending minimum holding periods. Generally, co-determination on the firm level and improved rights of other stakeholders in the firm should be strengthened in order to overcome short-termism and to increase the importance of investment into long-term projects improving productivity and developing new products.

Third, measures directed at containing systemic instability should be implemented. These should include equity regulation for all financial intermediaries, which should have countercyclical properties – different from Basel II regulation.[23] Improved equity requirements should reduce leverage on average, and thus require a higher capital base, which should make financial intermediaries more resilient in case of a financial crisis.[24] The introduction of asset-based reserve requirements (ABRR) for all financial intermediaries should also have stabilising properties for the financial system as a whole. (i) ABRRs have countercyclical properties: Reserves to be held with the central bank increase in an upswing with rising asset prices and they decrease in a downswing and recession when asset prices are falling and free reserves are needed most urgently by financial intermediaries. This stabilises the financial sector. (ii) ABRRs can also be applied by the monetary authorities in order to prevent over-heating and bubbles in particular markets by means of increasing the reserve requirements for assets generated in these markets. (iii) Differentiated ABRRs can be applied in order to direct credit and investment towards socially preferable areas.[25] Finally, in order to reduce speculation and volatility of short-term financial market flows, a general transaction tax for all financial transactions[26] and a general capital gains tax – also for corporations – should be introduced.

4.2 Re-orientation of macroeconomic policies

Macroeconomic policies, in particular in current account surplus countries, have to be reorientated toward improving domestic demand, employment, and hence also imports. Therefore, neo-mercantilist strategies will have to be abandoned, in particular in countries like Germany, Japan and China. In Hein and Stockhammer (2009, 2010) a blueprint for a Post-Keynesian macroeconomic policy mix – as opposed to the New Consensus model focussing on labour market deregulation in order to reduce the NAIRU and on monetary policy for short-run real and long-run nominal stabilisation – has been developed, which can be used as a theoretical foundation for our suggestions here. Macroeconomic policies should be coordinated along the following lines:

First, central bank's interest rate policies should abstain from attempting to fine-tune unemployment in the short run and inflation in the long run, as suggested by the New Consensus approach. Varying interest rates have cost and distribution effects on the business sector, which may be effective in achieving inflation targets in the short run, in particular if the economy suffers from accelerating inflation but not necessarily if accelerating disinflation or deflation prevails, due to the zero lower bound of the nominal interest rate. In the long run, however, rising interest rates, applied successfully in order to stop accelerating inflation in the short run, will feed cost-push inflation again. Therefore, central banks should focus on setting low real interest rates in order to avoid unfavourable cost and distribution effects on firms and workers, while favouring rentiers.[27] A slightly positive real rate of interest, below the long-run rate of productivity growth, seems to be a reasonable target: Rentiers' real financial wealth will be protected against inflation, but redistribution of income in favour of the productive sector and at the expense of the unproductive rentiers' sector will take place, which should be favourable for real investment, employment and growth. Further on, central banks have to act as a 'lender of last resort' in periods of liquidity crisis, and central banks should be involved in the regulation and the supervision of financial markets, as suggested in the previous sub-section. This includes the definition of credit standards for refinance operations with commercial banks, and the implementation of compulsory reserve requirements for different types of assets to be held with the central bank, in order to channel credit into desirable areas and to avoid credit-financed bubbles in certain markets.

Second, incomes and wage policies should take responsibility for nominal stabilisation, that is, stable inflation rates at a level consistent with a roughly balanced current account. In the end, accelerating inflation is always the result of unresolved distribution conflicts. With the degree of monopoly in the goods market and hence profit aspirations of firms given, nominal wages should rise according to the sum of long-run average growth of labour productivity in the economy plus the target rate of inflation set by the government. In order to achieve the nominal wage growth target, a high degree of wage bargaining coordination at the macroeconomic level, and organised labour markets with strong labour unions and employers' associations seem to be a necessary condition.[28] Minimum wage legislation, in particular in countries with highly deregulated labour markets and increasing dispersion of wages, will also be helpful for nominal stabilisation at the macroeconomic level, apart from its usefulness in terms of containing wage inequality. Further deregulation of the labour market, weakening labour unions, and reductions in the reservation wage rate by means of cutting unemployment benefits, however, will be detrimental to nominal stabilisation and will rather impose deflationary pressure on the economy.

Third, fiscal policies should take responsibility for real stabilisation, full employment and also a more equal distribution of disposable income. This has several aspects. By definition the excess of private saving (S) over private investment (I) at a given level of economic activity and employment has to be absorbed by the excess of exports (X) over imports (M) plus the excess of government spending (G) over tax revenues (T): $S - I = X - M + G - T$. Therefore, with balanced trade – or balanced current accounts – government deficits have to permanently take up the excess of private saving over private investment in order to assure a high desired level of employment.[29] As is well known from Domar (1944), a permanent government deficit with a constant long-run GDP growth rate will make the government debt–GDP ratio converge towards a definite value. Therefore, there will be no problem of accelerating public debt–GDP ratios. Further more, low real interest rates – falling short of GDP growth and hence of tax revenue growth – will prevent the redistribution of income in favour of rentiers. Permanent government deficits should be directed towards public investment in a wider sense (including increasing public employment), providing the economy with public infrastructure, and public education at all levels (Kindergartens, schools, high schools, universities), in order to promote structural change towards an environmentally sustainable long-run growth path. Apart from this permanent role of government debt, which also supplies a safe haven for private saving and thus stabilises financial markets, counter-cyclical fiscal policies – together with automatic stabilisers – should stabilise the economy in the face of aggregate demand shocks. Further on, progressive income taxes, relevant wealth, property and inheritance taxes, as well as social transfers, should aim at redistribution of income and wealth in favour of low-income and low-wealth households. On the one hand, this will reduce excess saving and thus stabilise aggregate demand – without generating problems of unsustainable indebtedness for private households. Progressive income taxation and relevant taxes on wealth, property and inheritance thus also reduce the requirements for government deficits. On the other hand, redistributive taxes and social policies will improve automatic stabilisers and thus reduce fluctuations in economic activity.

4.3 Re-construction of international macroeconomic policy coordination, in particular on the European level, and a new world financial order

In order to successfully implement the macroeconomic principles outlined in the previous section and to cure and prevent further global and intra-European imbalances – which have been at the roots of the severity of the present crisis – major changes are required in international macroeconomic policy coordination and in the world financial order.

On the European level, reorientation of macroeconomic policies and macroeconomic policy coordination along the lines sketched in the previous section requires major institutional reforms. The institutional setting of the ECB and its monetary policy strategy have to be modified such that the ECB is forced to take into account the long-run distributional, employment and growth effects of its policies, and to pursue a monetary policy targeting low real interest rates. In a first step, an adjustment towards the Federal Reserve's objectives might be helpful, which include stable prices, maximum employment and moderate long-term interest rates on an equal footing (Meyer 2001). In its monetary policy strategy the ECB should refrain from fine-tuning the economy in real or nominal terms and should keep interest rates low such that long-term real interest rates remain below Euro area average productivity growth in the medium run. This should be conducive to real investment in the Euro area. The ECB should focus on financial market stability. Instead of the blunt instrument of the interest rate it should introduce those instruments which are appropriate to contain bubbles in specific asset markets in specific countries or regions, i.e. asset-based reserve requirements.

The SGP at the European level has to be abandoned and needs to be replaced by a means of coordination of national fiscal policies at the Euro area level which allows for the short- and long-run stabilising role of fiscal policies. In Hein and Truger (2007b) we have suggested the coordination of long-run expenditure paths for non-cyclical government spending, that is, those components of spending which are under control of the government. Such expenditure paths could be geared towards stabilising aggregate demand in the Euro area at full employment levels, and automatic stabilisers plus discretionary countercyclical fiscal policies could be applied to fight demand shocks. In order to avoid the current account imbalances within the Euro area which have caused the present euro crisis, these expenditure paths would have to make sure that, on average over the cycle and the average tax rate in each member country given, as a first approximation the government deficits in each of the countries would have to be roughly equal to the excess of private saving over private investment in the respective country, such that the current accounts are roughly balanced at a high level of aggregate demand and employment. Since growth dynamics within the Euro area will vary for a considerable period of time due to the different levels in productivity and related (but probably incomplete) catch-up processes, it will be difficult to target exactly balanced current accounts. Coordinating fiscal policies and government deficits should therefore take into account tolerable current account deficits associated with catch-up processes. However, these would have to be strictly limited, in order to avoid a constellation as the one at the roots of the 2010 euro crisis.[30]

Given the present massive intra-Euro area imbalances reviewed in Section 2.2 of this paper, fiscal policies would have to contribute to overcoming these imbalances: Those countries with current account surpluses would have to increase their government deficits allowing those countries with current account deficits to reduce their current account and thus also their government deficits.

The orientation of labour market and social policies towards deregulation and flexibilisation still prevalent in the European Union and the Euro area will have to be abandoned in favour of reorganising labour markets, stabilising labour unions and employers' associations, and Euro area-wide minimum wage legislation. This could provide the institutional requirements for the effective implementation of nominal stabilising wage policies: Nominal wages should rise according to the sum of long-run average growth of labour productivity in the national economy plus the target rate of inflation for the Euro area as a whole. For a transitional period, during which the current account imbalances within the Euro area have to be corrected, in the countries with current account surpluses nominal wage growth should exceed the sum of national productivity growth plus the inflation target, whereas in those countries with current account deficits nominal wage growth should fall short of this norm. This would improve relative competitiveness in the deficit countries and stimulate aggregate demand in the surplus countries and thus contribute to overcoming the imbalances.

Finally, attempts at effective macroeconomic 'ex ante' policy coordination among monetary, fiscal and wage policies at the Euro area level will have to be made. For this the Macroeconomic Dialogue (Cologne-Process) supplies an institutional basis.[31]

On the international level, the return to a world financial order with fixed but adjustable exchange rates, symmetric adjustment obligations for current account deficit and surplus countries, and regulated international capital markets is required in order to avoid the imbalances that have contributed to the severity of the present crisis. Keynes's (1942) proposal for an International Clearing Union can be seen as a blueprint for this: As is well known, Keynes suggested an International Clearing Union in a fixed but adjustable exchange rate system, with the 'bancor' as international money for clearing operations between central banks, the Clearing Union as an international central bank financing temporary current account deficits, and selective controls of speculative capital movements between currency areas. What is most important for the present situation is that, according to Keynes (1942), whereas permanent current account deficit countries would be penalised in order to contract domestic demand (or to depreciate their currencies), also permanent current account surplus countries should be induced to expand domestic demand and thus to increase imports (or to appreciate their currencies), so that the whole burden of adjustment does not have to be carried by the deficit countries. This should give an overall impetus to world aggregate demand which will be needed in the future, not only in the short run but also in the long run.[32]

UNCTAD (2009, pp. 51–3) has recently proposed a system of managed exchange rates which aims at stable real exchange rates by way of nominal wage policies following long-run productivity growth, and an inflation target consistent with stable real exchange rates in each country. Nominal exchange rates would have to adjust if nominal wages and inflation failed to generate stable real exchange rates. In order to prevent speculation under the conditions of rather free movement of capital, the UNCTAD scheme argues that nominal interest rates should be set such that the interest parity conditions would be maintained. Speculative attacks should be countered symmetrically, by both the country under depreciation pressure and the country with an appreciating currency. A redesigned system should be a multipolar one, with several lead currencies linked to each other through symmetric, managed floating systems with exchange rates automatically adjusted by relative price differentials, and satellites linked to the lead currencies. Although the UNCTAD system seems to be a step into the right direction, it contains at least one major shortcoming: National interest rate policies have to be applied in order for the interest parity conditions to hold, and thus to counter currency speculation. However, this might contradict our suggestion of a policy of low interest rates geared towards domestic distribution targets. Therefore, the UNCTAD scheme would have to be further developed in order to solve this dilemma of monetary policies in a world of free capital mobility. As is well known, this dilemma can only be overcome if restrictions on capital mobility are imposed.[33] A related scheme will have to be developed.

5 Summary and conclusions

We have analysed the long-run imbalances of finance-dominated capitalism underlying the present crisis, with a focus on developments in the USA and Germany as representative countries and on the imbalances which have piled up in the Euro area. We have argued that, beyond inefficient regulation of financial markets, increasing inequalities in income distribution and rising current account imbalances at the global scale and within the Euro area should be considered the main underlying causes for the severeness of the global financial and economic crisis and for the recent euro crisis.

Against the background of rising inequalities and a falling labour income share the credit-financed consumption boom in the USA prior to the crisis was built on a highly fragile constellation. Domestically, it had to rely on ever-increasing property prices in order to allow for rising indebtedness fuelling steady increases in consumption demand. Regarding the relationship with the rest of the world, a sharp depreciation of the US dollar, which would have been required in order to improve international price competitiveness of USA producers and thus the current account, had to be avoided in order to guarantee steady capital imports without having to raise domestic interest rates, which in turn would have increased the possibility of a collapse in the domestic demand boom. The erosion of such a constellation in the subprime mortgage crisis and the following downswing did not only affect the USA, but also the rest of the world, in particular, the current account surplus countries. On the one hand, the capital exports into highly speculative USA markets were devalued by the financial crisis, and therefore the financial crisis quickly infected some of the surplus countries. On the other hand, their markets for exports collapsed and they were thus infected by the real crisis as well.

Whereas the dynamic consumption-driven model of the USA had to rely on the willingness and the ability of private households to go into debt – and of the rest of the world to supply credit –, the stagnating German neo-mercantilist model had to rely on the willingness and the ability of the rest of the world to go into debt. This German model was therefore as fragile as the USA model. On the one hand, the moderate growth rates were dependent on the dynamic growth of export markets, and hence on the expansion of the world economy. On the other hand, increasing capital exports to the more dynamic economies carried the risk of contagion in the case of a financial crisis in these markets. And both channels became effective during the crisis.

The German strategy was not only suboptimal for Germany; we have also identified the German neo-mercantilist macroeconomic policy regime to be a major reason for the current account imbalances within the Euro area which are at the roots of the euro crisis starting in 2010. Germany's consistently weak domestic growth, as well as its rising international competitiveness as the result of extremely moderate wage developments, has been a drag for some other Euro area economies, driving their balance of goods and services and ultimately also their current accounts into deficit. Of course, the bubbles, in particular in Ireland and Spain, as well as inadequate fiscal policies and wage developments in the deficit countries have also contributed to the current account imbalances within the Euro area. However, we have argued that the German neo-mercantilist policy regime has been a major underlying and still active force which is a massive threat to the coherence of the Euro area.

Although the breakdown of the world economy in the financial and economic crisis could finally be halted by monetary policy interventions providing liquidity on a massive scale to the money market – thus preventing a meltdown of the financial sector – and, in particular, by massive fiscal expenditure programmes, we have argued that due to the underlying imbalances the world economy is unlikely to return to its pre-crisis growth path. In particular, the USA will not be able to act as the driver for world demand, in the short or in the long term. The European Union or the Euro area are far from replacing the USA as a world demand engine and rather suffer from their internal contradictions, mainly caused by the German neo-mercantilist economic policy strategy. Therefore major parts of the world economy are presently threatened by a period of deflationary stagnation.

This analysis has major implications for economic policies far beyond immediate responses to the crisis. We have outlined the elements of a Keynesian New Deal at the global and the European level in order to prevent sustained deflationary stagnation in major parts of the world. The policy package of a Keynesian New Deal should address the three main causes of the severe crisis: inefficient regulation, increasing inequality in income distribution and imbalances at the global and the European scale. The Keynesian New Deal policy package should consist of the following elements: (i) the re-regulation of the financial (and the real) sectors in order to increase transparency and reduce asymmetric information and uncertainty, to generate incentives for long-run growth, and to contain systemic instability; (ii) the re-orientation of macroeconomic policies along (Post-) Keynesian lines with monetary policies by central banks being responsible for low real interest rates and for the stability of the financial sector, wage and incomes policies taking care of nominal stabilisation and stable income shares, and fiscal policies being in charge of real stabilisation in the short and the long run, and of redistribution of income and wealth; (iii) the re-construction of international macroeconomic policy co-ordination – in particular, at the European level – and a new world financial order, in order to allow for the implementation of the macroeconomic policy package outlined above and to tackle global and intra-European imbalances.

Among economists of different schools and also in public debate, there seems to be broad agreement with respect to the requirements of the re-regulation of the financial sector, however, not about the details of this re-regulation. But there seems to be far less or even no awareness about the requirements of a re-orientation of macroeconomic policies and a re-construction of international economic policy coordination.

However, from our analysis it follows that without this re-orientation and re-construction a turn towards a sustainable long-run full employment growth path is hard to imagine. Therefore, these are the areas (Post-) Keynesians have to focus on and to draw attention to, in particular.

Notes

1. The IMF (2010) reports the following GDP growth rates for 2009: world output: −0.6 per cent; USA: −2.4 per cent; Euro area: −4.1 per cent, Germany: −5.0 per cent, France: −2.2 per cent, Italy: −5.0 per cent, Spain: −3.6 per cent, Japan: −5.2 per cent, UK: −4.9 per cent, Russia: −7.9 per cent, Brazil: −0.2 per cent. Among the major countries, only in China (+8.7 per cent) and India (+5.7 per cent) GDP growth did not become negative in 2009, although these countries also experienced a decline in growth. The GDP growth rates projected by the IMF for 2010 and 2011 are: world output: 4.2 and 4.3 per cent, USA: 3.1 and 2.6 per cent, Euro area: 1.0 and 1.5 per cent, Germany: 1.2 and 1.7 per cent, France: 1.5 and 1.8 per cent, Italy: 0.8 and 1.2 per cent, Spain: −0.4 and 0.9 per cent, Japan: 1.9 and 2.0 per cent, UK: 1.3 and 2.5 per cent, Russia: 4.0 and 3.3 per cent, Brazil: 5.5 and 4.1 per cent, China: 10.0 and 9.9 per cent, and India 8.8 and 8.4 per cent.
2. See Hein and Niechoj (2007) and Hein and Truger (2005a,b, 2007a,b,c, 2009) for comparisons of the more restrictive German and Euro area macroeconomic policies with the more expansive versions pursued in the USA and the UK. These differences in the chosen macroeconomic policy mixes have contributed to the differences in GDP growth and unemployment since the mid-1990s, and in particular since the recession in 2000/01.
3. See, in particular, the overview in Akerlof and Shiller (2009, pp. 29–40, 149–56), but also Baker (2009).
4. On global imbalances and unequal distribution as causes for the present crisis see also, with different emphasis, Bibow (2008), Horn et al. (2009b), Fitoussi and Stiglitz (2009), Sapir (2009), UNCTAD (2009), and Wade (2009). In particular, see also the early pre-crisis analysis by van Treeck, Hein and Dünhaupt (2007) focussing on the effects of 'financialisation' on distribution, aggregate demand, global imbalances and the following potential for instability.
5. See Guttmann (2009) for a review of the changes in world wide financial markets and related imbalances which fed the financial crisis.
6. Epstein (2005, p. 3), for example, argues that '[...] financialization means the increasing role of financial motives, financial markets, financial actors and financial institutions in the operation of the domestic and international economies'.
7. See Krippner (2005), Palley (2008), and the contributions in Epstein (2005) for a detailed treatment of the development of 'financialisation' in the USA, van Treeck (2009a) and van Treeck, Hein and Dünhaupt (2007) for a more detailed comparison of the macroeconomics of 'financialisation' in the USA and Germany, and Stockhammer (2008) for the development in Europe.

8. Of course, there are major differences among the surplus countries. Whereas current account surpluses in China were accompanied by high growth rates, in Germany and Japan they were accompanied by mediocre growth and longer periods of stagnation, in particular in the 1990s (Japan) and the early 2000s (Germany).

9. For studies on the effects of increasing shareholder or rentier power and/or rising dividend and interest payments of the corporate sector on income shares see Argitis and Pitelis (2001), Dünhaupt (2010), Dumenil and Levy (2005), Epstein and Power (2003), Epstein and Jayadev (2005), and Hein and Schoder (2011).

10. For the effects of increasing shareholder power on investment see Crotty (1990) and Stockhammer (2005–6), and for empirical evidence regarding the negative effects of 'financialisation' on real investment via the 'preference channel' and the 'internal means of finance channel' see the estimations by Orhangazi (2008), Stockhammer (2004) and van Treeck (2008). For theoretical modelling within the tradition of Post-Keynesian distribution and growth models, see Hein (2010a, 2010b), Lavoie (2008), Skott and Ryoo (2008a, 2008b), van Treeck (2009a) and the overview in Hein and van Treeck (2010).

11. See Barba and Pivetti (2009) on increasing household debt as the result of redistribution of income and rising inequality. For a theoretical assessment of the potentially contradictory effects of household debt on macroeconomic dynamics see Bhaduri, Laski and Riese (2006), Dutt (2006) and Palley (1994).

12. For the wealth effect on households' consumption in the USA see for example the empirical studies by Boone, Giorno and Richardson (1998), Ludvigson and Steindel (1999), Davis and Palumbo (2001), Mehra (2001) and the more recent estimations by Onaran, Stockhammer and Grafl (2009).

13. The economic downturn in 2009 in the slowly growing surplus countries, in particular Germany (-5 per cent) and Japan (-5.2 per cent), was even more severe than in the USA (-2.4 per cent) where the crisis started (IMF 2010).

14. For Italy the picture is less clear. In this country the private sector balance was consistently positive. Therefore the government deficit could be financed partly by the private sector surplus and partly by the capital inflows associated with the moderate, but continuously rising, current account deficit. When the crisis hit, the improvement in the private sector balance was compensated mostly by a rather modest increase in the government deficit.

15. Note that these differences in inflation rates cause reverse differences in real interest rates within a currency union with a single nominal short-term and a high degree of convergence in nominal long-term rates. These differences may then feed back on the domestic demand differences further contributing to current account imbalances within the currency union.

16. For a more detailed analysis of the short-run macroeconomic policy reactions towards the crisis see our companion paper (Hein and Truger 2010b).

17. For a detailed exposition of the methods used by the European Commission see Denis et al. (2006) and European Commission (2005). The calculated cyclically adjusted measures can be criticised for a number of theoretical and empirical reasons and must therefore be interpreted with great care.

Theoretically, they are very close to the idea embedded in the standard NAIRU models: There is a long-run equilibrium, determined by structural characteristics of the labour market, which is independent of the short-run fluctuations generated by demand shocks or macroeconomic policies. We do not share this view (Hein and Stockhammer 2010). Empirically, these measures are very sensitive to the exact method used and to the choice of observation period: The separation of a cyclical from a potential or trend component will be biased because the potential component is endogenous. After some years of high (low) growth caused by 'short-term' demand side measures or shocks, the potential or trend growth will go up (down) thereby underestimating the cyclical component compared to a situation without such demand-side measures or shocks (Horn, Logeay and Tober 2007). Therefore, the cyclically adjusted budget deficits (surpluses) for low (high) growth countries may be considerably overestimated. For Germany it can be shown specifically that the calculated cyclically adjusted deficits are highly sensitive to forecast revisions (Horn et al. 2009a).

18. See also Godley et al. (2008) and Papadimitriou (2009) for similar conclusions with respect to the USA.
19. One might speculate whether China, India and other emerging countries could take over the role of the USA as world demand engine. However, the individual weight of these countries in world demand and output might be still too small, and the most important of these countries, China, has been following a neo-mercantilist economic policy strategy, too, aiming at continuous current account surpluses (Herr 2009, 2010).
20. For similar views see Fitoussi and Stiglitz (2009), Guttmann (2009) and Wade (2009), although with different emphasis on the various components.
21. Kregel (2009b), for example, shows that just bailing out the financial sector won't work in terms of stimulating the economy.
22. For a more detailed list of required regulation see, for example, Ash et al. (2009), Fitoussi and Stiglitz (2009), and Wade (2009). On the state of financial market reforms in the European Union see Dullien and Herr (2010).
23. On the problems of Basel II regulations see for example Springler (2007).
24. On countercyclical capital requirements see Goodhart (2009).
25. On the properties of asset-based reserve requirements see, in particular, Palley (2003, 2004, 2010) and Holz (2007).
26. See Schulmeister, Schratzenstaller and Picek (2008) for a recent proposal.
27. See Rochon and Setterfield (2007) for a review of Post Keynesian suggestions regarding the 'parking it' approach towards central banks' interest rate policies and the rate of interest central banks should target.
28. See Hein (2002) for a review of the related theoretical and empirical literature.
29. This is, of course, the 'functional finance' view, pioneered by Lerner (1943). See also Arestis and Sawyer (2004).
30. Dullien (2010) and Dullien and Schwarzer (2009) have proposed an 'External Economic Stability Pact' for the Euro area countries allowing for external deficits or surpluses of 3 per cent of GDP. For deficit countries this would stabilise foreign debt at 60 per cent of GDP, assuming that trend nominal GDP growth amounts to 5 per cent. The advantage of this suggestion is that it includes symmetric adjustment obligations for deficit and surplus

countries. However, the proposed target or threshold ratios would have to be differentiated for individual countries because tolerable current account deficits should be based on different growth dynamics. Further research in this area is required.

31. See Hein and Niechoj (2007), Hein and Truger (2005a) and the papers in Hein et al. (2005) for the deficiencies of macroeconomic policies and macroeconomic policy co-ordination in the Euro area and for an outline of required institutional reforms.
32. See Guttmann (2009) and Kregel (2009a) for a more detailed discussion of the needs for a reform of the international monetary system.
33. See Keynes's (1942, pp. 187–9) proposal for an International Clearing Union, in which he also allows for selective capital controls. See also Davidson (2009: 134–42) and Wade (2009).

References

Akerlof, G.A. and Shiller, R.J. (2009) *Animal Spirits: How Human Psychology Drives the Economy and Why It Matters for Global Capitalism*. Princeton: Princeton University Press.

Arestis, P. and Sawyer, M. (2004) 'On Fiscal Policy and Budget Deficits', *Intervention. Journal of Economics*, 1(2), pp. 61–74.

Argitis, G., and Pitelis, C. (2001) 'Monetary Policy and the Distribution of Income: Evidence for the United States and the United Kingdom', *Journal of Post Keynesian Economics*, 23, pp. 617–38.

Ash, M., Balakrishnan, R., Campbell, A., Crotty, J., Dickens, E., Epstein, G., Ferguson, T., Ghilarducci, T., Greisgraber, J.M., Griffith-Jones, S., Guttmann, R., Jayadev, A., Kapadia, A., Kotz, D., Meerepol, M., Milberg, W., Modeley, F., Ocampo, J.A., Pollin, R., Sawyer, M. and Wolfson, M. (2009) 'A Progressive Program for Economic Recovery and Financial Reconstruction', New York and Amherst, MA: Schwartz Center for Economic Policy Analysis (SCEPA) and Political Economy Research Institute (PERI).

Bach, S., Corneo, G. and Steiner, V. (2009) 'From Bottom to Top: The Entire Distribution of Market Income in Germany, 1992–2003', *Review of Income and Wealth*, 55(2), pp. 303–30.

Baker, D. (2009) *Plunder and Blunder: The Rise and Fall of the Bubble Economy*. Sausalito, CA: PoliPointPress.

Barba, A. and Pivetti, M. (2009) 'Rising Household Debt: Its Causes and Macroeconomic Implications – A Long-period Analysis', *Cambridge Journal of Economics*, 33, pp. 113–37.

Bhaduri, A., Laski, K. and Riese, M. (2006) 'A Model of Interaction between the Virtual and the Real Economy', *Metroeconomica*, 57, pp. 412–27.

Bibow, J. (2008) 'The International Monetary (Non-) Order and the "Global Capital Flows Paradox"', in E. Hein, T Niechoj, P. Spahn and A. Truger (eds), *Finance-led Capitalism? Macroeconomic Effects of Changes in the Financial Sector*. Marburg: Metropolis.

Boone, L., Giorno, C. and Richardson, P. (1998) 'Stock Market Fluctuations and Consumption Behaviour – Some Recent Evidence', OECD Economics Department Working Papers No. 208, Paris: OECD.

Brecht, M., Tober, S., van Treeck, T. and Truger, A. (2010) 'Squaring the Circle in Euroland? Some Remarks on the Stability and Convergence Programmes 2010–2013', IMK Working Paper 3/2010, Duesseldorf: Macroeconomic Policy Institute (IMK) at Hans Boeckler Foundation.

Cordonnier, L. (2006) 'Le Profit sans l'Accumulation: la Recette du Capitalisme Dominé par la Finance', *Innovations. Cahiers d'Economie de l'Innovation*, 23, pp. 51–72.

Crotty, J. (1990) 'Owner–Management Conflict and Financial Theories of Investment Instability: A Critical Assessment of Keynes, Tobin, and Minsky', *Journal of Post Keynesian Economics*, 12, pp. 519–42.

Davidson, P. (2009) *The Keynes Solution: The Path to Global Economic Prosperity*. Basingstoke: Palgrave Macmillan.

Davis, M.A. and Palumbo, M. (2001) 'A Primer on the Economics and Time Series Econometrics of Wealth Effects', Finance and Economics Discussion Series, 2001–09, Washington, DC: Federal Reserve Board.

Denis, C., Grenouilleau, D., McMorrow, K. and Röger, W. (2006) 'Calculating Potential Growth Rates and Output Gaps – A Revised Production Function Approach', European Commission Directorate-General for Economic and Financial Affairs Economic Paper No. 247, March 2006, Brussels: European Commission.

Domar, E.D. (1944) 'The "Burden of the Debt" and National Income', *American Economic Review*, 34, pp. 794–828.

Dullien, S. (2010) 'Towards a Sustainable Growth Model for Europe: Institutional Framework', *Internationale Politik und Gesellschaft*, 1/2010, pp. 36–44.

Dullien, S. and Herr, H. (2010) 'EU Financial Market Reforms. Status and Prospects', Spring 2010, International Policy Analysis. Berlin: Friedrich Ebert Stiftung.

Dullien, S. and Schwarzer, D. (2009) 'The Euro Zone Needs an External Stability Pact', SWP Comments 2009/C09. Berlin: German Institute for International and Security Affairs.

Dumenil, G. and Levy, D. (2005) 'Costs and Benefits of Neoliberalism: A Class Analysis', in G.A. Epstein (ed.), *Financialization and the World Economy*. Cheltenham: Edward Elgar.

Dünhaupt, P. (2010) 'Financialisation and the Rentier Income Share – Evidence from the USA and Germany', IMK Working Paper 2/2010, Düsseldorf: Macroeconomic Policy Institute (IMK) at Hans Boeckler Foundation.

Dutt, A.K. (2006) 'Maturity, Stagnation and Consumer Debt: A Steindlian Approach', *Metroeconomica*, 57, pp. 339–64.

Epstein, G.A. (ed.) (2005) *Financialization and the World Economy*. Cheltenham: Edward Elgar.

Epstein, G.A. and Jayadev, A. (2005) 'The Rise of Rentier Incomes in OECD Countries: Financialization, Central Bank Policy and Labor Solidarity', in G.A. Epstein (ed.), *Financialization and the World Economy*. Cheltenham: Edward Elgar.

Epstein, G.A. and Power, D. (2003) 'Rentier Incomes and Financial Crises: An Empirical Examination of Trends and Cycles in Some OECD Countries', Working Paper Series No. 57, Political Economy Research Institute, University of Massachusetts, Amherst/MA.

European Commission (2005) 'New and Updated Budgetary Sensitivities for the EU Budgetary Surveillance', Directorate General Economics and Financial Affairs, September 2005, Brussels: European Commission.

European Commission (2010) 'AMECO Database', http://ec.europa.eu/economy_finance/db_indicators/ameco/index_en.htm.

Fitoussi, J.-P. and Stiglitz, J. (2009) 'The Ways Out of the Crisis and the Building of a More Cohesive World', OFCE Document de travail, No. 2009-17. Paris: OFCE.

Godley, W., Papadimitriou, D. and Zezza, G. (2008) 'Prospects for the U.S. and the World: A Crisis That Conventional Remedies Cannot Resolve', The Levy Economics Institute of Bard College, Strategic Analysis, December.

Goodhart, C.A.E. (2009) *The Regulatory Response to the Financial Crisis*. Cheltenham: Edward Elgar.

Guttmann, R. (2009) 'Asset Bubbles, Debt Deflation, and Global Imbalances', *International Journal of Political Economy*, 38(2), pp. 46–69.

Hein, E. (2002) 'Monetary Policy and Wage Bargaining in the EMU: Restrictive ECB Policies, High Unemployment, Nominal Wage Restraint and Inflation above the Target', *Banca Nazionale del Lavoro Quarterly Review*, 55, pp. 299–337.

Hein, E. (2010a) 'Shareholder Value Orientation, Distribution and Growth – Short- and Medium-run Effects in a Kaleckian Model', *Metroeconomica*, 61, pp. 302–32.

Hein, E. (2010b) 'A Keynesian Perspective on "Financialisation"', in P. Arestis and M. Sawyer (eds), *21st Century Keynesian Economics*. Basingstoke: Palgrave Macmillan.

Hein, E. and Niechoj, T. (2007) 'Guidelines for Sustained Growth in the EU? The Concept and the Consequences of the Broad Economic Policy Guidelines', in J. McCombie and C. Rodriguez (eds), *The European Union: Current Problems and Prospects*, Basingstoke: Palgrave Macmillan.

Hein, E., Niechoj, T., Schulten, T. and Truger, A. (eds) (2005) *Macroeconomic Policy Coordination in Europe and the Role of the Trade Unions*. Brussels: ETUI.

Hein, E. and Schoder, C. (2011) 'Interest Rates, Distribution and Capital Accumulation – A Post-Kaleckian Perspective on the U.S. and Germany', International Review of Applied Economics, forthcoming.

Hein, E., Schulten, T. and Truger, A. (2006) 'Deflation Risks in Germany and the EMU: The Role of Wages and Wage Bargaining', in E. Hein, A. Heise and A. Truger (eds), *Wages, Employment, Distribution and Growth. International Perspectives*. Basingstoke: Palgrave Macmillan.

Hein, E. and Stockhammer, E. (2009) 'A Post-Keynesian Macroeconomic Policy Mix as An Alternative to the New Consensus Approach', in P. Arestis and J. McCombie (eds), *Unemployment: Past and Present*. Basingstoke: Palgrave Macmillan.

Hein, E. and Stockhammer, E. (2010) 'Macroeconomic Policy Mix, Employment and Inflation in a Post-Keynesian Alternative to the New Consensus Model', *Review of Political Economy*, 22, pp. 317–54.

Hein, E. and Truger, A. (2005a) 'Whatever Happened to Germany? Is the Decline of the Former European Key Currency Country Caused by Structural Sclerosis or by Macroeconomic Mismanagement?', *International Review of Applied Economics*, 19, pp. 3–28.

Hein, E. and Truger, A. (2005b) 'Macroeconomic Coordination as an Economic Policy Concept – Opportunities and Obstacles in the EMU', in E. Hein, T. Niechoj, T. Schulten and A. Truger (eds), *Macroeconomic Policy Coordination in Europe and the Role of the Trade Unions*. Brussels: ETUI.

Hein, E. and Truger, A. (2007a) 'Germany's Post-2000 Stagnation in the European Context – a Lesson in Macroeconomic Mismanagement', in P. Arestis, E. Hein and E. Le Heron (eds), *Aspects of Modern Monetary and Macroeconomic Policies*. Basingstoke: Palgrave Macmillan.

Hein, E. and Truger, A. (2007b) 'Fiscal Policy and Macroeconomic Performance in the Euro Area: Lessons for the Future', in J. Bibow and A. Terzi (eds), *Euroland and the World Economy: Global Player or Global Drag?* Basingstoke: Palgrave Macmillan.

Hein, E. and Truger, A. (2007c) 'Monetary Policy, Macroeconomic Policy Mix and Economic Performance in the Euro Area', in E. Hein and A. Truger (eds), *Money, Distribution and Economic Policy: Alternatives to Orthodox Macroeconomics*. Cheltenham: Edward Elgar.

Hein, E. and Truger, A. (2009) 'How to Fight (or not to Fight) a Slowdown: Lessons from France, Germany, the UK and Sweden, 1996–2005', *Challenge*, 52(2), pp. 52–75.

Hein, E. and Truger, A. (2010a) 'Finance-dominated Capitalism in Crisis – the Case for a Global Keynesian New Deal', Berlin School of Economics and Law, Institute for International Political Economy, Working Paper 6/2010.

Hein, E. and Truger, A. (2010b) 'Financial Crisis, Global Recession and Macroeconomic Policy Reactions – the Case of Germany', in S. Dullien, E. Hein, A. Truger and T. van Treeck (eds), *The World Economy in Crisis – The Return of Keynesianism?* Marburg: Metropolis.

Hein, E. and van Treeck, T. (2010) '"Financialisation" in Post-Keynesian Models of Distribution and Growth – a Systematic Review', in M. Setterfield (ed.), *Handbook of Alternative Theories of Economic Growth*. Cheltenham: Edward Elgar.

Herr, H. (2009) 'Global Imbalances and the Chinese Balance of Payments', *Intervention. European Journal of Economics and Economic Policies*, 6, pp. 44–53.

Herr, H. (2010) 'Credit Expansion and Development – A Schumpeterian and Keynesian View of the Chinese Miracle', *Intervention. European Journal of Economics and Economic Policies*, 7, pp. 71–89.

Holz, M. (2007) 'Asset-based Reserve Requirements: A New Monetary Policy Instrument for Targeting Diverging Real Estate Prices in the Euro Area', *Intervention. Journal of Economics*, 4, pp. 331–51.

Horn, G., Logeay, C. and Tober, S. (2007) 'Estimating Germany's Potential Output', IMK Working Paper 2/2007. Düsseldorf: Macroeconomic Policy Institute (IMK) at Hans Boeckler Foundation.

Horn, G., Truger, A. and Proano, C. (2009a) 'Stellungnahme zum Entwurf eines Begleitgesetzes zur zweiten Föderalismusreform (BT Drucksache 16/12400) und Entwurf eines Gesetzes zur Änderung des Grundgesetzes (BT Drucksache 16/12410)', IMK Policy Brief, May, Dusseldorf: Macroeconomic Policy Institute (IMK) at Hans Boeckler Foundation.

Horn, G., Dröge, K., Sturn, S., van Treeck, T. and Zwiener, R. (2009b) 'From the Financial Crisis to the World Economic Crisis. The Role of Inequality', IMK Policy Brief, October 2009, Dusseldorf: Macroeconomic Policy Institute (IMK) at Hans Boeckler Foundation.

IMF (2010) *World Economic Outlook, April 2010: Rebalancing Growth*. Washington, DC: IMF.

Joint Center for Housing Studies (2006) 'The State of the Nation's Housing'. Report of the Joint Center for Housing Studies of Harvard University, Cambridge, MA.

Kalecki, M. (1954) *Theory of Economic Dynamics*. London: George Allen and Unwin.

Keynes, J.M. (1942) 'Proposal for an International Clearing Union', in *The Collected Writings of J.M. Keynes*, vol. 25, London: Macmillan 1980.

Kregel, J. (2009a) 'Some Simple Observations on the Reform of the International Monetary System', The Levy Economics Institute of Bard College, Policy Note 2009/8.

Kregel, J. (2009b) 'Why Don't the Bailouts Work? Design of a New Financial System versus a Return to Normalcy', *Cambridge Journal of Economics*, 33, pp. 653–63.

Krippner, G.R. (2005) 'The Financialization of the American Economy', *Socio-Economic Review*, 3, pp. 173–208.

Lavoie, M. (2008) 'Financialisation Issues in a Post-Keynesian Stock-flow Consistent Model', *Intervention. European Journal of Economics and Economic Policies*, 5, pp. 331–56.

Lazonick, W. and O'Sullivan, M. (2000) 'Maximizing Shareholder Value: A New Ideology for Corporate Governance', *Economy and Society*, 29(1), pp. 13–35.

Lerner, A. (1943) 'Functional Finance and Federal Debt', *Social Research*, 10, pp. 38–51.

Ludvigson, S. and Steindel, C. (1999) 'How Important is the Stock Market Effect on Consumption?', *Federal Reserve Bank of New York Economic Policy Review*, July, pp. 29–51.

Mehra, Y.P. (2001) 'The Wealth Effect in Empirical Life-cycle Aggregate Consumption Equations', *Federal Reserve Bank of Richmond Economic Quarterly*, 87(2), pp. 45–68.

Meyer, L.H. (2001) 'Inflation Targets and Inflation Targeting', *Federal Reserve Bank of St. Louis Review*, 83(6), pp. 1–13.

OECD (2008) *Growing Unequal? Income Distribution and Poverty in OECD Countries*. Paris: OECD.

OECD (2009) *Economic Outlook: Interim Report, March*. Paris: OECD.

Onaran, Ö., Stockhammer, E. and Grafl, L. (2009) 'The Finance-dominated Growth Regime, Distribution and Aggregate Demand in the US', Working Paper No. 126, Department of Economics Working Paper Series, Vienna University of Economics and Business.

Orhangazi, Ö. (2008) 'Financialisation and Capital Accumulation in the Non-financial Corporate Sector: A Theoretical and Empirical Investigation on the US Economy: 1973–2003', *Cambridge Journal of Economics*, 32, pp. 863–86.

Palley, T. (1994) 'Debt, Aggregate Demand, and the Business Cycle: An Analysis in the Spirit of Kaldor and Minsky', *Journal of Post Keynesian Economics*, 16, 371–90.

Palley, T. (2003) 'Asset Price Bubbles and the Case for Asset Based Reserve Requirements', *Challenge*, 46(3), pp. 53–72.

Palley, T. (2004) 'Asset-based Reserve Requirements: Reasserting Domestic Monetary Control in an Era of Financial Innovation and Instability', *Review of Political Economy*, 16, pp. 43–58.

Palley, T. (2008) 'Financialisation: What It Is and Why It Matters', in E. Hein, T. Niechoj, P. Spahn and A. Truger (eds) *Finance-led Capitalism? Macroeconomic Effects of Changes in the Financial Sector*. Marburg: Metropolis.

Palley, T. (2009) 'America's Exhausted Paradigm: Macroeconomic Causes of the Financial Crisis and the Great Recession', IPE Working Paper 2/2009, Institute for International Political Economy, Berlin School of Economics and Law.

Palley, T. (2010) 'Asset Price Bubbles and Counter-cyclical Monetary Policy: Why Central Banks Have Been Wrong and What Should Be Done', *Intervention. European Journal of Economics and Economic Policies*, 7, pp. 91–107.

Papadimitriou, D. (2009) 'Global Imbalances: Strategic Imbalances for the US and the World', *Intervention. European Journal of Economics and Economic Policies*, 6, pp. 53–60.

Piketty, T. and Saez, E. (2003) 'Income Inequality in the United States, 1913–1998', *The Quarterly Journal of Economics*, 143, pp. 1–39.

Piketty, T. and Saez, E. (2006) 'The Evolution of Top Incomes: A Historical and International Perspective', *American Economic Review. Papers and Proceedings*, 96, 200–5.

Rochon, L.-P. and Setterfield, M. (2007) 'Interest Rates, Income Distribution and Monetary Policy Dominance: Post-Keynesians and the "Fair Rate" of Interest', *Journal of Post Keynesian Economics*, 30, pp. 13–42.

Sapir, J. (2009) 'From Financial Crisis to Turning Point. How the US "Subprime" Crisis' Turned into a World-wide One and Will Change the Global Economy', *Internationale Politik und Gesellschaft*, 1/2009, pp. 27–44.

Schulmeister, S., Schratzenstaller, M. and Picek, O. (2008) 'A General Financial Transaction Tax. Motives, Revenues, Feasibility and Effects'. Vienna: WIFO.

Skott, P. and Ryoo, S. (2008a) 'Macroeconomic Implications of Financialization', *Cambridge Journal of Economics*, 32, pp. 827–62.

Skott. P. and Ryoo, S. (2008b) 'Financialization in Kaleckian Economics with and without Labor Constraints', *Intervention. European Journal of Economics and Economic Policies*, 5, pp. 357–86.

Springler, E. (2007) 'Bank Lending and Regulation in Insider Financial Systems: A Theoretical Assessment', in P. Arestis, E. Hein and E. Le Heron (eds), *Aspects of Modern Monetary and Macroeconomic Policies*. Basingstoke: Palgrave Macmillan.

Stockhammer, E. (2004) 'Financialisation and the Slowdown of Accumulation', *Cambridge Journal of Economics*, 28, pp. 719–41.

Stockhammer, E. (2005–6) 'Shareholder Value Orientation and the Investment–Profit Puzzle', *Journal of Post Keynesian Economics*, 28, pp. 193–215.

Stockhammer, E. (2008) 'Some Stylized Facts on the Finance-dominated Accumulation Regime', *Competition and Change*, 12, pp. 189–207.

UNCTAD (2009) *The Global Economic Crisis: Systemic Failures and Multilateral Remedies*. New York and Geneva: UNCTAD.

van Treeck, T. (2008) 'Reconsidering the Investment–Profit Nexus in Finance-led Economies: An ARDL-based Approach', *Metroeconomica*, 59, pp. 371–404.

van Treeck, T. (2009a) 'The Political Economy Debate on 'Financialisation' – a Macroeconomic Perspective', *Review of International Political Economy*, 16, pp. 907–44.

van Treeck, T. (2009b) 'A Synthetic Stock-flow Consistent Macroeconomic Model of Financialisation', *Cambridge Journal of Economics*, 33, pp. 467–93.

van Treeck, T., Hein, E. and Dünhaupt, P. (2007) 'Finanzsystem und wirtschaftliche Entwicklung: neuere Tendenzen in den USA und in Deutschland', IMK Studies 5/2007, Duesseldorf: Macroeconomic Policy Institute (IMK) at Hans Boeckler Foundation.

Wade, R. (2009) 'From Global Imbalances to Global Reorganisations', *Cambridge Journal of Economics*, 33, pp. 539–62.

Index